Assassinations
& Conspiracies

From Rajah Humabon to Imelda Marcos

Assassinations
& Conspiracies

From Rajah Humabon to Imelda Marcos

Manuel F. Martinez

Anvil
Manila

Assassinations and Conspiracies: From Rajah Humabon to Imelda Marcos
by Manuel F. Martinez

Published and exclusively distributed by
ANVIL PUBLISHING, INC.
2/F Team Pacific Bldg., 14 P. Antonio St.,
Barangay Ugong, Pasig City
1604 Philippines
Telephones: 671-1899, 671-9235 (sales & marketing)
Fax: 671-1308
Email: pubdept@anvil.com.ph

First printing, 2002
Second printing, 2003

The National Library of the Philippines CIP Data

Recommended entry:

Martinez, Manuel F.
  Assassinations & conspiracies: from Rajah
Humabon to Imelda Marcos / Manuel F. Martinez –
Pasig City : Anvil Pub., c2002
  1 v

  1. Assassinations – Philippines. 2. Conspiracies –
Philippines. I. Title.

HV6278 364.1524 2002 P021000001
ISBN 971-27-1218-4

Book design by GERRY R. BACLAGON

Printed in the Philippines

To the innocent victims of political gangsterism...

... and, as the ancient Greeks said, "to tame the savagery of man, and make gentle the life of this world."

Author's Note

The English word *assassin* came from the Middle East at the time of the Crusades. Its root word is *hashshash,* which means "hashish," under whose influence certain killers were led by a secret order to eliminate their enemies.

Of course, this is only the origin of a word in a modern language. Assassination as an act has existed since the dawn of humanity itself — from as far back as Cain and Abel. Assassination — not prostitution — is the world's oldest profession.

Some assassinations treated in this book are fairly recent, and I have been careful not to cause any harm — emotional, legal, or otherwise — both to the families of the victims and to the suspects who have not been convicted.

This book is not only about assassinations but also about certain "legal" executions and conspiracies.

As in any nation, so many assassinations and conspiracies have occurred in the Philippines. There have been a lot of them, indeed hundreds through the decades. What I have included in this book are those characters and cases that have made an impact on the national consciousness.

Acknowledgment

The author thanks Ben Rodriguez, editor in chief of *The Manila Bulletin*; Rudy Romero, president of the Journal Group; Lolita Montano, Norma Carmona and Marcelo Bajan of the Journal library; former Congressman Oscar Santos; Edgardo B. Olaguer of the Light-a-Fire Movement; Elvie Iremedio, Mercy Servida, Maria Fe Marpa and Rod Enano of the Lopez Musuem; the libraries of the University of the Philippines, Ateneo de Manila University, *Manila Bulletin* and the *Philippine Inquirer*; Karina Bolasco and Ani Habulan of Anvil Publishing, Inc.; and the late public relations executive, Philprom Vice President Elmer Carreon, who was as great a friend as anyone can find.

Table of Contents

1. The First Conspirators

LAPULAPU WAS NOT the only village chieftain in Mactan island when Magellan came.

There was another one with the forbidding name of Zula. We can say he was Lapulapu's sworn enemy because he was the one who reported to Magellan that Lapulapu was defiant and would not pay tribute to the king of Spain.[1]

We don't know the reason why there was hostility between Lapulapu and Zula. But two hotheads living together in so tiny an island could not but produce one big quarrel.

Zula blatantly asked Magellan for a boatload of Spanish soldiers to help him, Zula, subdue Lapulapu. Magellan refused, probably regarding the proposition as a monumental impertinence because it appeared that Zula was making him only a junior partner.

Magellan regarded himself as the conqueror and claimant of the islands. How dare a pip-squeak native chief relegate him to a secondary role? No one may preempt a conquistador. Anyway, nice try by Zula to exploit Magellan.

Humabon was the richest and most powerful of the village *datus* then, to whom other native chieftains deferred and paid tribute. Even those foreigners from other parts of the Orient and from faraway India, who seasonally anchored in Cebu's waters to trade, gave him tribute. This gives us a hint not only of Humabon's power but also of his enterprise and humor.

But the Spaniards were something else, and the relationship went the other way around. Faced with the persuasive nature of superior might, it was now Humabon who was only too willing to pay tribute to the foreigner.

Humabon was also Lapulapu's bitter enemy. We may wonder why he had failed to subjugate the Mactan ruler even if the latter was not as rich and as powerful as he. Maybe Lapulapu was simply more courageous — and more willing to wage a sudden death battle against him, Zula or anyone.

When Magellan decided to attack Lapulapu, Humabon reversed Zula's gambit. Instead of inviting Magellan's soldiers to join him, he made it clear it was he who was joining Magellan — he offered to contribute to Magellan some 25 of his own best warriors to join the Spaniards in their Mactan war party.

Another impertinence, but this time it was at least respectful of Magellan's primacy. Magellan again refused. But he kindly allowed Humabon and his warriors to sail along with him in their boat — under the instruction that at no time would they intervene or participate in the battle. They were to be mere observers of a historic moment in what we call today front-row seats.

Magellan found it necessary to demonstrate Spanish valor and Spanish arms to the Indios; he showed his capacity to crush anyone who chose to defy his king. That he set out to quell Lapulapu by himself made him the only Spanish commander in history who refused to conspire and use Indios to fight against their own kind.

Filipinos have always complained that the Spaniards succeeded in conquering and colonizing the Philippines by applying the policy of divide-and-rule. Indeed, no Spanish military or political leader (except Lapulapu) ever dealt with the Indios without the support of other Indios willing to collude with the foreigner against their own lifetime neighbors.

The Spaniards in all their military operations utilized only a handful of Spanish soldiers. These few armored, well-armed Iberian tough guys mobilized numerous natives under their command in their wanton attacks against native communities. The latter consequently lost most of the time in more than three centuries of bloody struggle, biting the dust of defeat and subjection up to the outbreak of the Philippine Revolution.

In refusing the help offerings of Zula and Humabon, Magellan, one of the bravest leaders in history, was therefore a sensational exception. And look what happened to him.

With Magellan outclassed by Lapulapu, Humabon must have been exceedingly embarrassed by his having bet on the wrong horse. And as Horacio de la Costa says, "Magellan's defeat and death changed Humabon's attitude towards the strangers from hospitality to hostility."[2] Humabon disenthralled himself, and proceeded to ruminate, and apply, his own gimmick.

He politely invited the surviving Hispanics, led by Magellan's unworthy replacement, to leave their ships for a while and join a banquet ashore. Although the Spaniards may have had suspicions of Humabon's motive, they presumably had a low regard for his capabilities and manhood, since he had earlier welcomed them and embraced their religion with alacrity.

Alas, they failed to reckon with Oriental cunning, however unimaginative. Conspiring with his followers, Humabon offered good food and titillating wine, waited for the foreigners to get drunk to excess, and then with Mafioso dispatch signaled the implementation of the massacre.

The horrified Spaniards who were left watching safely from the ships must have heard in the night the pained cries of their expiring comrades ashore. They immediately fled to the Moluccas, this time with little thought of spices.

They continued their voyage back to Spain for a first circumnavigation of the world that was treated by the enraptured medievals with much greater wonder than 20th-century mankind contemplated the astronauts' first banal orbits in outer space.

Lapulapu and his men had eviscerated only eight Spaniards and have been celebrated as heroes ever since. Humabon extirpated almost three times that number — 22 Spaniards — but has always been regarded with disdain.

Lesson: A big first mistake may be irreparable.

The sad phenomenon of being divided against one another and thus losing their battles, their freedoms, their dignity and happiness must not have been lost to the Filipino natives.

But what could they do, their society being always riven by petty rivalries and jealousies centuries before the white man came. That was a given, and it was therefore not a question of capacity for wisdom but of incapacity to change their state of things.

Indeed, many leaders of subsequent revolts — Rajah Soliman, Magalat, Sumuroy, Malong, Maniago, Diego Silang, etc. — were not impervious to the thought of unity. They urgently sought the help of leaders in other provinces.

But not even the Katipunan could stop the greater number of able-bodied Filipino men from joining the Spanish forces.

That the native leaders were not so stupid as to be mentally unaware that unity, even among only a part of them, was vital could simply be deduced after Legazpi conquered Manila. It was here that the first conspiracies in Luzon against the Spanish rulers were forged.

In this episode figured one swashbuckling character whom an admiring Nick Joaquin calls "the nameless king of Macabebe."[3] He writes that after Soliman, Lakandula and Rajah Matanda had initially sworn allegiance to the Spanish sovereign and asked other chieftains to do likewise, the Macabebe chief "exploded with fury."

According to the National Historical Institute's multivolume work, *Filipinos in History*, "King Macabebe" furiously confronted Lakandula and Soliman after the latter two had allowed the Spaniards to settle in Manila — without bloodshed or without so much as raising the dirty finger.

"He clandestinely went to them and other rajahs of the neighboring towns and incited them to take up arms against the foreigners."[4] Then later, regardless of the effects of his conspiratorial come-ons to other *datus*, he sailed with solitary intrepidity down the Pampanga river to Manila Bay — with 2,000 troops on 40 war boats. It appears that his numbers were not inadequate to his courage.

The Spaniards knew of the daredevil's efforts because they sent a Spanish officer to negotiate with him. He thundered in reply:

"May the sun split my body in half and may I become shameful and hateful to my women if I ever befriend the Kastila. Tell your master we have come to make war, not peace, and are challenging him to meet us in battle in the waters of the bay."[5]

It was a great song of freedom rarely equaled in Philippine literature.

He jumped out of the small window of the nipa hut and stormed away to his boat to prepare for battle, in which he soon fell stone-dead. Nick Joaquin concludes, "On that day fell the nameless king of Macabebe. Among the first of us was he to die for freedom. He should be listed among our heroes as Lakan Macabebe."

In some later negotiations with the Spaniards, Soliman was often defiant while Lakandula was often conciliatory. We use the word *often* because both blew hot and cold, sometimes fighting, sometimes accommodating, sometimes just plain startled.

Later, after agreeing to a pact with the Spaniards in which the natives would yield to Spanish sovereignty and pay tribute with the exception of the chiefs and their families, Soliman reversed himself and became a conspirator, determined to drive out the white rulers who had overstayed their unwelcome. Knowing the firepower and rapacity of the Spaniards, he asked help from other tribal chieftains:

From Navotas, where Soliman and Lakandula were entrenched, the word went up the river to Bai, and across the bay to Cavite, that every Tagalog or Pampango worth his riverbank was to rise up against the white devils. On the instant, a fleet of *paraos* manned by some 10,000 warriors appeared on the bay to blockade Manila. On the roads swarmed guerillas sent out to ambush the hated colonizers. Churches were raided and the friars terrorized.[6]

A battle of unprecedented magnitude and bloodbath ensued. The Spaniards won a great victory with the support of swarms of short-legged native warriors they had earlier brought from Cebu.

Before that great battle began, the raging Soliman proudly screamed to the Spaniards that he and his men "would repay with death the least thing that touched our honor... for my people are not like the *pintados* [the Visayans] who are subservient."[7]

The victorious white men offered a settlement with the surviving chieftains, among whom were, again, Lakandula — and Soliman, now no longer screaming, but chastened and maybe contrite. A peace agreement was signed, with the payment of tribute and the acceptance of Spanish sovereignty naturally enforced.

Spanish colonial rule was now militarily unchallenged in the Manila Bay area, at least for the short while before the appearance of the dreaded Limahong — and, almost two centuries later, of the British who vanquished Spain in Intramuros itself.

Note that in this beginning of colonial rule, a peace agreement was signed between the natives and the Spaniards, with the natives agreeing to make payments. But at the end of this same colonial rule three centuries later, a peace agreement was also signed, the Pact of Biak-na-Bato. This time it was the other way around — it was the Spaniards who agreed to make payments to the Filipinos amounting to 800,000 pesos.

How times had changed — but slowly, after more than three centuries.

Finally, a word about the latter-day Macabebes, who gained a notoriety unworthy of their early king mentioned above. This is not to generalize on them, much less on other Pampangos, who throughout Philippine history have shown themselves to have produced heroic and enterprising men, like Jose Abad Santos and Ninoy Aquino, for example. It is simply to refer to those who had actually conspired with and worked for the Spaniards and then the Americans and the Japanese against their own countrymen. No one will ever forget that the Macabebes, to no one's surprise, helped the Americans capture Aguinaldo not on the battlefield of honor but treacherously in his own office, where he had welcomed them — a humiliating end for a world-famous, legendary revolutionary's struggles against foreign oppressors.

Indeed, during the Revolution, the Macabebes were such a hideous bane to the Filipino cause that the revolutionaries planned to burn to ashes the whole hometown of the Macabebes. Aguinaldo himself took note of the problem. He later wrote in his memoirs:

> We ourselves had no Macabebes in our forces. It is said that the original paternal ancestors of the Macabebes were western Mexican Indians brought to the Philippines as recruits of the Spaniards and later permitted to settle. The original Indians naturally felt foreign among the Filipinos and looked upon the Spanish government for assistance and protection.
>
> This feeling seems to have been transmitted from generation to generation to their descendants who continued to serve the Spaniards. After the Spanish defeat, they transferred their loyalty to the Americans almost instinctively.[8]

Back to the great Lapulapu. Pigafetta's story is the only eyewitness account of the Battle of Mactan, and it is a brief tale. It offers no description of Lapulapu's personal character or physical attributes.

But from the story itself, it can be gleaned that the Mactan ruler was not a mere accident of history who won simply by overwhelming numbers, but a towering personality who was brilliant, strong, deliberate and splendid. He knew exactly what he wanted — freedom — and would not compromise it in any way.

Indeed, Napoleon G. Rama, publisher of *The Manila Bulletin* and a fine historical writer, believes that even from the scanty Pigafetta account Lapulapu looms as a truly great Filipino — next only to Rizal and therefore greater than Bonifacio, Quezon, etc., as he never tires of telling those who would care to listen.

Pigafetta was Magellan's official chronicler — not exactly like a presidential campaign spokesman today but certainly a partisan — and he had only good words for his captain. To him Magellan was truly a great hero, and Lapulapu was the enemy, the villain. But though he never praises the Mactan ruler, his account is not tilted against Lapulapu who comes through as an impressive personage.

In his Mactan attack, so the account goes, Magellan brought only 60 soldiers, amply protected with metal, although he had twice that number in his ships. He underestimated the strength, and obviously the courage, of Lapulapu.

Lapulapu turned out to be tougher — and more intelligent and deliberately and cautiously prepared — than those powerful Aztec and Inca kings that Spanish conquistadors like Cortes and Pizarro had subjugated in Mexico and Peru.

It is probable that Lapulapu, befitting an exceptional leader, had spies in Humabon's territory who had sent him reliable intelligence, because he seemed to have had a good estimate of the Spaniard's attacking force.

Before the battle, Lapulapu also had his men furiously digging pits on the shore to entrap the Spaniards. He then proceeded to try outwitting the renowned Spanish commander by sending him a perplexing message — do not attack us at nighttime.

But Magellan was equal to Lapulapu's cunning at least on this one instance, because he considered it a ruse for him to attack precisely at night. Had he done so, then certainly he and his men would have been more easily routed because in the dark they would have ignominiously fallen into the pits.

To attack by day, however, was too literal a response that would have exposed him to raucous ridicule — or the tender mercies of whatever tactical plays and ploys Lapulapu may have conceived in case he proved to be unprofound in his interpretation of the tricky message.

Not disrespectful of the Mactan chieftain's tactical wit, of which Humabon may have grudgingly told him, the equally crafty Magellan attacked neither at night nor in the daytime but at dawn.

According to military historian Uldarico Baclagon:

Lapulapu showed better judgment when he did not take chances but instead gathered as much as he could and applied the principle of concentration of combat power. When he finally encountered the enemy, he immediately saw in his numerical superiority the opportunity to execute double envelopment and weaken the enemy's center.[9]

He concludes by saying that Lapulapu displayed tactical skill, leadership and the ability to make quick decisions.

Lapulapu's rare greatness of character showed not only in his defiance, but also in the fact that he was the only one who exhibited that defiance — a singular attribute which through the centuries has kept his stature at great heights.

He was not a brute who won without imagination or valor, or who won only because of an excessive manpower advantage, besides profiting from Magellan's grievous tactical and strategic errors. He had class.

That other chieftains regarded Lapulapu's personal strength and character could be gleaned from the fact that he had only 1,500 warriors or so — much less than the swarms of lancers and other warriors Humabon had in Cebu. And yet Humabon, as we said, was not able to vanquish him, or possibly never attempted to attack him.

Parenthetically, Spaniards invading Mexico and Peru, with the same technology and weapons as Magellan, smashed with a small number of soldiers those screaming, mouth-slapping Aztecs and Incas who often numbered by the tens of thousands in one battle.

Montezuma, for example, had at least 100,000 battle-tested warriors specially held in reserve in Tenochtitlan, now Mexico City. Even these the Aztec warrior-emperor failed to use well against the tiny advancing force of Hernando Cortes — and lost.[10]

So why would Lapulapu's measly 1,500 forces, in comparison, even be reckoned as a "superiority in numbers?" Was his superiority not in courage — tempered with perspicacity?

A Spanish soldier in those days was heavily covered with armor, unlike the Aztec, Inca or Filipino warrior who was half-naked and therefore not so difficult to mutilate.

Can one imagine a more unequal contest? It was like the slim Luisito Espinosa facing on the ring an armored Tyson.

The Filipinos' weapons were made mostly of bamboos while the Spaniards' swords were long and made of Toledo steel, the finest in the world.

It may be noted that while in the Americas and in the Orient, a bunch of Spanish soldiers could kill scores of native warriors in one continuous combat while sustaining only a few casualties, with only minor wounds on their own survivors, they could not do the same feat against their continental enemies in Europe, since they were more or less at the same level of technology.

The Battle of Mactan did not go as usual for the Spaniards. One reason was that with the weakening of Magellan's center from Lapulapu's double envelopment, the natives, probably the best and the fiercest of them, whom we may call Lapulapu's *pambato*, went straight like a juggernaut for Magellan himself, an unexpected tactic.

This scene, however modest, is reminiscent of the Battle of Arbela where Alexander the Great concentrated his vicious attack on the exact spot where Darius and his general staff were standing, and sent the Persian king running for dear life. Lapulapu's men smashed through and dealt the person of Magellan an overkill of cutlasses and spears.

Unlike Darius, Magellan was in knee-deep water and could not run away as fast as the armorless natives who, like all Mactanese since their childhood, must have been used to horsing around on seawater and romping around on their fabulous beaches that have now become lucrative tourist spots.

Moreover, the natives aimed their lances and arrows at the flesh in the Spaniards' anatomy that were unprotected by armor. According to Pigafetta:

> When morning came we leaped into the water to our thighs and walked through for more than two crossbow flights before we could reach the shore. The boats could not approach nearer because of certain rocks in the water. When we reached the land, the [native warriors] had formed three divisions to the number of more than 1,500 persons. [The number may have been exaggerated to impress the Spanish king's court and increase the rewards for Magellan and his men, as many such reports by the conquistadores in those times were in parts exaggerated — Ed.]
>
> When they saw us they charged down upon us with exceeding loud cries, two divisions on our flanks and the other on our front. When the captain [Magellan] saw that, he formed us into two divisions and thus did we begin to fight.

So many of them charged down upon us that they shot the captain through the leg with a poisoned arrow. On that account he ordered us to retire slowly, but the men took to flight, except six or eight of us who remained with the captain.

So we continued to retire for more than a good crossbow flight from the shore, always fighting up to our knees in the water. The natives continued to pursue us, picking up the same spear four or six times to hurl it at us again and again.

So many turned upon the captain that they knocked his helmet off his head twice, but he always stood firmly like a good knight together with some others.

An Indian hurled a bamboo spear into the captain's face, but the latter immediately killed him with his lance, which he left in the Indian's body. Then trying to lay hand on sword, he could draw it but half-way, because he had been wounded in the arm with another bamboo spear.

When the natives saw that they all hurled themselves upon him. One of them wounded him on the left leg with a large cutlass which resembles a scimitar, only being larger. That caused the captain to fall face downward, when immediately they rushed upon him with iron and bamboo spears, and with their cutlasses killed our mirror, our light, our comfort and true guide.[11]

Thus did crimson European blood commingle for the first time in the shallow waters — clear, warm, soft waters — of the Orient.

Besides overconfidence and lack of preparation and information, Magellan apparently committed a grave error in proceeding with his attack — actually it appears later he was the one attacked. He was not prepared for low tide and the discovery that their boats could not approach the shore nearer because of the rocks.

Lapulapu's singular triumph must have made him the awesome superstar and topic in every *tuba*-drinking party in the archipelago, in the Moluccas and beyond, indeed even among some people in Europe.

Aguinaldo in his time became the toast of liberal elements in Europe for fighting a war of independence against superpower America and holding it at bay for a good while. Even in the United States, he had many such admirers. It is known that, in a Chicago theater, when an image of him was flashed on the movie screen it was greeted with applause.

Another instance of a world-renowned Filipino was, of course, Ninoy Aquino. But before Aguinaldo and Ninoy, no single Filipino, not even Rizal in his own lifetime or shortly thereafter, had ever caused a global sensation except Lapulapu.

Professor Gabriel Fabella, former head of the history department of the University of the Philippines and of the Philippine Historical Association in the 1950s, said Aguinaldo was the first Filipino ever to be mentioned in world encyclopedias. Should he have instead read much earlier editions?[12]

The greatness of a historical personage may be measured by his value and impact on his time.

Lapulapu delayed the colonization of the islands by more than 40 years, thus protecting his countrymen at least for that period from the terrible horrors that were to visit latter-day Filipino generations. No pip-squeak, *patay-patay* leader could be of such decisive importance in the long-term unfolding of events.

If he were not Lapulapu, he could not have beaten the Spaniards. But he was Lapulapu, and he stayed the course of history to an extent no other Filipino ever did.

While other personages adjust to or ride on events, he defied and surged onto them. He was a creator, not just a creature, of history.

2. The Tondo Conspiracy

LEGAZPI TOOK Manila in the year 1571. The great Tondo Conspiracy was crushed less than 20 years later, in 1588. To us today, that was more than 400 years ago.

No doubt, historians are correct when they say that the Tondo Conspiracy was the largest — or shall we say, in terms of territory traversed, the widest — conspiracy against Spanish rule next to the Katipunan itself. This was because it spanned Manila and some nearby provinces. It reached the Calamianes islands located in the middle of the sea between Zamboanga, Palawan and Borneo.

It was supposed to involve the Borneans themselves. And the conspirators, hearing that Spain's enemy, the English, were in some warships in the Visayas, also expected the latter to get involved in the effort to topple the brutal colonial regime.

Like the ill-starred Katipunan, it was prematurely discovered by the Spaniards. And like the Katipunan, its betrayer was a native informer. But unlike the Katipunan which went on with the Revolution in spite of the mass arrests of its members, the Tondo conspirators were caught with their pants — or their *bahag*s — down.

And they lost their heads, literally.

Like alleged conspirators to assassinate Ferdinand Marcos who signed confessions about who plotted what, with whom and how, the Spaniards left a written account of the Tondo Conspiracy, presumably from confessions and trial testimonies of the imprisoned putschists.

Isn't it curious that signed confessions under the Marcos regime are regarded by many today to have been forcibly extracted from the arrested plotters, and were probably false, while no one seems to question the truth of the confessions given by the ancient Tondo putschists?

A quirk of history? Ask Abadilla.

The Spanish account of the confessions made by the plotters is detailed. It includes a meeting that lasted for three straight days in a village called Tambobong, with details like how they got drunk recalling those good old free days before the Spanish conquest.

Filipino students for generations have heard of the name Magat Salamat — although who this fellow was, and what he did, is vague to most. Simply, he was one of the Tondo conspirators.

He was the son of Lakandula — some say of Rajah Matanda. Others play it safe and state that he was simply the son of a Manila rajah. Someone said he was the son of Rajah Soliman, but this is unlikely, for Soliman was much younger than Lakandula and, no pun intended, Rajah Matanda.

No matter. Fact was many *datus* or rajahs in those days were close relatives, of course, for noble blood didn't marry *aliping saguiguilid* — just as modern Manila's 400 before martial law times and the cronies later would not allow their kin to marry someone with an address of "9 Ipil Street, Lot 24, Block 3, People's Home-site, San Mateo, Rizal."

In the folded tortilla of vanished times, Magat Salamat certainly belonged to the generation that immediately followed the slam-bang era of Lakandula, Matanda and Soliman, rulers of Manila and Tondo when Legazpi came land grabbing like crazy.

Magat Salamat's noble lineage may help explain why he has often been promi-nently mentioned by academically ill-equipped historians. But he was neither the founding spirit nor the top leader of the movement, as we shall see.

There were about 8,000 natives living in Tondo and other villages outside the formal Manila city limits in 1588. This is roughly the equivalent of a sixth-class mu-nicipality today.

Inside the city were only some 80 Spaniards, 50 of whom had Spanish wives, the rest having native wives, and 200 Spanish soldiers.[1]

"At this time only 20 Chinese trading ships were calling Manila each year although, for two years running, some merchants had been coming from Japan, Macao, Siam, and other countries."

On June 20, 1582 — five years before the beginning of the conspiracy — the bishop of Manila wrote the king of Spain a pro-people letter. It was about a group of native chiefs from Tondo led by one Martin Pangan and his cousin, Agustin Legaspi, who had submitted a petition for redress of grievances. The bishop said in his letter:

> Without doubt, it would break your Majesty's heart if you could see them as they are, and how pitiable their appearance and the things they relate.
>
> The alcaldes bought up the people's rice and other produce cheap, and then sold them back dear. They impressed the people as rowers at all times; after a month as oarsmen they would be required to get ready for another without having been paid wages.
>
> Yet the other people left in the pueblos would be made to pay the wages that were supposed to have been paid to the rowers! Many of the chiefs' people

had left their villages, but the chiefs would be made to pay the tributes of those who had left.

When they failed to pay, they would be placed in the stocks and flogged.[2]

Also, prisoners were required to spend for their own food in jail — like today's kidnap victims in the south whose exorbitant ransom money is called "board-and-lodging fees" in camps crawling with poisonous snakes and leeches.

As with so many other petitions in those colonial days, nobody knew what happened to this one.

Later, in the signal year of 1587, Martin Pangan had become *gobernadorcillo* in Tondo but he was still, or again, in jail. A historian spells his name without the letter *n* — *Panga*, meaning "jawbone." How a Filipino today may wish that, like Samson in the case of the 1,000 Philistines, he managed to kill just as many Spaniards with the jawbone of an ass.

He was in a *karsel* along with constant companion Agustin Legaspi, no doubt also a Christian convert as can be gleaned from his Christian name, and other chiefs who were also their relatives in the Tondo *principalia*.

As was usual in those days, they were in prison probably because they had protested, not committed, injustice. With their hands idle, their minds worked. They pledged to stand together against the Spaniards. In what manner they were not certain yet.

Misery loves company — and freedom, too.

Release from prison expanded, not diminished, their feelings to be free. They got in touch with the *datu*s of Pandacan, Navotas, Taguig, Maysilo, Catangalan and many others in the Manila area and nearby provinces like those in Candaba, Pampanga, who wished there was an uprising.

Besides their having been reduced to vassalage by the iron might of Spain, they mourned that their own former native slaves had been freed from them; "their gold was being taken away...even the old gold that the natives wore as ornaments....Some had also lost their wives, because it was determined that these had been married to others first.

"They yearned to be chiefs again. They were drinking a lot. They swore to act as one should an opportunity arise...."[3] Who said the Indios never had a notion of unity?

We have in the Tondo Conspiracy a curious parallel to the Katipunan where Bonifacio got in touch for help with a Japanese naval officer, one named Kanimura, who was no less than an admiral with a warship in Manila Bay. The Agustin Legaspi we mentioned above told his brooding companions in Tondo that there was this Japanese, Juan Gayo, captain of a trading boat whom he had often entertained in his house — presumably with meals and with the local version of saki, and with some creeping conversation that revealed the dark conspiratorial secret.

The ninja Gayo was probably more than entertained, he was enthused, by the *tuba*. He precipitately promised to provide the conspirators some weapons just as the latter-day Jap promised Bonifacio. The chiefs said they would gather among themselves more arms, including provisions and other necessities.

A historian writes that Gayo vowed to provide Japanese warriors also, for which he was promised "one-half of the tribute to be collected in the Philippines"[4] by the contemplated new dispensation. That would have made him richer than any Spaniard.

That they did not have any fine print saying how long Gayo would receive his share helps to show that the conspiracy was haphazard. What if the Jap later insisted getting his part of the tribute collection for years and years?

And yet, had they started talking about the period, good old Gayo could have insisted on ten years, while the Filipinos would be ready to grant only one and one-half years — and from that impasse the conspiracy would have already broken up from a premature quarrel.

At this point it appears Agustin Legaspi had primacy, because from an indefinite, shapeless plot they now decided that after exterminating the Spaniards they would crown him king. No other detail agreed upon!

Parenthetically, historian Gregorio Zaide says Legaspi was no less than the son-in-law of the Sultan of Brunei! And he fingers the awesome *manugang* as the mastermind of the plot.

Unlike Bonifacio's Jap, who later vanished into thin air and was never heard from again, good old Gayo stayed with the Indio chiefs to the very end until he, too, was arrested and hanged. Or was it involuntary — that is, was he surprised in his Manila lair, along with his Filipino interpreter who was also hanged, since the arrests were sudden and unexpected?

The insurrection was hazy in terms of means — or in terms of what engineers today would call a blueprint, or mechanism with identifiable nuts and bolts. But the plan was unanimously adopted. After all, they were probably drunk again, and enjoyed the subject matter for *pulutan*.

The Tondo plot remained only a plot for a good while because although he was also from Tondo, Agustin Legaspi was no Andres Bonifacio.

The year 1587 passed and in February 1588, a new factor obtruded. The English pirate Thomas Candish (also known by other historians as "Cavendish") captured a Spanish galleon, with all its awesome riches intact. The news was like an oasis in the desert of their parched plan — except that Candish was in the middle of the sea.

Their plan had not gained any headway, and had not even started to be implemented for they did not bother to determine the first step. But the conspirators regarded Candish as a new card.

They decided to await the swashbuckling Englishman's coming to Manila to unleash hell on the Spaniards from the sea — however unlikely that eventuality could happen — during which they, the Tondo putschists, would overpower them from behind on land.

They dared to dream this congenial and salutary development although they had not contacted Candish. In any case it was impossible to do so. Not one of them was capable of psychic communication.

And so they waited — for nothing — in animated suspension even as Candish, unaware of the plot which he could have exploited for his king and country, and already overloaded with easily liquifiable booty, guffawed his way to India with an English accent, and soon ensconced himself comfortably in his home in England.

After the Candish nonstarter, a Bulacan chieftain named Esteban Taes sought Martin Pangan in Tondo and the vision of an all-Tagalog uprising started to form and crystallize — involving Bulacan, Pampanga, Laguna and Batangas, to which secret agents were later sent. Now they were going somewhere.

Once they approached a group of Pampango *datus* who were on their way to the governor-general to present a petition, and were rebuffed. O. D. Corpuz, in his massive two-volume work, *Roots of the Filipino Nation*, writes:

"Unwittingly, Panga was talking to people who were soon to become the Spaniards' staunchest military supporters. They replied they had no quarrel with the Spanish king, and declined a second invitation to visit Tondo after their business in Manila was concluded."[5]

A pity, because Tagalogs and Pampangos are close blood relatives. They had descended from what Nick Joaquin calls "twin Malay migrations" that came to the archipelago during the great migrant wave in the 10th century, huddling together wet and exhausted in their frail but unsinkable *barangay* crafts.

It was through the span of many centuries that their language and customs eventually diverged even as they lived as neighbors.

Apparently, after the quick Pampango rejection of the Tondo conspirators, the latter turned their hopes on another group of relatives, this time the ones in Borneo.

It is said without much fear of contradiction or laughter that Manila's blue bloods were related to the Bornean rulers. In fact, some people in the University of the Philippines' history department claimed in the 1960s that those rulers were illegitimate descendants of Alexander the Great.

The Macedonian conqueror, they said, took a concubine while he was in India, not minding reports that he was gay. Her far descendants migrated to the Orient, then later to the Philippines presumably with the twin migrations, and produced a president, Kapampangan Diosdado Macapagal. In other words, Gloria Macapagal-Arroyo is a descendant of Alexander the Great.

But let us continue with our ancient subject. Lakandula was a descendant of an early Tagalog ruler, King Balagtas.[6] King Balagtas was the son of Prince Soledah, an heir to no less than the grand Madjapahit throne who had migrated to the archipelago in his youth and married a Tagalog princess.

So the DNA link was heavy — Magat Salamat, a son of Lakandula, was a descendant of the southern Islamic royalty, while Agustin Legaspi was the son-in-law of the Brunei sultan who introduced his blood participation into the illustrious line.

There are more indications of the apparent truth of the Borneo connection. A Franciscan friar in the 18th century wrote that "about the year 1365, during the archipelago's pre-Christian era, the Shri-Visayans and later those of the new empire of Madjapahit came to Lucban, Quezon province. They introduced the use of *sigay* shells, which were exported from Lucban to Hindustan where they were used as money."[7]

Another priest, one Fray San Antonio, wrote in his "Philippine Chronicles" that "fine seashells called 'sigueys' are used as currency in Siam and Bengal."[8]

The year we just mentioned, 1365, was within the span of time in which Prince Soledah is estimated to have migrated to the Philippines. It is possible he brought along a coterie of cronies to Manila who proceeded to Quezon and other nearby provinces in their search for local wherewithal.

While the Madjapahit throne was not necessarily situated in Borneo, some of the empire's royals or their close relatives may have settled there.

It is said it was from the arrest and investigation of the Tondo conspirators that the Spaniards were startled to discover for the first time the very close connection between the Manila native rulers and those of Borneo.

This was no idle trivia to them. Halfway around the world, in their own home in the rough Iberian Peninsula and in the Mediterranean, Christian Spaniards had clashed in deadly wars for centuries with the rampaging forces of Islam.

And now they were in an eyeball-to-eyeball confrontation again in the Orient with their former enemies — indeed a blood-soaked armed confrontation that lasted through all the centuries of their dreadful regime in the Philippines and has its present-day echoes in the south.

Not only for reasons of blood relationship, but also for historical momentum, the Bornean rulers were deemed by Martin Pangan and the others as not predisposed to ignore the plight of their Manila cousins groaning under the heavy yoke of Islam's old Christian foes.

Of course, Miguel Lopez de Legazpi himself much earlier may already have had more than an inkling of the Borneo — or a southern — connection outside of Mindanao simply because Soliman and the others were Muslims.

And so with Candish evaporating into thin air without having precipitated in the first place, where else could the conspirators turn but to the more reliable Borneans? After all, they were more powerful and had the resources for a strong military expedition.

The plan was "to invite the Borneans to attack the Spaniards. They anticipated that when the Bornean fleet reached Cavite, the Spaniards would call on them to help defend their city. The chiefs would be waiting, but they would turn around and kill the Spaniards."[9] A treacherous, but plausible, idea.

Of course, the first step was to send a delegation to Borneo, and Magat Salamat was chosen chief envoy. It would be both a mistake and an injustice to say this was his initial role, for he had been in the heroic conspiracy from the beginning.

On the way to Borneo Magat and his *rondalla* stopped at Cuyo island in far-flung Calamianes. Ever the fervent *filibusteros*, they persuaded a native chief named Sumaclob to join the simmering rebellion.

Here the often logical O. D. Corpuz fumbles by wondering, somewhat condescendingly, "what Sumaclob could do in far off Cuyo in an attack [on Manila] from Tondo."[10] Simple — he could have joined the Bornean fleet.

In another Calamianes island they enlisted an Iscariotic man named Antonio Surabao, who joined the movement. To him Magat Salamat, probably drunk, gave some details of the plan. Surabao was a native servant of a Spanish *encomendero* in the area named Pedro Sarmiento who promptly had the visitors arrested, no thanks to Salamat.

It was now only a matter of time before the plotters in Manila were rounded up.

According to Zaide, on October 26, 1588, some 15 months after the conspiracy was first hatched without the Spaniards getting wind of it, Sarmiento sailed from the Calamianes for Manila to report the conspiracy to the authorities. In the same ship, of course, were his distraught captives, now contemplating with disillusioned eyes their most unfavorable vicissitude of fortune.

Thus the sultan of Brunei did not receive the historic letters and the conspirators' gifts of weapons and other things.

The leading conspirators in Manila were promptly tried and just as promptly executed. Martin Pangan and Agustin Legaspi were hanged, their properties confiscated, their houses burned and their residential lands plowed and sown with salt to keep them barren, as in the case of traitors in Hebrew scripture.

The Spaniards did not deem it superfluous to cut off the two leading conspirators' heads and exhibit them in iron cages for the two *T*'s — terrify and teach (a lesson to) — the Indios.

A few others were also hanged, their corpses left dangling from the rope. The rest were banished to distant Mexico, some of whom jumped ship off California without a green card and from them germinated the first branch of brown Americans from Manila.

As if to show that they were not summary, unjust or merciless in their gruesome tantrum, the threatened Spaniards set one conspirator free as *consuelo de bobo*. Corpuz laces his primary-sourced account with some obvious but tolerable observations:

1. The Indios, instead of immediately fighting for freedom when the Spaniards arrived, quickly surrendered — and it was only after they had lost their freedom, with them now hideously disadvantaged, that they tried to regain it. Talk of doing it the hard way.

2. Because of this, they were different from the Muslims who never surrendered. Hence, when the Christian Filipinos defied the Spaniards, it was already in the category of *rebels* who wanted to throw off their acquired yoke. When the Muslims fought the Spaniards, they were not rebels but *antagonists* [terminology mine — Ed.], simply because they had not become subjects in the first place.

3. With the extirpation of the Tondo Conspiracy and its Borneo connection, "the influence and memory of Islam effectively disappeared from the Manila and Tagalog area, and Christianity's future in Luzon was assured."

4. Unlike the scores of conspiracies and uprisings where "the objectives of the revolt were [supposed to have been] attained when the tribute collector or alcalde or friar was killed, to the Tondo conspirators the goal was the overthrow of Spanish rule itself."

5. Thus began the abominable role of the traitor who through three centuries of uprisings would betray various Filipino patriots.

6. The Tondo cabal was not an isolated case. Almost at the same time, as the Spanish records show, other plotters like those in Cebu and Panay arose.

Parenthetically, primary sources written by the friars reporting to the king of Spain relate so many more revolts by Filipinos than those major ones reported in today's history textbooks.

The truth is that there was hardly any considerable length of time during the Spanish tyranny in the Philippines when there was not one, or even two or more, revolts occurring in one region or another, some of them so much localized that they have not gained notice from classroom historians.

Spanish rule in the Philippines was really demonic in spite of the good intentions of the Spanish kings and governments in Madrid.

But on so many occasions, even as the crushed Filipinos suffered unbearably, individual Spaniards like friars and *alcalde mayores* and *guardia civil* chiefs experienced uprisings that produced conflagrations no less painful and despicable than hell.

And hell is what this book is all about.

3. The Sumuroy Assassination

THE TONDO plotters, assiduous but unspecific, believed that the Pampango delegation to the governor-general which we mentioned earlier would help in their planned coup d'etat. Could we blame them for expecting support from the Pampangos?

After all, many Pampangos were neither cowards nor unpatriotic. Only two years earlier, in 1585, "the Pampangos connived with some people of Manila and the Borneans, who used to trade with the city, to rise in revolt. According to their plot, they would secretly enter the city of Manila one dark night and massacre the Spaniards."[1] That simple.

But its very simplicity in the face of the Spaniards' superiority in technology and cruelty seemed to foredoom it, since reason teaches that the superiority of an enemy could be overcome, not with simplicity, but with creativity and imagination.

Although it was not actually a revolt because it never got off the ground, some historians call it "the first Pampango revolt" — a looseness in words that no one has bothered to correct.

With such a track record, added to the memory of the much-lamented, hyper-courageous King of Macabebe, an enthusiastic Pampango input to the struggle was therefore not unexpected.

In the Kapampangan plot, a native woman married to a Spaniard "happened to learn of it and warned the Spanish authorities." Unlike the Tondo conspirators, the leaders of this earlier collusion were executed without trial, without delay, without mercy, without memory.

O. D. Corpuz, as we pointed out in the previous chapter, writes that in the Tondo Conspiracy the native traitor, who through the centuries was to often rise as a grim and gruesome apparition in the Philippine scene, first appeared. But with what happened with the above woman in the Pampango revolt, how could Corpuz be correct?

Moreover, it does not require the most rigorous intellect to see that the first recorded native traitor who sided with the foreigner had lived and devegetated more than 50 years earlier. His name was Zula (or Humabon?).

A little-known uprising in the years following the Tondo Conspiracy was the revolt of Magalat, which happened in the far north, in the province of Cagayan.

This Magalat was truly a brave and skillful leader who with his men managed to kill some Spaniards by surprising them in the *poblacion*. This was a very rare achievement in those hard-pressed early colonial days when each and every Spaniard was very highly valued and well-protected by the *guardia civil* — while the Indios were expendable for any Spanish purpose, big or small, and could not much defend themselves because they had inferior weapons.

Magalat and his kinsmen were later captured and jailed in Manila, where as country bumpkins they felt uncomfortably like ducks taking to no lake water. It is a wonder why they were not summarily tortured and executed, having stained their hands with precious Spanish blood.

Did they have friends in low places? It appears so. The poor and self-sacrificing original Dominicans of Cagayan, who were truly of heroic stuff compared with the abusive latter-day friars, demonstrated unaccustomed pity besides their accustomed piety. They asked the governor-general to pardon the rebels.

The governor-general acquiesced in the liberation of so despicable a biped as an Indio ringleader. Magalat was freed along with his fellow troublemakers.

Back in his lush native turf in the valleys of the north, the irrepressible Magalat, unwilling to compromise freedom for *utang na loob*, again revolted with much more gall and fury than before. This time he asked, and received, the help of other native chiefs.

Magalat was "too good a leader to be crushed in battle."[2] So some Spaniards, probably nonfriars, with their ample resources which they had sucked from the Indios themselves for decades, hired native assassins to extirpate him. Which they did.

And the Cagayan revolt, being coterminous with Magalat's considerable talents in inciting people to vehemence and sedition, ended without further fuss. His gross annihilation was the first major orthodox assassination in Philippine history.

But events were not to be one-sided. In 1601 the Igorots conspired to resist any effort to Christianize them. Of course, to the ethnics, the imposition of any religion on them was revolting, and they revolted.

The governor-general from Manila sent a military expedition to quell them. It was accompanied by a most holy friar named Esteban Marin who, in his desire to qualify for the gates of heaven, stubbornly absorbed all hardships in accordance with his missionary renown. His admirable obstinacy included the scholastic effort to learn the Igorot dialect, which he eventually spoke with Manglapus fluency.

Alone and unafraid, the brave Fr. Marin went to the tempestuous pagan villagers to mollify, if not to enchant, them. But the Igorots quickly assassinated him. The score now was: one assassination (Magalat's) in favor of the Spaniards, another assassination (Fr. Marin's) in favor of the natives, or one to one.

Still in Cagayan, the ethnic Mandaya natives executed a friar in 1625 — while in the rebellion of Sumuroy in his own hometown of Palapag, Samar, they killed the parish priest.

Sumuroy and company also eliminated the *cura*'s unfortunate and probably cautious replacement without ceremony or remorse. They had burned the old convent and now they also burned the new one without feeling monotonous.

It would be a laborious occupation to sum up the exchange of so many assassinations on both sides through the infernal centuries. But with reference to our subject, Renato Constantino points out that the Sumuroy rebellion was significant in that it triggered sympathetic tumults in other places, a spontaneity that gave a greater meaning to them than their merely individual local character.

Some kind of an embryonic seminational sense of commonality emerging here? The Sumuroy initiative led to the following secondary explosions:

A Franciscan father was banished [by the rebels] from Sorsogon, an *alferez* chief was put to death in Masbate, an officer was killed in Cebu, natives of Camiguin tied up the father prior and humiliated him by placing their feet on his neck, several priests were killed in Zamboanga, and the entire coast of Northern Mindanao revolted.[3]

Since this book is only a short and perfunctory work, let us content ourselves with summarily saying that through the centuries, almost all Indios who led revolts were assassinated or executed — either shot, hanged or decapitated.

Among them were Almazan who had proclaimed himself king of Ilocos, Malong who had proclaimed himself king of Pangasinan, Hermano Puli who had proclaimed himself king of the Tagalogs, and scores of other energetic rebel leaders who never proclaimed themselves anything but inborn heirs to freedom.

Of course, returning the favor, the Indios killed many Spaniards in different localities, as in the 1589 Ilocos-Cagayan revolt, the same year when the Tondo conspirators were being exterminated. And so many friars were executed during — and before — the Philippine Revolution.

Let us mention one rebellion because its leader — Bankaw — suffered earlier than the great Sumuroy, our main subject of this chapter, the same horrible fate of having his severed head placed on the higher end of a stake for public exhibition and communal rumination. Displaying the severed head of a rebel on a stake was an excessively malicious penalty which the threatened Spaniards not infrequently inflicted so as to warn the living of the hazards of insubordination.

In 1621 — 100 years after Lapulapu and 28 years before Sumuroy — Bankaw the village chieftain vibrated in rebellion in Leyte because of his reconversion from Christianity to the old native religion. Because of this ambiguous oscillation in piety, the revolt was considered a religious one, although there was nothing pious about its violence and havoc.

Parenthetically, the Spaniards, ever the devoted trustees of the one true God whose Scriptures said He was a jealous God, often sought to abolish all remnants of the old native religion.

They did it with beastly intensity, not without the natives' determined resistance and tactical deception of pretending to adopt the foreign religion while still doing in secret the same old *anito* practices and rituals of their forebears.

This was true in the case of other peoples ravaged by the Spaniards. For example, in Mexico, at about the same era, the Jesuit scholar Ernest Gruening wrote:

> Fear of punishment rather than the desire that their children shall be Christians makes the Indians bring them to baptism. It is common practice for a woman, no sooner out of the church in which her child had been baptized, to rush at all speed to her house and there, placing her mouth on that of the infant, to suck with all diligence and extract the salt put there in baptism.
>
> Then she washes the child's head, changing the water six or seven times, with which she feels she has removed every trace of Christianity.[4]

It should be stressed that Sumuroy's father was a priest of the old native religion. Presumably Sumuroy himself, who was an assistant of the Spaniards in the coastal fort built to help repel Muslim raids, was a staunch believer in the native religion, and this may be considered to have contributed not only to the decision to revolt but also to the extent of its fury.

Note that he did not carry a Christian name, and may have resisted Christian baptism.

In any case let us cite Tagalog historian Elsie S. Ramos who notes a phenomenon in the Philippines not dissimilar to the example in Mexico that we stated above:

One time in 1595, while the curate in thoroughly Catholicized Lucban in Quezon province was blessing the bodies of dead epidemic victims in the town's magnificent cathedral he found out that they were *"nagtatago ng mga anitos at anting-anting, na bumibilang sa isang daan at animnapu't tatlong (163) klase; ang ilan ay nababalot sa ginto, ang iba naman sa pilak, at ang iba'y pinalalamutian ng mga sinsing, bato at kahoy, tinatangi nang higit pa sa kanilang buhay. Hinakot [ng pari] ang mga ito sa teheras at iniutos na sunugin.* [5]

At another time, says Elsie Ramos, while Lucban had become the center of the friars' missionary penetrations in Quezon, the celebrated friar Juan de Plasencia, overjoyed by the success of the Christian conversion programme, later complained in extreme frustration about the persistence of the old religion:

Idinadaan [ng mga Indiong paniwala pa rin sa dating relihiyon] sa pagdiriwang ng mga kasiyahan ang kanilang pag-aalay ng sakripisyo, at inihahain sa demonyo kung ano man ang kinakailangan nilang kainin. Pinababanguhan nila ang mga anito, at inaawitan ng matatalinhagang awitin, sa pamumuno ng lalaki o babae na tinatawag nilang katalonan [priest].

Ang mga naroroon ay sumasagot sa awit, hinihiling sa mga anito na ibigay ang kanilang pangangailangan. Sa ilang mga distrito, laluna sa kabundukan, kapag nasa-tao na ang demonyo sa katauhan ng katalonang namumuno (diabolic possession) *sa harap ng sumasamba, ang nabanggit na katalonan ay kinakailangang itali sa puno ng kanyang mga kasama upang di siya mapinsala ng pangangalit ng demonyo.*

The point is that while the conscription for the Cavite shipyards was the immediate and main reason for the Sumuroy revolt, many of the rebels may have remained *babaylan* believers even if they had already adopted the Christian practices — or at least they believed in both religions through internal syncretic accommodation.

In resorting to a rebel explosion, such men had a short fuse.

Back to Bankaw before we go further on Sumuroy. Bankaw must have been very old already when he took to the hills and possibly stubbed his toe once or twice — he had enthusiastically welcomed Miguel Lopez de Legazpi himself some 60 years earlier.

Perhaps he was the oldest rebel ever in rebel-infested Philippine history — maybe older than the conspirator Artemio Ricarte rummaging with the Japanese in the Cordilleras in the 1940s for the mysterious residual elements of the Katipunan Revolution.

How did ancient Bankaw look doddering around with ferocious fellow Warays as young and as truculent as our latter-day Waray OXO and Sigue-Sigue gangs?

Soon the other towns in Leyte rose up too, like a blistering flame leaping from the phosphorescent heat of a common oppression. A Jesuit fled from the tumultuous island to warn his fellow Spaniards in Cebu. A strong expedition of 40 vessels brought a handful of armored Spanish soldiers in command of hundreds of half-naked native warriors who crushed the rebellion.

The aged head of Bankaw as well as that of his second son was lopped off and, as we said, displayed to the townspeople as a warning against anyone tempted to translate into external action his dangerous internal reflections of insurrection.

When Sumuroy revolted the Spaniards asked anyone who would want to bother to kill him. Sumuroy's followers in response sent them the cut-off head of a pig instead, without making it *lechon* first.

Alas, a little more than a year later, during which the Sumuroy rebellion raged on, implacable and unbowed, these same native followers turned traitor and assassinated him — and delivered his own severed head to the Spaniards, who naturally displayed it with more relish than the pig's.

This hideous sort of medieval advertisement was a favor returned by Filipinos with impunity. For example, in the Pangasinan revolt of 1660, Andres Malong's forces sacked a town, "caught up with the fleeing Spanish *alcalde mayor* and...killed him and his guard."[6]

The following year, 1661, the rebels killed more Spaniards and in Lingayen "they entered the town at sunset to see the heads of the new [Spanish] alcalde, his wife, sister-in-law and of two other Spaniards impaled on stakes for public view."

At least Bankaw died in battle against the enemy, however slow-moving and flat-footed he had become, while the young and agile Sumuroy was wiped out by his own fellow natives — like Bonifacio, like Luna, like Mrs. Aurora Quezon, like Ninoy Aquino.

The details of the Sumuroy killing, done away from the bleary-eyed Spaniards who often wrote what they saw, and who are our only primary sources about that long and tragic colonial era, naturally have been lost to history.

A most moving part of the historic pandemonium was that Sumuroy's mother fought valiantly in battle and perished with Leonidan significance — the first Filipino woman fighter followed by many other great women who struggled on the battlefield heroically during the Revolution against Spain, and later in the war with the Americans and then the Japanese, and much later in the vexatious times of martial law.

The story of Sumuroy — some spell his name Sumoroy — bears retelling because of its magnitude, its character and its pathos. It was a rebellion that was large — and gripping, literally and figuratively.

It all began in Palapag, a big Pacific-facing town also in Samar. As we said, Sumuroy's father was a seething native priest of the old *babaylan* religion of the *anitos* who told his son to send the Spanish curate to heaven — forcibly, for many friars, however optimistic, were not in a hurry to go to paradise in spite of its come-ons. The euphoria of living in the Philippine archipelago where they reigned and ruled was good enough for the meantime.

Without delay, drama or delirium, Sumuroy committed the deed before the friar could say *dandansoy*.

He presumably did it with mixed volumes of filial piety and existential impiety — to the resounding jubilation of many of his compatriots who promptly joined him in his slam-bang revolt. For the duration of his triumphant but precarious rebellion, he was celebrated by the Warays as a conquering hero.

As pointed out, the uprising he ignited scraped and oscillated all the way to Leyte and Guimaras and Northern Mindanao up to faraway Zamboanga — and Masbate and Camiguin.

In Cebu and Bohol the first stirrings of sympathetic unrest were effectively pacified by the friars. But most ominously for the Spaniards, the commotion also traversed and lacerated Bicol, from where the scintillating Waray writer Pete Goudin Jr. says Sumuroy was supposed to march on to Manila, seat of Spanish tyranny and grandeur.

That meant that Sumuroy and his coterie, not just the Bicolanos, wanted to pummel and sack Intramuros itself, and for this they must undertake the formidable effort of crossing San Bernardino Strait from Samar to Sorsogon at a time when today's ferry was not yet envisioned even in their most phantasmagoric dreams.

It is tempting to call Sumuroy's struggle a revolution because in its wake so many towns rose up in revolt — related to one another in time, in sentiment and in the reasons for their revolt.

The reasons were many — from the backbreaking tribute to war conscriptions to exile and torture and the innumerable caravan of injustices wrought by the Spaniards even for so petty an infraction as insufficient respect.

But the immediate reason was the rounding up of men to serve as workers in Cavite's famous, or infamous, shipyards — perhaps the biggest in the world for many decades, what with the galleon trade and the need for ships in Spain's many overseas wars.

Parenthetically, the galleons were also the biggest ships in the world at that time, and therefore the prized targets of marine highwaymen.

It all meant forced labor — one that even Hercules himself would not have sneezed at. Samar, in spite of its distance, was chosen as the site of recruitment because through the decades the manpower of nearby Pampanga, Bataan, Laguna and Batangas had been piteously depleted, and in fact some of their villages had revolted because of it.

The grinding process of shipbuilding began with the felling of gigantic timber in virginal forests — so gigantic that they would have been impervious even to the mechanized smuggling of today's illegal loggers. The poor wretched Indios, without the help of Mitsubishi cranes, were whipped and kicked to drag the huge logs across jungles and ravines and craggy wooded valleys, amid much heckling by snakes and mosquitoes and leeches.

They may have suffered more than the weather-beaten workers who built the pyramids in Egypt or the Great Wall of China.

Not a few of those hard-pressed Filipinos expired a few days after starting work, long before they reached the shipyards, where tedious nonstop work also awaited them, and where many more perished.

Even if the workers — or slaves — survived a season of work which spanned a few weeks, they went home to their villages only to be threatened with the subtle squeezes of individual starvation and internal corrosions of communal famine. This was because the menfolk, having gone to Cavite, were not around to till the soil at home.

The Spaniards were aghast at the scale of the Sumuroy-inspired uprisings. They organized a three-pronged counterattack from Manila, Cebu and Zamboanga, with the usual handful of Spanish soldiers in command of hundreds of native warriors. Now they included the so-called Lutaos of Zamboanga, many of whom were part-Muslims and were particularly ferocious in their service of the Spaniards.

In spite of their having organized an enormous expeditionary military shebang, the Spaniards were conciliatory and able to persuade most of the fearful rebels to lay down their arms — except Sumuroy and his men in Palapag, who would not receive mercy for setting a bad example, and who of course did not ask for any.

That all had surrendered even in Bicol while Sumuroy had not — this only showed a rare occasion when a movement's palpitating center of gravity was in the Visayas rather than in Luzon.

They built a defiant redoubt on top of a hill which could be ascended by the enemy only at great risk of disaster. Their lair could be approached only through a very steep slope for a frontal attack, in which any army could be repulsed by a rain of unmanageable boulders.

And the only other approach was a narrow pass on the rear side which only one man could squeeze through at a time — and get easily punctured by the *talibong* of the defenders.

As the awesome, newly arrived Spanish forces bivouacked in their camp one night, the enterprising Sumuroy, acknowledged by yesterday's Spaniards and today's historians as a great leader, decided to give them a taste of Filipino valor and Filipino arms.

He and his courageous band assaulted the numerically and technologically superior enemy like a swarm of mad *tamaraws*. The result was one of the bloodiest encounters

counters ever, where the attackers had to eventually withdraw carrying with them their dead and wounded.

The enraged Spaniards unleashed a vicious counterattack on the rebel stronghold on the hill, only to be castigated with heavy losses on their part — and on Sumuroy's.

Since it was June-July of 1650, it was rainy season, and it exacerbated the hardships and agonies on both sides. And finally the Spaniards used the rains as cover.

On July 2, it didn't rain, it poured, as in the apocalyptic Ormoc flood of recent times (1993), where more than 4,000 Leyteños perished in a few minutes of unexpected deluge. The Spaniards and their Filipino lackeys were able to move unnoticed one by one through the narrow pass behind Sumuroy's lines, overeager to slit insolent Indio throats. Sumuroy's sentinels had taken cover and probably indulged in a midnight siesta because of the rains that approached biblical proportions — and of the fatal presumption that in such formidable circumstances it was foolhardy to attack.

And yet, it was wise precisely because it was foolhardy. It surprised beyond salvation the rebels, who were slammed from behind and damned in front. They had no choice now but to succumb.

It is not known exactly how the followers of Sumuroy killed their own leader, or why they were persuaded to do the deed, or at what ignoble moment they cut his head off. Did the Spaniards bribe them, as in the case of Magalat's assassins?

Did they kill him while in a later skirmish? It is said he was still alive after the last decisive battle, but from his new lair he refused overtures of surrender until he was decapitated and was forced to surrender his soul to his *babaylan* Creator — shortly after which it may be presumed he engaged the friar he had assassinated in divine conversation in the presence of St. Peter stroking his cock, no pun intended.

What is known is that his assassins personally delivered his head to the Spaniards, although no Salome had demanded it.

Of course, besides John the Baptist, there was another parallel to Sumuroy. It was the unfortunate general Pompey, whose decapitated head was offered to the advancing Julius Caesar and his legions in a jar by the nervous Egyptians who thought they could ingratiate themselves with the Roman conqueror by assassinating his sworn enemy and rival.

Instead of being exhilarated, entertained, Caesar wept.

Many wept for Sumuroy. Some of his brooding lieutenants managed to escape from the debacle. But the Spaniards, stunned by the scale of the uprisings his reverberating revolt had triggered in other places, were unwilling to provoke another such defiance. They offered the hand of conciliation to the rebels, especially those in other towns whom they considered less infamous and less threatening.

They gave some of them full pardon although others, when caught, were promptly executed. But in the hearts of his countrymen, particularly of Warays, Sumuroy lives.

4. The Diego Silang Assassination and Gabriela Execution

LET US look back to what we have seen on the previous pages:

1521 —   Lapulapu slew Magellan.
1571 —   Legazpi occupied Manila and
           the king of Macabebe perished
           in battle.
1588 —   The Tondo Conspiracy was crushed.

In the exact midpoint of the next century, meaning the year 1650, Sumuroy was assassinated and his rebellion extinguished, as we have seen in the previous chapter.

Another century later, in 1763, Diego Silang was assassinated. After four months his wife Gabriela, who had continued his revolt, was captured and hideously executed.

This is the story of the heroic Silang couple — one of the most sensational, and the saddest, in Philippine history.

Sumuroy and Silang lived more than 100 years apart. While Sumuroy and his people did not leave any records written by themselves, it was the Spaniards who customarily wrote about the events of their day.

In the case of Diego Silang much later, there are additional materials in that a few of his letters have been preserved. And they help us take a closer look at him.

Also, the ruling Spaniards among themselves — from Governor-General Anda to the Spanish provincial administrators and friars in Ilocos — wrote and corresponded more about Silang than was much earlier done about Sumuroy.

These writers were Spaniards and some of them mortal enemies of Silang in Vigan, and therefore could not be expected to sing hallelujahs for him. And yet events as events could not be denied. Their narration, even if colored, could not entirely conceal what was good in him and his revolt from the viewpoint of the oppressed and of Filipinos today.

Silang belonged to a higher social category than Sumuroy, who worked for a living in the coastal fort keeping it tidy and watching grimly for the slightest signs of those dreaded Moro raiders from the truculent south.

Silang lived as a houseboy serving the curate in the Vigan convent. He stayed on to rise much later as a trusted messenger perambulating among the local communities. This could only mean he was personally known not only in Vigan but also in many towns and this may have helped him when he revolted.

He must have been familiar with the terrain. But in his revolt later he was immediately victorious in Vigan, and did not have occasion to fight in the other towns. It was Gabriela who later had to deal with the larger terrain as a factor in the struggle.

Also, he was so busy in his headquarters in all the months of his administration that he failed to visit the countryside although he wanted to attend to many things there.

In the years before the revolt, his tasks under the employ of the curate included taking letters and other things from Vigan to Manila and back, with both outgoing and incoming mail carried by the galleon to and from Mexico. And, of course, letters to and from Spain itself.

He remained in this capacity as mailman even after the *cura* was transferred to Manila when he, Silang, was 25 years old.

His trips took many days at a time, by ship or by land. Or much longer, since the galleons' schedule was often delayed by piratical attacks, withering storms, execrable corals and navigational nincompooperies.

Despite his friar connection, he was of low stature — he was not a friend but somewhat a little higher than a servant, possibly with informal compensation which we could venture to guess was measly.

This shows he was not exactly of the *principalia* whom he later fought to the death, that he personally was neither landed nor engaged in some lucrative business or trade.

He did not have much formal education, and could not read as well as the local clerks. But from all indications he was highly intelligent and resourceful.

He could speak good Spanish — apparently because he lived in the *cura's* house and there, in addition to his messengerial excursions, met many Spanish-speaking people. And one who spoke good Spanish enhanced his own stature in those days just as speaking good English was a wow during the days of colonial mentality in the Commonwealth era up to the 1960s.

He lived in a milieu where women married only men of more or less the same means, or at least whose distance in socioeconomic status was still bridgeable in spite of the embarrassing odds which, to confront, called for great moral — or immoral — courage.

Therefore his marriage to Gabriela could mean he was not a specimen of poverty. On their wedding day Gabriela was about 26 years old and, more important, propertied. Her wealth was from a previous marriage with a doddering old man into whose waning marital clasps she was brought by his parents at the age of 20.

With his long absences due to his postal errands, during which he left the childless Gabriela in Vigan, Diego did not remain ignorant of the political or socioeconomic landscape of the capital itself. And in those days, anyone who had gone to the Great City and returned to the rustic countryside somehow acquired, or at least was bestowed, an enviable mystique and was thus more inclined to assume leadership.

In later times Spaniards were to comment that any *provinciano* who had gone to Manila, especially students, came back to his rustic pueblo a *filibustero*, meaning a subversive.

Presumably Diego did not suffer from an inferiority complex in his home province at a time when the Spaniards and, under their blessing, the mestizos and *principalia* and the businessmen and the big landed people were lording it over as in other wretched places in the Philippines.

As he planned to organize his revolt, he meant to be leader not just of Vigan but of the whole of Ilocos. Before he unfurled his flag of rebellion, he talked first with the leaders in the southern towns, whom he probably knew well from his messengerial days, to expand his intended jurisdiction, at the same time feeding their already half-open mandibles of rebellion.

He thought from the start that his clout and his understanding of the issues were wide, as we shall see. Was he some kind of an Oriental Midas — of whom it may be said that for a time everything he touched turned into a revolt?

A historian claims Diego Silang did not correctly estimate the extent of the upper class hierarchy's collective power which he gored, and this contributed largely to his mortal difficulties.

That historian is New Zealander David Routledge, who in 1979 came out with a book about Silang. Although difficult to read because of its peristaltic incoherence and constipated paragraphs which are often so kilometric that they look like a Bicol railway accident, it is more substantial and substantive than anything published about the rebel leader.

He had the benefit of researching in the academic catacombs of Seville, Spain.[1]

There he found materials that were previously unknown. With the encouragement of his penniless peers in the University of the Philippines who otherwise could have done a better, bigger job, the precious materials increased his English-speaking temerity to spin a scholarly production from Spanish-written scrolls.

We shall go back to him later. In the meantime let us look at an outline of what is commonly known about Diego Silang's life and insurrection.

He was, probably, born in Pangasinan and, certainly, baptized in Vigan, where his birth year is recorded as 1730. This means he was 33 years old when assassinated, two years younger than Rizal and fellow Vigan-born Fr. Burgos when they were executed.

As an example of historical clumsiness, others say he was born in Manila where he became a *cochero*.[2] His mother was from Vigan.

In 1755, seven years before he as rebel leader harangued his compatriots, intimidated the Spaniards and discombobulated the *principalia*, he suffered a shipwreck off Bolinao in Pangasinan while transporting his friar's hardwood furniture to Manila. The surviving passengers and members of the crew who escaped drowning or shark's teeth vigorously swam ashore — only to be dispatched also to Kingdom Come by the waiting Aetas.

Somehow those Aetas made a solitary exception by allowing Diego Silang to live as their hostage.

The then 25-year-old postman was spared "on account of his engaging personality and handsome physical appearance"[3] — a description that may be apocryphal, but may have been near the truth considering that he became the leader of a major revolt.

Or the fellow who invented the story — how did he know the Aetas' reason for sparing Diego Silang, was he a mindreader or did the Aetas tell him? — may have himself known Silang was engaging and handsome, or that this was the common knowledge of him. Would he have had the humor to say so if Silang was, in fact, well-known in past tradition to be ugly and dumb?

It appears those were a different sort of Aetas — assuming they were really the killers — who according to anthropologists have been known throughout the centuries to be friendly, peaceful and nonviolent up to our present day, unlike other incredibly ferocious ethnics in the Luzon highlands. Could it be a case of mistaken identity — not of the victims but of the victimizers?

For six months Silang lived with them, augmenting his familiarity with Manila hustle with an intimacy of the Aeta way of life.

Not long after, the Bolinao curate — some say a Recollet friar lumbering around in Pangasinan — ransomed him. This was not exactly an omen of things to come where the friars helped arrange his assassination. Since the Aetas were not as a rule greedy, and the hostage was a pure Indio and, further, the friar sacrificed for someone who was nothing to him the money he could have kept in his *kaban*, the ransom must have been a pittance.

His old *cura* in Vigan, now stationed in Manila, may have given the Bolinao friar an encouraging long-distance nudge, for after all the hostage was his sidekick. And friars in those days, especially those who had been in the same region, knew one another. They scratched each other's backs. We may recall that Silang since his childhood had been with the *cura*, who may have learned to value — even love — him apart from the other Indios.

Silang upon release trudged straight to his father's original hometown of Lingayen and met his relatives. One of them became a Pangasinan rebel leader himself — Andres Lopez, whom we will meet again on the eve of Silang's Ilocos bedlam.

The British landed in Malate, Manila in September 1762, when Silang was in Intramuros waiting for the galleon to arrive from Acapulco. Then in a month's time they attacked Intramuros itself and Governor-General Rojo surrendered the city — only the city, it was later stressed, not the rest of the islands where Spain's flag kept on flying proudly. By this time Silang had left Manila.

At the same time Rojo appointed the energetic Simon de Anda, soon to become governor-general — and soon to play a role in the Spaniards' dealing with the Silang revolt — as commander of Spain's armies outside the city.

From Manila Silang first went to Pangasinan again. There he found the people, as in many other places, alternately brooding and agog about the humiliation dealt the Spaniards by the British. It disposed them to rise against the dastardly Spanish rule.

We may safely presume that Silang himself, in the face of the Spaniards' eggregious Intramuros debacle, spent much of his rustic journey entertaining dangerous thoughts of rebellion and freedom.

Silang's relative whom we mentioned before, Andres Lopez, was about to lead a revolt in Lingayen. His men had successfully demanded from the intimidated Spaniards his formal appointment as master-of-camp — maybe this meant chief of town chiefs, or *cabo mayor*, or *cabo* of *cabo*s, or provincial commander.

Routledge loudly states that Silang helped conceive, and instigate, the Pangasinan rebellion of Lopez.[4] Corpuz only says that Silang left for Ilocos to start his own rebellion there "with Lopez's consent or knowledge."

Later, when Silang had launched his uprising, he "extended his rebellion to as far as Pangasinan and the Cagayan Valley," says Teodoro Agoncillo.[5] Horacio de la Costa writes the same thing: "Silang spread [his] revolt to Pangasinan and Cagayan Valley on his own initiative."[6]

Let us go back to the time when the British had landed in Malate and had not yet conquered Intramuros. As we said, Silang at that time was in Manila, where he habitually lodged with the Augustinians. They were the rulers of Ilocos and his *cura*'s religious order. He slept probably in some uncomfortable part of the big house reserved for functional Indios, not far from the functional horses.

That Silang had extraordinary possibilities could be gleaned from the fact that he at times stayed in the house of a dignitary who had become his friend, one Santiago Orendain, apparently an intellectual progressive, a nonracist and nonsnobbish lawyer "who belonged to the highest level of mestizo society."[7]

More important, he was *asesor*, a Spanish title which means legal adviser to no less than the governor-general himself in preparing judicial decisions. Routledge claims that:

> Orendain discussed the imminent Spanish defeat with his young friend from Ilocos, particularly the declaration of [the British commanding general] Draper and [the naval commander] Admiral Cornish which promised that if the people should give their allegiance to the king of England, freedom of religion and freedom of trade would be assured — something which carried weight in both Pangasinan and Ilocos.[8]

When Pangasinan under Lopez, and Ilocos under Silang, massed and confronted their respective local Spanish rulers prior to their armed revolt, they presented some significant demands which led Routledge to say: "The influence of Orendain's trained legal mind and ill-disposition towards the friars and the Spanish government is to be detected. The Pangasinan leaders would have listened with close attention to Silang's account of what had happened in Manila, and the views of Orendain would have figured...."[9] Really?

Note that the British took Intramuros in October 1762, when Silang had left the city and was now in Pangasinan. He left for Ilocos the following month of November and openly took up arms in December. In another month's time, or January of the incoming year of 1763, he was master of Ilocos. In May, five months later, he was dead.

Leaving Lopez in Pangasinan for Vigan, Silang tarried in the southern towns talking, as we said, with local leaders who were also predisposed to revolt like the Pangasinenses. When he arrived in Vigan, conspiracies had in fact already been slithering around but only on the discursive level.

On December 14, some 2,000 men recognizing him as their chief gathered on Vigan's fringes but did not find it necessary to attack. Events were now to move fast.

The bishop fled to Bantay, where he was held prisoner by Silang's charges in the convent beside the big church. The *alcalde mayor*, the equivalent of today's provincial governor, who was a Spaniard escaped, clutching silver and gold coins.

The *principalia* in Vigan and nearby towns were in confusion and disarray. They were mostly pro-Spanish. As a class Silang had called them enemies of the people collaborating with Spanish oppression and exploiting the lower classes along with the *alcalde mayor*. They organized from Laoag a bristling military expedition craving for Armaggedon against Silang.

They assaulted him southeast of Vigan early on Christmas Day — an inappropriate timing, but whose inappropriateness they may have hoped would help them catch him leisurely eating garbanzos with Gabriela. No such luck.

They were repulsed, and scattered nqt like sheep but like the wolves that they were, beyond regrouping. With this victory Silang established control of Vigan and many towns, and he received many more volunteers to join his steadily burgeoning forces.

On that same Christmas Day a few hours later, a gigantic concentration of some 6,000 men was seen in front of the great church in Vigan, now under control by Silang's forces who were also dominant in many Ilocos towns.

They included ethnic Tinguians, who were much dreaded as the fiercest warriors of the robust North. Gabriela's mother was a Tinguian, and her relatives on one hand and the Silang movement on the other therefore had a psychological affinity.

A massacre began. Seven people were killed, including one whose body was thrown from an open window on to upraised stakes, and then dismembered. Benito Estrada, a half-brother of Gabriela on the Tinguian side of her family, ate the heart, saying that it belonged to a brave man.

Silang sat under a tree outside the church ... and watched impassively without taking part in the proceedings. It is not clear whether he ordered the massacre to rid himself of the most actively pro-Spanish elements in Vigan .... Silang certainly accepted that he could do nothing to stop the killing once it started, and may well have been content not to try.[10]

Silang had himself acclaimed by the people as *cabo mayor*, in the same rank as Lopez, a parallel which could mean that Routledge's Silang-Pangasinan theory may not entirely be impertinent. Note that Silang wanted only to be *cabo mayor*, not king as his detractors charged.

He had a house in Vigan besides the fomidable camp in a nearby redoubt which is now called Silang Hill, which he used as headquarters. From this ancient home settlement of the grand conquistador Juan de Salcedo now governed the new ruler of Ilocos, an Indio, finally.

Because his was a revolt of the people, by the people and for the people, and why not throw in the rest and say also with the people, Silang through his village criers promptly drumbeated his incredibly propeople reforms — drumbeated literally, for in those days drums were used to catch the people's attention for public announcements.

First he jettisoned the rapacious age-old tribute and the gruelling forced labor. With the swish of a feather pen he abolished decades-old taxation on the poor! He then decreed taxes for those able to pay, and this meant the *principalia*, who all the more resolved to help the Spaniards end Silang's rule.

Since it took months to collect taxes, how on earth did he finance in the meantime his government and army which numbered by the thousands? He simply took from the rich, like cattle, and confiscated church property.

His new soak-the-rich taxation scheme included a collection of 100 pesos from every friar, a huge amount which had come from the people anyway. Perhaps he was only trying to recover the ill-gotten wealth. Later this was reduced to 80 pesos upon request of a miserly friar friend.

Earlier, before the uprising, he led a group which demanded from the religious authorities led by the bishop named Bernardo Ustariz the removal of the "extortion-ate [Spanish] alcalde."

Silang declared that forced personal labor, like work in the convent and in Spanish/ *principalia* households and in ships as rowers and so on, was

illegal so long as Spanish sovereignty remained less than complete by virtue of the occupation of the capital by a foreign power. The provinces were to be estab-lished on a military footing in defence against the English, with command in the hands of a *provinciano*.

Silang insisted that the people wanted that their loyalty to Two Crowns [God and the king of Spain] should be formally acknowledged, and in a sepa-rate statement declared his intention to wrest power from the *principalia* and restore it to the people[11]

Wow!

To Routledge, there was in other promulgations of Silang "a subtlety of expres-sion" that revealed the Orendain hand — they declared a revolt, yet they impinged on a legal interpretation of a state of affairs. He points out: "The rebels did not say that they refused to pay tribute or to render personal services, but rather that these were made illegal by the surrender of power by the [governor-general]." Also, they were rebels fighting the king's forces, but in the very act of rebelling insisted on a formal recognition of their loyalty to the king!

Like Disraeli's opposition, they were His Majesty's most distinguished and ever-loyal rebels!

With the threat of eternal hellfire hanging over their heads, they were of course all loyal to the Christian God, but promptly imprisoned in the convent beside the big Bantay stone church not only Ustariz but other friars. Yet they did not touch most town parish priests and allowed them to continue with their sacerdotal services to the people, like saying mass and making available the other sacraments.

Otherwise they would have lost both popular — and unpopular — support. In those days, almost everybody was Catholic.

In this, Diego Silang was different from other rebel leaders like Sumuroy and some Katipuneros during the Revolution more than 200 years later who executed, sometimes after the much-desired torture, the friars. To use the word Richard Nixon popularized in policy debates when he was a young rising congressman damning those who were "soft on communism," Silang was "soft" on friars.

This was because Silang wanted to get their support for his movement — after all, he was not against Christ or the king, he was against local Spanish officials and the native *principalia* only. In fact his *pronunciamiento* said defense preparations would be made against the Protestant English.

Of course he did not know that the Spanish king himself as a matter of policy regarded the friars as indispensable to Spanish colonization, which included the subjection of Ilocos to local Spanish rulers against whom he was revolting.

With undiminished contempt for the Indio Silang, the bishop Ustariz kept urging anyone who would listen to fight the rebellion with all might and means.

In fact he ordered that Silang and his supporters be deprived of the sacraments, like Communion and Christian burial. The most feared was the withdrawal of absolution of sins, a denial which meant one would surely go to hell and forever burn like crazy.

Silang tried his best to stop the pestilential communication between Ustariz and his parish priests, but the bishop still succeeded in regularly sending out messages to overthrow Silang, even to Governor-General Anda who was in Pampanga organizing forces to launch against the British in Intramuros.

Curiously Silang, still overflowing with the milk of human kindness, did not kill him.

In fact, it was because of Ustariz' missives, full of intrigues and falsehoods against Silang, that Anda finally "invited" Silang to report to him in Pampanga within nine days. This was actually a command and a trap because at the same time he secretly ordered his arrest.

Like Hermano Puli of Tayabas more than a hundred years later who was confronted by another governor-general with the same backbreaking choice, he ignored Anda.

That the governor-general himself wanted to smash him was one of the reasons why Silang finally turned to the British for help. Other reasons were: one, the ecclesiastical authorities in Ilocos were hopelesssly hostile to him in spite of his reaching out his hand to them and finally planned to kill him; and, two, he could not stand up alone against the Spanish armies.

Ustariz and the friars stood fast with the *principalia* who were anti-Silang because Silang was anti-*principalia*. This was what Routledge called the solid hierarchy whose power to remain united was the controlling factor that sprang out of their common interest to remain in power — not because of devotion to God and king — which Silang had underestimated.

He allowed the Holy Week rites to go on, not really because of the friars but because the people, common and uncommon, were begging for it. Lo and behold, it was at this time that he learned of the murderous plot. He heard that the friars wanted his assassination on that Holy Thursday, a plan different from the latter one that finally succeeded in killing him.

Another curiousity was that even if Silang was the provincial ruler and ensconced mightily in Vigan, and had appointed town *cabo*s all over who were ruling effectively, there were some prevailing anti-Silang, pro-Spanish official elements and outbursts.

For example, in January 1763, one month after Silang had seized power, two "Silanistas" in Paoay were tried by pro-Spanish *principalia* officials and promptly executed. The uproar was such that those who issued the sentence fled to Cagayan.

On the other hand, some of Silang's followers sowed terror. In Laoag, where there were many pro-Spanish *principalia*, "a decapitated head was thrown into a jar of rice wine to entertain the Tinguian warriors, and the tumult was allegedly so great that women miscarried."[12]

The British could not fight in the provinces, for they lacked manpower and logistics to extend their conquest beyond the walls of Intramuros. Silang had written them of his desire to accept the sovereignty of the English king, pointing out that he had heard about their announcement proclaiming freedom of religion and of trade. He made it clear he did not wish to desert his Catholic religion.

But when the British wanted the Augustinian friars to be sent to Manila, Silang agreed, but time ran out on him before he could carry this out. However, he was able to issue an instruction to gather the friars in the Bantay convent, and some of them expressed fears in a subsequent meeting there that Silang wanted to execute them together.

The British sent a small ship, or boat, to Vigan carrying his appointment as "Maestro de Campo General y Teniente de Justicia Mayor," with a regalia of office composed of a hat, a robe and a gold-tipped baton. But the British lacked weaponry, and all they could send was a small bronze cannon.

At least they also sent printed paper forms for the appointment of town officials under Silang's government — these forms were of no mean use in those eras long past when written documents were regarded among the illiterate common people as an unearthly phenomenon almost with mystical power.

No one needed to tell the British how important Silang was to them because of his position in Ilocos. Besides, throughout the Philippines, no other person, let alone a successful rebel leader, had offered to support them.

Although some Filipinos who considered themselves loyal to the church were not loyal to the Spaniards, most Filipinos were, of course, loyal to their God, meaning their Church, and were therefore loyal to the Spaniards in the face of the visiting Protestants.

Why, even Silang who was disloyal to Spanish rule was actually a good Catholic who was often seen praying the rosary and always wore it around his neck.

Somehow the British commander, while saying in his letter that under the British-Silang dispensation freedom from taxation and personal service and freedom of religion will continue, also sensed a personal danger to Silang. In his letter he "laid emphasis on the importance of security to Silang's own person."[13]

Was this a simple reminder of how important Silang was to the situation — or a long-distance premonition of death?

The wretched Ustariz, with some friars gathered in his convent in the Bantay church, hatched another plot to kill Silang. During their unchristian deliberations, a Spanish mestizo, Miguel Vicos, came. In the northern towns he had led an anti-government uprising in sympathy with Silang's southern revolt.

But Silang had become a towering personality and Vicos was regarded only as one of his secondary supporters.

It is said Vicos felt he was not amply rewarded by Diego, which meant that like many others, he had joined the revolt with palpitating courage but for material or personal aggrandizement. Besides, this mongrel was probably envious of the preeminence of Silang, who was only an Indio.

Furthermore, one of Silang's original plans was to expel from the province Spanish mestizos along with pure Spaniards.

Vicos' demon-eyed companion in the conspiratorial confab was one Pedro Becbec, another envious malcontent who had led the Silang forces in Abra, and whose onomatopeious name did not inspire confidence in the abodes even of the non-paranoid.

From Vicos' own medieval mouth first came out the words that he would personally kill Silang, saying it was God's purpose. In short, God had become a ventriloquist communicating through Vicos' tongue.

This must have impressed the detained friars even though they were possibly jaded from a long concatenation of sinful but unfulfilled plots. In describing the killing, it is better to give Routledge's account which is based on the writings of a Vigan friar during Silang's time, Fr. Pedro Vivar, in his "Relacion de las Alzamientos de la Ciudad de Vigan": "Ustariz gave his blessing to the venture and produced a holy relic to ensure its success. The deed was first scheduled on May 30 but then advanced a couple of days for fear the plot would be discovered and thwarted by Silang's bodyguards."[14]

The fact that both Vicos and Becbec had been known as loyal assistants of the uprising allowed them to reach Silang's presence without arousing suspicion. Becbec pretended to wish for advice on certain questions relating to funds, and brought his account book. Vicos loaded a blunderbuss [a short-barreled pistol — Ed.] and put it under his clothes.

The two made their way to Silang's headquarters accompanied by a considerable crowd to add conviction to the supposed reason for the visit. Not all, however, were allowed to approach close. Vicos placed himself among some bamboos where he could see into the *sala* as Silang came out of his chamber.

As soon as Vicos saw Silang he wished him good afternoon — Silang returned the greeting, at the same time turning as if to go back to his room. Vicos promptly raised the blunderbuss and discharged it to such effect that Silang, taking the entire charge in his body, staggered and fell dead.

Several *principalia* from Santa gave the body a number of stabs, saying it still lived. Vicos assured them that [Silang] was dead, but did not stop them as they said Silang had been responsible for the death of some of their relatives [Others] tested their weapons on the corpse.

The assassins returned in triumph to report their success to Ustariz, who congratulated them [and] directed an order to Silang's town heads reminding them of the offer of pardon to all who repented and returned to the fold.[15]

Vicos, fearing reprisal, fled to Cagayan. Becbec remained in Vigan, with more than ample opportunities to protect himself because he was promptly rewarded with the post of *justicia mayor*. He immediately abused his powers by restoring taxes on the poor and the old tribute! With the friars' instruction or consent? Parenthetically, these abuses by Becbec helped Gabriela rouse the people to continue the revolt.

After helping pacify the North, Vicos later returned to Vigan and, of course, was also rewarded with the same post.

Was Gabriela present when Diego was shot? A few days later in the same Vigan house she openly talked to her loyalists of continuing the struggle. No one dared to arrest or kill her.

Then she and her late husband's uncle, Nicolas Carino, managed to organize a neither-small-nor-big army of 2,000. On June 24, a month after Diego's elimination, they attacked the Becbec forces in the small town of Santa, won the battle and released two former top lieutenants of Diego who had been held as prisoners and who now happily rejoined the insurrection.

But Becbec, who was visiting Santa and whom they planned to capture, escaped.

Three days later, on June 27, somewhere between Sinait and Cabugao, they clashed with a big force organized from Batac by pro-Spanish *principalia*. It was the biggest battle then, fought mainly by Filipinos against Filipinos.

The bloodbath was staggering on both sides, with Gabriela's forces suffering some 200 casualties and 600 taken prisoner. It was a major blow to Gabriela and her forces, but because of their courageous persistence it was not conclusive.

Two more bloody clashes occurred — one in Sinait on July 3 and another in Bantay on July 9 — and again both sides sustained huge losses. This time Gabriela and her forces were dispersed. It appears that the Gabriela stage of the rebellion was more gruesome and decisive and had more major encounters with the enemy than the Diego stage.

After the agonizing Bantay bloodletting, the Diego-Gabriela rebellion, which had started only some nine months ago, practically was over because of its enormous casualties on the battlefield wrought by the better-equipped, more numerous enemy.

Gabriela sadly went back to her Tinguian territory of Pidigan, in whose high mountains the pursuing pro-Spanish forces, accompanied by Vicos, captured her. Some 90 of Gabriela's lieutenants and men were hanged in Vigan and in other towns where they were caught. The rest were imprisoned or flogged.

And why was that diabolical Vicos there? It may be recalled that Diego had confiscated properties and money from the rich and the friars, and it was rumored that after he died, Gabriela was in possession of a huge trove of wealth.

But how could this be true? It was never said that Gabriela paid her lieutenants or army handsomely. Or was this because she was an Ilocana? Perhaps Vicos tortured the captured Gabriela in a worse fashion than Agapito Bonzon allegedly tortured Gregoria de Jesus over so-called Katipunan funds. Who knows?

But apparently Vicos heard nothing or found nothing, and no story or rumor persisted in those days or in later times about a so-called Gabriela wealth deeply buried in the Tinguian mountains or elsewhere. Or maybe some people today may start digging for it in Abra besides searching, again, for the Yamashita gold.

Neni Sta. Romana Cruz describes Gabriela's last moments in words that are powerful because they are simple:

Because Gabriela's men were the most defiant among the rebels, a special kind of death was planned for them. One by one, each soldier was hanged, lined along the coastal towns for everyone to see. Their bodies were left hanging to sway along with the breeze from the sea.

This was to serve as a reminder to anyone who dared fight the Spaniards. And to Maria Josefa Gabriela Silang was given the doubly painful experience of being the last one to die. The Spaniards wanted her to see how each of her men would go.

She had fought like a man. Thus, she also deserved a man's sentence, according to the Spaniards.

Gabriela was taken to the plaza of Vigan early in the morning. She was hanged before a curious crowd of Spaniards and Filipinos, all in a holiday mood. They were celebrating the capture of a dreaded enemy of the government.

What sorrow she must have felt during these last few moments as her very own countrymen shouted, "Long live Spain!"

It is said that the 32-year-old Gabriela stayed calm and courageous during her final moments as she took the 13 steps that led to the scaffold.

Even in death, Gabriela was treated as an enemy who did not deserve a decent burial. No one bothered to take care of her body days after the execution. Today the final resting place of this extraordinary woman remains a mystery.[16]

The marriage of Diego and Gabriela occurred some five years before the revolt. If her previous marriage to the old man was not enviably ecstatic, theirs in all probability may have been an exceedingly happy one in spite of Diego's long absences.

Just like Diego, Gabriela grew up under the care of a Vigan friar. This is because her mother was a Tinguian, and her parents followed the Tinguian custom of entrusting daughters to persons with authority. "This did not mean they no longer loved their own children. The children just had two sets of parents — the real and the foster parents."[17]

She therefore learned to read and write. In this alone, she was already an exceptional woman in an age where women were usually destined only for the household and for childbearing.

She was a woman warrior not because she was a tomboy or wanted to do things done only by men. She was beautiful. "She drew attention at social gatherings. It is said that when she rode a horse she was very poised and dignified."[18]

Although there is nothing extant today to give us a hint of how either Diego or Gabriela looked and comported themselves, their breathtaking monuments, particularly of Gabriela, are not entirely without basis in tradition.

Of course, Gabriela Silang is regarded as the Filipino Joan of Arc.

What we know is that besides being religious, as practically every wife in that Age of Faith was, she was generous by nature. A story goes that one night, on the way to visit a sick friend, she took along a bowl of *dinengdeng*, an Ilocano dish. She was wearing a new shawl in the chilly air.

Along the way she met an old woman shivering in the cold. She gave the dish to her. She also placed her shawl on her and more — she went back home to prepare another dish for her friend.

Her acts of generosity increased after she married the wealthy old man, and she became known as "the good rich woman."

"Courage," said someone, "is the most admirable of all human virtues." Of course, to say that Gabriela Silang was courageous would be exquisitely superfluous.

Renato Constantino in his rigidly argumentative book, *A Past Revisited,* gives a different and derogatory picture of Diego Silang[19] which sounds unfair .

He says that the rebel leader had "messianic tendencies which blended with religious fanaticism." Yet when Silang wrote to an Ilocano town leader whom he was persuading to join the rebellion, he cited in his letter only political reasons and advantages. No millenarian is like that.

Constantino says that Silang was a messianic fanatic who cast himself as "defender of King and Church, [declaring] Jesus of Nazareth to be the Captain-General and he as Christ's *cabo mayor*."

But all that he could summon to support this accusation of messianic fanaticism was that Silang had his house filled with images of saints and, according to Constantino's own words, "urged his followers to hear mass on Sunday, go to confession and receive the Sacraments and also to see to it that their children went to school."

To repeat, this was all Constantino could say to prove his particular point of messianic fanaticism. But what's so messianic or fanatical in that? Weren't so many of the enemy, the Spaniards themselves, like that in the Age of Faith?

Besides, others say that Silang himself was the one who was first acclaimed by the people themselves as "general," but he refused it. Later, after his death, Gabriela was called "*generala*" — by the people, not by herself, and it is possible she also discouraged them from it, without success.

Parenthetically, Silang's involving Jesus by acknowledging him to be his general may sound amusing to us today, but people were deadly serious in things like that in those times when religion was the main fact of life, the governing principle and purpose and devotion.

Constantino has a self-stated motive in downgrading Silang, and that is to cast the latter as the "*ilustrado* prototype" of later collaborators of colonial rule. Diego Silang a collaborator? C'mon.

It is not irrelevant to note that Constantino regards himself as a committed nationalist historian and is devoted to historical class analysis — which makes him sound like a Marxist. This shows through in his criticism of Silang.

When a handful of nationalists/leftists talk today of *ilustrado* collaborators, they mean those characters during the late 19th-century Katipunan and during the first years of the American colonization who sided with the foreigners, or otherwise undermined the Revolution by talking about, and advancing, the cause of peace.

These turn-of-the-century *ilustrados* are the whipping boys of leftist/masses-oriented historians in our own time, or at least in the tumultuous and ideology-crazed decades of the 1950s and 1960s.

Of course, during Silang's time there were no *ilustrados* yet. As a class or as individuals they were identified only more than 200 years after Silang, meaning in the second half of the 19th-century when Filipino classes and subclasses had only recently risen in Philippine society and the nationalist struggle had yet to reach a more mature stage.

Constantino forgets that Silang did not "change masters" as a matter of opportunism or cowardice, as some latter-day *ilustrados* did. For if he was an opportunist or coward, why revolt — in the way, under the circumstances, and for the reasons that he did, as shown by his declared reforms?

There are more indications than otherwise that it was more a means to preserve his rebellion and its thrusts, and in addition it was no affront to him — or any man — to secure his own physical self-preservation *under certain circumstances*.

Besides, the British promised to abolish the tribute, forced labor, personal services, and to respect freedom of religion, and actually backed up these promises with example. Wasn't anyone like the 18th-century Silang reasonably, or at least understandably, expected, though not necessarily or absolutely justified, to change allegiance under the circumstances?

He could have revolted again, at a later time, against the British, if a new set of circumstances arose.

Secondly, it is rather too much for Constantino to expect Silang to have mature notions of kingless nationalism, i.e., no masters at all, for he lived in the age of kings who all over the world were regarded to be blessed with the divine right to rule, and even to misrule — more often the latter.

Nationalism, by the way, did not come to the Filipino consciousness suddenly as a complete, well-wrapped package. It had to undergo stages of development just as a man develops from fetus to baby to child to adult.

Imagine having a childbirth, or an adult offspring, five minutes after copulation. It would have astonished Diego and Gabriela.

Was it Silang's fault — of course it was his misfortune — that he lived in so early an age when the Filipino nation, as it was understood and declared in Malolos in 1898 or earlier during the Katipunan or the Propaganda Movement, did not yet exist?

Why, even today, people quarrel on who or what is a true nationalist, in spite of all those debates, useful and enlightening to a certain degree, in the days of Rectonian nationalism and Marxist infection of UP in the 1960s and 1970s, the era when Constantino researched and wrote his book.

He was in fact one of the most fervent spokesmen for the nationalist/class analysis/masses-fixated sector, which is not to say that I disagree with him on this general point. What I disagree on is his coming on much too strongly against a chronologically situated Silang.

Constantino says in his book that Silang was a reformist and not a revolutionary. These were fashionable words of cant and canticle in those UP days, whose distinctions were meaningless to Silang, who just went ahead with his nationalist, anti-*principalia*, propeople job without any ideological fuss.

Is it correct, or at least kind, for Constantino to put Silang under the yardstick of ideological standards more than 200 years later, although as a committed historian he has the scholar's privilege to employ historical analysis to the service of knee-jerk class ideology or ideological constructs?

In any age or clime where race crosses race, and mind penetrates mind, and culture copulates with culture, it is not appropriate to apply wooden standards. Things are not as simple as they is made to appear by leftist bifocals.

In the medieval era, it was not wrong *per se* to change allegiances to kings, just as communists today would change tactics at the drop of a circumstance. Many medievals did it in Europe, and each one must be judged on a case-to-case basis — and with understanding of the times in which he lived.

The great Ferdinand Magellan, for example, was a Portuguese who by definition owed his allegiance to the Portuguese potentate, but whose willfully chosen master was the Spanish king. But how could one say that he necessarily debauched himself simply because of this somersault?

Shouldn't we be kind to our heroes rather than be unkind to them, for after all they made great sacrifices and we are the ones who are beholden?

Beholden? Yes, because Diego Silang revolted against Spanish rule as Bonifacio did. It's the revolt, stupid!

Constantino also says in his book that Silang represented "elite servility" — note his derogatory terminology, "servility" — because of the "kowtowing" and "flattering" words in his letters to the British. But if we closely analyze the content of the sentences which he, Constantino, quoted from Silang to prove his point, two thoughts arise:

The "kowtowing" tone and the "flattering" vocabulary must have been a matter of form in those days and cannot be justly measured with surface 20th-century semantics. The language is not the message.

Indeed, there was a time even in English history when language was effusive, not to mention Spanish rhetorical extravagance and lavishness to which Filipino leaders in their time naturally adjusted — just as today our own manner of language is affected by contemporary forms and usages.

The British in their replies addressed Silang as "Your Grace." This could be flattery now, but only simple usage then according to the circumstances. In any case Diego must have been thrilled.

Could it not be said that even dialectic materialists exercise subjective interpretation — although in their serviceable ideological constructs they obstinately, even serenely, call it objective?

Constantino's ruthless derogation of Diego Silang as "flattering" cannot really be considered seriously because, form aside, the substance of that "flattery" was germane to the reasons for his revolt — like the promise to free the natives from the detestable tribute, the despicable taxes and the abominable forced labor.

It would have been a different case if the British vowed, or were seen, to impose the same things that the Spaniards did, or were silent about them, and Diego Silang still changed his position in spite of that.

Anyone in those early days who made decisions with a nationalist content in an age when the nation as we know it now did not yet exist, however immature or imperfect his nationalism may be, deserves not only understanding but the most deafening applause.

One like Silang who felt most intensely about certain things to which he had committed his life and happiness within the framework of 18th-century perceptions could not be expected to talk about them to the British in terms of 20th-century nationalist configurations.

To prove his derogatory point, Constantino quotes from Silang's letter to the British commander to show the "flattering" style, and let us consider it here with the reminder to today's reader not to take it in the context of today's lingo but that of yesterday, which was so different, just as Chaucer's language was so different in sentiment from that of Victorian, or later Elton John's, England:

> With the greatest pleasure and satisfaction imaginable have I received the news of your having conquered the Capital by Force of Arms and with so much ease which has undoubtedly been an effect of your good conduct and the permission of the Almighty, I have [been] informed that notwithstanding the fatal misfortune of that city your Lordship [who] is endowed with so many great qualifications and compassion has behaved in a most generous manner to the poor Indians who were within and out of the Town paying them punctually for their labour without requiring any other acknowledgement than that they should obey and be loyal as they should to his Majesty George III, King of Great Britain (whom God preserve) and for such obedience Your Lordship has been pleased to allow them their Freedom to enlarge their Trade and Commerce, for their own benefit to caress them and prevent their being hurt by the Spaniards or by your own Troops all which I have [been] minutely informed of.[20]

In short, Diego was in effect telling the Brits, "Hey, you guys really made short shrift of those bastards. Congratulations! Besides, I am told that you have behaved well to the poor Indians in and out of downtown, promptly paying their wages without strings attached except to regard your Georgie as their king. Thanks also for your trade offer, that can do us both a lot of good."

Of course, in terms of style, his writing would have received a grade of 5, even 6, in UP's freshman English course today. But should this be taken against Diego Silang, who was not in the position to enroll in the great Republic of Diliman?

Although the letter was crucial to his purpose in getting British support, Silang did not evade a most sensitive point, which Constantino grossly ignored, that could have been a source of irritation to the Protestant recipients whom he was wooing. He said that "all my Countrymen of the Province of Ilocos ... beg is that your Lordship will condescend to let them maintain their Parish Priests and live as Christians and Catholicks...."

Constantino is somehow sarcastic even about Silang's harmless talk of trade, saying that the rebel leader had the "alacrity to take advantage of the new opportunities, [for] his contact with the Manila galleons as a courier, and the fact that his wife was a property owner in a prosperous town, prepared him for these new possibilities." Was this malicious or not?

Of course, trade is a capitalist or bourgeois activity, and automatically the leftist/class analytic/masses-oriented ideology is automatically against it.

But to condemn a courageous, activist leader of a Spanish era revolt just because he saw trade opportunities — not only for his "prosperous town" but, to assume without conceding, for his wife — in those dangerous and often fatal times may be ideologically correct but is rather too much to swallow.

How many of UP's leftists and "objective interpreters of history" remained professors, and in their moral bankruptcy and cowardice kept a sedentary existence, dealing with nothing but words, words, words, words, and never joined the NPA revolt?

If the above discussion tends to establish an indiscriminate ideological prejudice of Constantino against Silang, it may explain why he, Constantino, in his derogatory premises, mentions Orendain only in one sentence: "In Manila Silang lived in the house of a lawyer," and·he quotes a Spaniard writing the words, "the traitor Orendain."

Shouldn't Constantino at least have shown why Orendain was called a traitor? Was he not foisting the impression that Silang was conniving with an out-and-out traitor and thereby also deserved disrepute?

The fact is that good old Orendain was legal adviser to Governor-General Arandia, who was perceived to be antifriar. When Arandia ceased to be governor-general Orendain was removed and charged in court. The case was dismissed by the succeeding governor- general, Rojo, who reinstated him as legal adviser.

When the British arrived, Orendain expressed his opinion that the city should be surrendered to them because of the obvious odds which he may have discussed with Silang, and to save both Spaniards and Filipinos from suffering and dying — just as MacArthur declared the same Manila an open city when the Japanese hordes came.

No American branded MacArthur a traitor to America as Orendain was called by Spaniards a traitor to Spain. Rojo himself eventually followed Orendain's advice to surrender, but was not accused of treachery.

If Orendain was a traitor, as Constantino unceremoniously says without explanation, then he was not a deplorable traitor. He was not a traitor in the first place, he was only committed to his own strong opinions, and he may have had Spain's real interests at heart.

But have the readers of Constantino's book then been misled, because the author saw his subject all the time through a thick ideological prism in which Silang through no fault of his did not fit, a prearranged prism where the other shafts of light in the reality spectrum are blocked from human sight?

In contrast to these derogatory words from a bona fide Filipino nationalist is what the foreigner Routledge said — that Diego Silang, for all his shortcomings, was one of those who stoked the first early embers of Filipino nationalism.

Constantino ends his commentary on Silang with one last cruel blow: "Silang was the prototype of future leaders who would capitalize on the genuine grievances of the people. [But the people themselves in] each successive uprising took a step in their political awakening. Each local revolt was a contribution to the national consciousness."

Poor Diego Silang did not only fail to get credit for all his pains and hardships, he was one who "*capitalized* on the genuine grievances of the people." An evil, greedy, exploitative man, whose "capitalism" sought monetary profit, not danger and death from superior Spanish arms? He "capitalized" on danger and death? Were danger and death a good investment?

But what about those who did nothing about "the genuine grievances of the people?" What about those who, in fact, were responsible for inflicting grievances on the people? What about those who, then and now, have not invested a single drop of blood for their country or for their own convictions?

Did Constantino, in his ideological obstinacy, fail to remember that Silang, like him, was promasses, that Constantino of all people should have been the first to applaud the propeople Silang movement?

Incidentally, Constantino was a high school student when woman Sakdal leader Salud Algabre, another Gabriela, became a sensation during the Sakdal uprising in the 1930s. When captured and later interviewed, she uttered the immortal words, which became a sacred nostrum in the decades to come: "No uprising fails. Each one is a step in the right direction."

Is this not what Constantino says in his book in slightly different words, but in exactly the same progression of thought, published almost 40 years later than Salud? Was he not drawing from her original remark without giving her credit — even as a footnote, or even just in quotation marks — for the brilliant and beautiful thought?

But if he could not give much nationalist credit to Silang, why should he give any intellectual credit in the case of Salud Algabre? In fact, in his whole book, *The Past Revisited*, a nationalist book, he never mentions Salud even once.

Postscript: It would not be a surprise had Bishop Ustariz recommended Miguel Vicos to the Pope for canonization as a saint for shooting a fellow Christian on the back. Actually, less than two years after the assassination, the Spaniards erected in Bantay a huge monument — in honor of Vicos. In 1914, it was turned into a monument for Diego Silang.

Would Constantino have hated that change in the monument as he did Silang's "change of masters?"

5. The Extermination of Hermano Puli

WE HAVE dealt with the Tondo Conspiracy in the 16th century, with Sumuroy in the 17th century and with Diego Silang in the 18th century. Now we come to the 19th century.

Apolinario de la Cruz, known to history as Hermano Puli, or Brother Puli, was born in Lucban, Quezon in 1814. It is said that he came from peasant stock.

Of course the word *peasant* may have meant that his parents — and siblings, if any — lived on subsistence farming, and that without working in the fields they would have had little to eat, or clothe themselves with.

Such is the painful lot of peasants, for the land must be tilled to produce, unlike today's lucky-devil rich who capitalize on land values in Manila and government treasury warrants whose monetary stock increases on its own like magic.

A historian though claims that Apolinario was "of an established family in the pueblo, with an old surname before the 1849 decree requiring family names."[1]

Reynaldo Ileto further confuses the issue by claiming that he had "relatively well-to-do peasant parents."[2]

Now we know that a peasant is a peasant — the word has a more or less definite meaning: one who personally tills the soil, has thick-skinned hands and, besides, is uneducated or uncouth, drinks *tuba* or *sioktong*, and is buried not with a wooden or metal coffin but with his cadaver wrapped only with a *banig* even when raining and with mud in the ground.

There cannot be a "well-to-do peasant" because *well-to-do* and *peasant* are a contradiction in terms. A word that has a more elastic meaning would be *farmer*.

A farmer could be a peasant, or he could be a self-tilling small landowner, or a big landowner, or a gentleman farmer like the superrich ones in the proud aristocracies of Central Luzon and Negros.

As for the claim that Apolinario's was a "pueblo" family, this does not mean much. There were people in Quezon province, as elsewhere, whose class or status could not be determined with the use of one word indicating location.

There were families who, for their own safety from ferocious and pitiless bandits who were common in those times, worked in their far fields by day, but had a hut in the *poblacion* where they slept at night.

After the bandits and the *guardia civil* came the haphazard *insurrectos*, then the angry Colorums, the atrocious Japanese, the shameless Makapilis and Ganaps, the peripatetic wartime guerrillas, the civilian guards, the deluded Huks and the even more deluded NPAs and dastardly counterinsurgency constabularies and political warlords big and small and what-have-you, and only heaven knows how the innocent, fun-deprived farmers or peasants quavered in the crossfire.

What is certain is that Apolinario did not come from the *principalia*.

It is almost superfluous to say that his mother Juana was a devout Catholic, and this impacted on Apolinario deeply for he was even more religious than she. That she was devout is a cliche said of practically every Filipino hero's mama in Spanish times, when being an assiduous Catholic was the only way to go for a housewife or mother startled by her lack of options.

Apolinario's formal education presumably was nothing more than the primary subjects rigidly taught by the town friar's rudimentary school. It enabled Indio *poblacion* kids — even hill peasants' children? — to have some degree of literacy. A little more than enough to say their brief religious prayers and obey the Kastila commands.

Apolinario was exceptional. He wanted to be a local poor boy who made good. He aimed, not to go to the hill nearby, but to the stars.

Instead of remaining an Indio, he wanted no less than to become a "regular priest," meaning a member of a religious order like the Jesuits or Franciscans or Dominicans, as differentiated from a "secular priest," who is usually a parish priest and is under the supervision of the bishop. Unfortunately, Indio and regular priest in those days did not mix, like oil and water.

But there were stars not only in heaven, but in Manila. It is the mark of his resolute spirit that in 1830, at the very young age of 15, he proceeded to the Great City.

Subsequent events show that his interest was not in a typical livelihood job but in so unusual an occupation as religiosity. He worked as a servant, and it may not be a mere coincidence that it was first run by the Franciscan fathers, who also reigned in his hometown of Lucban.

Servant is the term used by some authors to describe his station in the San Juan de Dios complex.

But the translated version in Blair and Robertson uses the word *donne*. This is derived from the word *donare*, which means "to give." But what could he give, he was penniless. But he could serve, or "give" service.

Another word, *donee*, which is slightly different in spelling, means the opposite — "the recipient of a gift." Could it also mean one who is served?

But Apolinario was never called this. Historian Elsie S. Ramos uses the Spanish/Tagalog word *donado*, which means "lay brother." Now we are going somewhere. Spanish writer Leandro Tormo in fact directly calls him "lay brother" who lived with the friars in the convent of San Juan de Dios Hospital.[3]

He was therefore not a servant in the low sense that we usually understand the word, although in a moment of Christian effervescence a *donado* or lay brother may proclaim himself the lowest of lowly servants in the tradition of Jesus, who came not to be served but to serve.

After all, one of the breathtaking titles of the Pope, besides Vicar of Christ, Supreme Pontiff, Bishop of Rome, Successor to the See of Peter, and Pastor of the Universal Church, is Servant of the Servants of God.

A Lucban quadcentennial publication — that's how old the town is — says that: "Apolinario avidly read the Bible, Christian catechism, and novenas, and attended many sermons in the churches of Intramuros, thereby improving his desire to reform the dogmatic practices of the friar-controlled Catholic faith and to promote greater freedom of worship."[4]

Such was his *apog* that, if the above statement is to be believed, he defined the state of no less than the Church and held himself responsible! A not self-overrated ambition, as we shall see in his effectiveness later.

He was exposed to the best books, and "listened attentively to distinguished preachers and came to learn many things about Catholic theology."[5]

And so he became a preacher in later years. There is no record of his manner of talking, his posture and visage, but it may be granted he had considerable oral skills. One word used to describe him in public speaking was "thrilling."[6] In other words, he was not a congressman.

In 1915, or some 73 years after the Hermano's extirpation, one Gabriel Beato Francisco interviewed elderly people in Quezon and here are some of the things he heard:

When he became a brother in San Juan de Dios, Apolinario took it upon himself to carry an alms box as he went from house to house in the Manila area. In doing the rounds of begging, he never took off the black cloak draped about his body as a sign of piety and dedication to the Lord.

He never let go of the alms box until it was filled and too heavy for his hands to hold. In the early days of service, he used to return to the orphanage every afternoon with the box full of picking from nearby towns.

Later he received permission to take to the province the box filled with pachouli and balsam scent, which was placed before portraits to be kissed by those who had pious interests.

Day by day, Apolinario journeyed farther and farther away from Manila. In spite of his exhaustion, he reflected that "if San Juan de Dios is poor, even more abject is the condition of the country."

Driven by those thoughts he reached, in his journeys, the lake of Bae and from there headed for his hometown in Tayabas [province]. He made himself even more lowly, or *nagpakababa*. He attended mass every day.[7]

Later the Hermano said, as quoted by Ileto, that "he devoted eight years of toil and exhaustion, day and night, so that the *cofradia*, which already had 5,000 pesos in its coffers, could fund its masses and rituals."[8]

Previously, in 1832, while still working in San Juan de Dios Hospital, he had decided to organize, and maintain by long-distance maneuvers, a *cofradia* in Lucban, whose first members reached 19.

A *cofradia* was an organization of which there were many in the Philippines in Spanish times. Among these were sodalities which the friars introduced to help consolidate the Christianization of the natives.

How he did it — we don't know exactly. Maybe he set up the first meetings on his Lucban trip from Bae, as stated above. His Cofradia de San Jose of course had its catechetical and other religious goals and practices like the recitation of the *pasyon* of prayers which he himself crafted, and daily praying of the full 15 mysteries of the rosary every day; and aimed to promote social intercourse among its members.

It also provided personal and social counsel and discussed mystical theology, whatever that was, and presumably nothing, not a single sentence or word, of the superstitious and the subversive, of which he was later accused. This can be shown by some copies which are being kept in the National Archives, says Ileto.

He did not teach in person for he was always in Manila. But he sent regularly a torrent of letters to be read to the congregations with their fast-growing numbers of devotees and catechumens and multiplying branches.

Many of these letters were like *Paulinian epistles* in the New Testament; in short, Hermano Puli's followers had their own *Puli-nian epistles*.

But there were some curious features. Unlike other sodalities, it was kept secret. And it forbade membership to Spaniards, Chinese and mestizos of both kinds.

Why? Presumably because when the crunch would come, they could not be absolutely trusted to side with the *maralita*, as we shall see later when the Hermano was vindicated in this by the turn of events.

And yet there was a handful of rich persons, including a priest, who pierced the shroud of secrecy and sympathized with them and were willing to help them when they got into trouble.

And the *principalia* they disqualified, too. It was in fact a poor man's sodality that was more radical than the Katipunan itself, which was said to be a plebeian club but did not disqualify or ostracize the rich, hence such members and officers as Dr. Pio Valenzuela.

And while Hermano Puli's Cofradia de San Jose shied away from the rich, the Katipunan craved for their support, as advised by Rizal and machinated by Bonifacio and Jacinto.

Elsie Ramos points out that at the founding of their *cofradia* they enunciated that their vision was "*para makamit ang liwanag, tulungan ang katulad nilang kapus-palad at magbigay ng kawanggawa para sa kapwa nila maralita.*"[9]

Did the Katipuneros, or the Sakdals, or the Huks, or the NPAs, have a more definite and explicit propoor statement in their vision or mission?

They kept their Cofradia de San Jose's existence from the knowledge especially of the friars, the town officials and the *principalia*. Whatever were their fears that, like subversive movements, they had to be underground?

Did they fear for their movement because it was, as far as membership was concerned, anti-Spanish, anti-Chinese, antimestizo, and antirich?

Unlike other sodalities, the *cofradia* had no *cura* or *principalia* as adviser, naturally. The Hermano had shut them out completely, except when the curate or someone else was needed to officially perform common ceremonies — a lousy, hopeless way of keeping a secret.

They may have tried to anticipate the priests' suspicions by pretending it was only one of those minor neighborhood organizations for catechetical circumlocutions.

"The parish priest of Lucban knew about the existence of this society simply because he was the one celebrating the mass ... and also [he was present] in the meetings in a certain house in which the picture of Apolinario hung on the wall."[10]

In other words, the friar was not stupid. And, as we shall see, he was truculent.

Besides, as an organization they still attended mass in the *poblacion* itself, although no one knew exactly what their group was, and the curate did not seem to mind.

But like rats burrowing into the lion's mouth, they sometimes asked permission to pray a novena in the big *poblacion* church, paying the usual dues. They also continued to observe a monthly fiesta by themselves.

The Lucban curate and other friars in Tayabas, Laguna and Batangas, where the *cofradia* had spread with amazing speed presumably because of amazing grace, may have been infuriated by reports that the fast-growing brotherhood regularly collected huge monetary contributions from members.

The amount of P5,000 which we said the Hermano had collected all by himself a few years back, was already a small, or more precisely a big, fortune in those days. So the cofradia as a whole may have already accumulated a treasure that was not only Solomonic but, shall we say, astronomic?

Mulls a historian, "Each member of the cofradia was paying one real in monthly dues, which was more than the one-and-a-half reals per tribute-payer yearly that the friars received for the religious fiestas. In sum, Apolinario de la Cruz was not only making more money; he was besting the friars."[11]

The friars and their *principalia* acolytes first tried to stem the tide of the *cofradia*'s enviable expansion by organizing their own in Lucban and Mahayhay, naming it the Cofradia de San Francisco Xavier, to compete with Hermano Puli's Cofradia de San Jose.

It was a failure. There is nothing in the records to suggest that the people realigned their financial contributions from St. Joseph to St. Francis Xavier, thus depriving the friars of another hefty serving of pork barrel.

That the Cofradia de San Jose prevailed was probably due to the fact that San Jose was no less than the husband of the Virgin Mary herself, while St. Francis Xavier was only a Jesuit.

The humbled friars may have investigated who on earth was this formidable Apolinario de la Cruz, now called Hermano Puli by thousands upon thousands of members although he remained in Manila as a lowly, inconspicuous lay brother.

They must have discovered that he had applied for entrance into a religious order for education as a future priest but, tough luck, was rejected because only pure Spaniards were accepted.

And what gall, the friars may have thought, when Hermano Puli, with his *cofradia* now a gigantic organization, applied for official recognition by the ecclesiastical authorities in Nueva Caceres in Bicol, which had jurisdiction over Lucban.

By this time, what had happened to the policy of secrecy?

Due to vehement resistance by the Lucban *cura*, one Fr. Manuel Sancho, the archbishop rejected the application for official recognition. In addition, this *cura* doubled the fees for the *cofradia*'s monthly mass.

When he heard that the *cofradia* balked, the *cura* turned from *santong dasalan* to *santong paspasan*. He ordered the dissolution of the *cofradia* and its members' expulsion from Lucban. From then the brotherhood, which defied the order by continuing to meet, was in turn harassed at every turn.

Hermano Puli, laying down a peace policy at all cost, further distanced himself from his policy of secrecy and submitted a petition to be allowed to continue with his brotherhood this time before the archbishop of Manila, for he had lost faith in Nueva Caceres.

Being enterprising, he also filed a petition with Governor-General Marcelino Oraa, who would soon become one of his tormentors — and finally still another petition with the Royal Audiencia itself.

Although he was a poor man who probably did not know well the intricacies of correct petition making, he could do all these high-level moves because he was supported by a few upper-class Filipinos besides his faithful friend, Indio secular priest Ciriaco de los Santos.

These rich Filipinos were the well-known Domingo Roxas and businessmen and landlords like Jose Florentino, Felipe Vidal Marifosque, Toribio Pantoja, Jose Ramires and Florentino Felipe.[12]

In vain were his petitions, simply because Spanish rule — meaning the political (the governor-general), the religious (the friars) and the police (the *guadia civil*) — was monolithic.

In fact, like Diego Silang more than a century before, the Hermano instead was ordered to appear before Governor-General Oraa, who had already secretly issued an arrest order.

Like Diego Silang, Hermano Puli rightly did not trust Oraa and did not appear. He went underground, prepared to go back to Lucban and his endangered flock.

So the unimaginative Oraa arrested Fr. De los Santos and the Hermano's rich supporters, whom they sentenced to prison but years later, when Puli was dead, were exonerated in Madrid itself and ordered released.

In the province they also captured the *cofradia*'s secretary and Hermano's trusted aide, Ignacio San Jose, from whom they seized a long list of *cofradia* members — they now knew whom to arrest.

Good old Fr. Manuel warned the archbishop and maybe also the governor-general that the *cofradia* would soon become a big headache. The Spanish government decided to settle the problem once and for all.

Governor Oraa was already having enough problems from Philippine-born Spaniards, called creoles, who had mutinied in Intramuros under Andres Novales, whom we will meet in a later chapter.

He had vexations also with the Filipino secular priests who were defying the religious orders and advocating the Filipinization of the parishes. And the Carlistas, supporters of one Carlos, claimant to the royal throne then occupied by his niece, Queen Isabella, then only a child.

Why should he allow the *cofradia* to aggravate his problems? The noose was now tightening around Hermano Puli's neck.

Spanish soldiers raided a *cofradia* meeting in Tayabas town and arrested 243 out of some 600 persons attending — even if they had no jail large enough to accomodate them. They sent some of the prisoners to Lucena.

But the no-nonsense Tayabas *alcalde mayor*, or provincial governor, one Spaniard named Joaquin Ortega, was no friars' fool and immediately ordered their release, saying it was an ecclesiastical and not a police problem.[13]

Fr. Manuel the *cura* vehemently snarled at Ortega, telling him that if the problem became violent and fatal, "You will be the first victim!" — a hysterical but prophetic warning.

The many events above happened only within a few weeks. In September 1841, a big *cofradia* meeting again in Mahayhay was broken up and arrests were made. Some escaped and gathered around the Hermano who had landed in Bay, Laguna from Pateros in Manila across the lake by sailboat.

For the first time, some of them were now armed with bolos, bamboo spears, bows and arrows.

The Hermano had no thought of deserting his disadvantaged followers. He now intended to lead them in a time of crisis.

From the Tayabas capital, Governor Ortega went to Manila. Either Governor-General Oraa had summoned him or he, cornered by events, went on his own volition. When he came back to Tayabas he had decided, maybe upon orders of the vicious Oraa, to suppress the brotherhood in a most unbrotherly way.

From Laguna, Hermano Puli marched overland with his armed Indios. They passed through San Pablo, Tiaong, Sariaya, and when they reached Barrio Ilayang Sabang some 5,000 *cofradia* men and women had gathered to meet him. Fantastic. Wasn't 5,000 the number that often gathered around the preacher Jesus centuries ago?

It was now October 23, 1841, some 30 years before Gomburza were to be executed. Governor Ortega, with a force of 300 troops, appeared before the undaunted *cofradia* members who steadily and fearlessly looked at them from afar, their bolos glistening in the sun.

Ortega had three cheerleaders in his ranks — friars Vicario, Antonio Mateos and Victorino del Pareja. Before they could cheer their compatriots, they ran away because the battle immediately began.[14]

Ortega's troops attacked in full strength and fury. Somehow the *cofradia*'s untrained band of half-armed men, fighting with remarkable valor, won the battle. They killed Governor Ortega himself, a feat with hardly a parallel during Spanish times.

We have a historical vignette in a man from Tiaong, Joaquin Quizon de los Santos, an Indio. He served as a soldier under Governor Ortega. He was there in the historic battle against Hermano Puli.

Ortega, after being hit by a spear — one proof that the Indios had lowly spears for weapons, among others — cried for help and it was De los Santos who ran to try to save him. But it was too late. He expired from the spear wound.[15]

Teodoro Agoncillo, in his textbook, lugubriously says, "In 1841, Apolinario de la Cruz and his followers took up arms in Tayabas and murdered the [provincial] governor."[16]

Small wonder there have often been complaints about Agoncillo's biases and untruths. "Murdered?" The *cofradia* brothers did not murder Ortega. They killed him fighting in battle, fair and square.

Indeed, much as Ortega deserves historical respect for his hesitation in quelling disadvantaged Filipinos, and for his lack of canine subservience to the friars, it was not the *cofradia* people who attacked Ortega, it was Ortega — probably on orders from the governor-general, in which case he had no alternative as a soldier — who attacked them.

But Agoncillo may have only adopted and embraced the Spanish attitude. In those days, if the Indios killed Spaniards, it was murder. If the Spaniards killed Indios, it was pacification.

The Hermano and his people knew the Spaniards would avenge their incalculable humiliation. They moved to Alitao, at the foot of Mt. San Cristobal, beside Mt. Banahaw, which was protected by natural barriers — a hill on one side and two rivers on the other.

The tyrant Oraa, weighing the Spanish defeat with a disillusioned heart, now nurtured a grudging respect for the strength and courage of the *cofradia*.

In the old and historic palace of the viceroys of the Spanish king, as huge Intramuros flies noiselessly but insolently hovered in his face, he licked himself with the gnawing humiliation of the Ilayang Sabang debacle, which became a sensation in the Great City where he ruled proudly as a potentate.

He contemplated revenge and planned an apocalyptic overkill of what to him were traitorous subhuman Indios whose lives were no more valuable than those of wild boars scampering aimlessly in the Tagalog jungles.

Under the arrogant command of a mentally twisted butcher, Spanish veteran combat commander Lt. Col. Joaquin Huet, he sent a stultifying force of 1,000 crack troops from Manila, reinforced by scores of perfunctory Indios contributed by servile alcaldes from some provinces.

This last battle occurred on November 1, 1841. As the whole Christian Philippines venerated All Saints' Day, in Alitao it was All Demons' Day.

The encounter was said to be a massacre — some 500 of Hermano Puli's followers were killed, including women and children. A massacre? Why not? Huet the butcher did not suffer a single casualty.

A Spaniard who lived in Manila, from his own personal sources in Tayabas, said "more than 1,000 men, women and children were killed."[17] But let us be conservative in weighing the limitless horrors of colonial rule, otherwise we would become mentally deranged.

It is said that many of the great Hermano's disciples, in spite of their *anting-anting*, ran away at first sight of the huge force of Huet, the likes of which they had never seen before. But there were contrary reports that they fought with great valor.

With the disaster, Hermano Puli's personal fate was sealed — tragically on earth as it was gloriously in heaven.

Elsie Ramos, who uses the most reliable primary sources, says that Puli, separated from his followers, stayed that night in the dense jungle, exhausted and forlorn, unmindful of the beasts and snakes from which no latter-day Aladin would rescue the latter-day Florante.

Instead of a triumphant return to the Albanya of his affections, he was captured the next day, November 2, at ten a.m., in Barrio Kalachuchi.

And he was executed without ceremony or bluster on November 4, along with 200 of his followers, near the Tayabas town hall. All records agree that he was decapitated after being shot dead.

And more. Since barbarism was difficult to satisfy even in triumph, his severed head was placed in a cage, like merchandise in a pet market, and hung there — not impaled on a stake as it is said — and exhibited to the terrified public in the street in front of his parents' house in Lucban.

There is no record of how his parents reacted. They were probably still alive, since the Hermano was only 27 years old when meted out the extreme penalty, and most probably were forced to witness the indescribable hanging horror that must have lasted for days — until they would have found it unbearable and begged to be allowed to leave.

Or did they courageously and defiantly choose to stay and suffer with their son, like the Virgin Mary?

The Hermano's two feet and two hands were brutally cut off like pig's feet and displayed in all the four corners of Lucban's *poblacion*.

Many of the doomed *cofradia* men were interviewed with great interest, naturally, before being dispatched to eternal life. "The 200 men, when questioned by Spanish officers as to their objectives [in gathering in Alitao], answered, 'To pray.'"[18]

And so they were executed — all 200 of them, perhaps the most numerous among victims of Spanish rule who fell in a single encounter as their fellow Indios watched with intense but indefinite feelings.

There are other stories about how the Hermano was captured. It is said that the noble, trusting brotherhood leader, after having escaped the Spanish inundation of Alitao, entered alone a hut owned by an ex-*cofradia* couple in Barrio Ibanga and, being exceedingly hungry, was given some food by the housewife.

The demands of simple decency, humanity and mercy, not to say Indio commonality, should have led the owners of the house to eschew the perversity of treachery and, instead, helped him further to escape.

But while he was eating, the darkest impulses of Judas Iscariot activated the humor of the scheming husband. He went out to call for some men and, together, rushed and wrestled the great Hermano down and proudly presented his live but ravished body to the authorities in the provincial capital of Tayabas.

Is there some truth to this version because the names of the captors were curiously identified — Pedro de la Concepcion, Francisco de San Agustin, Leonardo de San Juan, Atanacio Bautista Reinoso, Ventura de la Cruz, Matias Bonifacio and Juan de la Cruz?.[19]

But there is a third version:

"A flying column of Spanish troops pursued the fleeing Hermano Puli and overtook him in the barrio of Ibanga, Sariaya. The religious crusader and his handful of courageous followers resisted, but in vain. He and his surviving men were captured alive, after furious combat."[20]

Here is another account:

Kay lungkot na kapalaran ng isang bayaning ang pinamuhunang buhay ay ang kaapihan ng bayan. Sa kabilang dako ay kay gandang kapalaran ang tinamo ng tatlong naghandog ng tulong sa pamahalaang Kastila sanhi sa ipinamalas nilang kabayanihan, upang sila'y gantimpalaan at tawaging Alferez de Milicia.

Ang mapapalad na mga taong ito ay sina Macario de San Juan, Joaquin Reyes de San Agustin at Patricio Juan de la Concepcion, *at ang mga anak ng mga ito'y hangga't hindi pa nag-aasawa ay hindi pabubuwisin at hindi rin mag-aatag na katulad ng isang kawani o empleado.*

At gayon din, nagtamo ng pabuyang salapi ang dalawang ginoong nagpamalas ng kabayanihang di pangkaraniwan sa pakikipagbarilan at sa paghawak ng armas de mano, at ang dalawang ito ay dili iba't sina Juan de Leon at Silvestre San Jose.[21]

Spanish tyranny, of course, employed not only murder and devastation, steel and annihilation, to quell the natives. It often paid the proverbial 30 pieces of silver. And, as in any society, there were clammy Indio palms that were eager to grasp them.

Here is a description of the aftermath of the battle:

"Sa labanang ito ay masasabing bumaha ng dugo sa Alitao, *pagka't saan mang pook ay may nakikitang bangkay, mga naghihingalo na lamang na dumaraing, mga sinalanta ng sandata kung hindi man naliligo sa sariling dugo."*[21]

Indeed, who would bury the bodies and treat the wounded? Not the Spanish army.

We shall talk at some length about Hermano Puli because some historians have not given him his due. He belongs not to Quezon province alone but to the nation as a whole. If there is one wrong that should be rectified, it is the dark oblivion to which the luster of his name has been consigned.

Teodoro Agoncillo in his textbook limits the Hermano story to only eight sentences.[22] In Santiago Alvarez's book, which deals extensively with the mystical revolutionary struggles of Filipinos, especially the Banahaw rebel tradition that started largely with the Hermano, Puli is not mentioned at all.[23]

In Renato Constantino's volume, he is dealt with only in four summary paragraphs.[24] And heaven knows how many national history books have treated him with superficial attention or forgetful disdain. But it should be recognized that Hermano Puli was a historical figure of great stature.

It is not fitting to regard Apolinario de la Cruz/Hermano Pule as just another one of those numerous minor rebel chieftains who led more than 100 revolts in the 300 years of the diabolic Spanish regime — or at least one revolt every three years.

Of course, others say there was one revolt at any time in one province or another all throughout the Spanish centuries but their cases are still hidden in largely untouched documents in dusty archives in Manila and in Spain.

A correct historical perspective demands that Hermano Puli be honored as a leading light of the country's struggle for freedom. This is because his life represented not just a challenge to colonial rule, but the most determined aspiration to the highest form of liberty — freedom of religious worship.

And he was faithful to it unto death.

He is well-documented enough and the basis for his elevation to his deserved place in the totem pole of history can be justified.

Of course, a large part of the neglectful bias against him is due to the fact that he is seen as a challenge to the mainstream orthodox religion. This prejudice existed against sects and their self-determined and self-crafted practices and their beliefs — at least in the rank-and-file members, not necessarily in their top leaders — in unearthly miracles like physical invulnerability through the *anting-anting* or colorful costumes.

Because of this, Western people and most educated Filipinos of all classes summarily regard them with contempt, and dismiss them as ignorant and misdirected.

Our task is not to condemn Hermano Puli for the nuances of his superstitious followers' beliefs. It is unlikely that he himself had the same superstitions, since he was well-versed in theology and had stayed for many years in Manila itself, and he was too spiritually well-grounded or, to use a glossy but approximate word, sophisticated.

Our task, instead, is to take the imperishable value of his struggle for religious freedom, and in his substantial contribution to our nation's overall fight for liberty and independence from foreign rule.

His historic role may be gleaned even from the words of the enemy. Some two years after his death, the Spanish military chief of the islands, Juan Manuel de la Matta, wrote a report to Governor-General Oraa:

"The sedition of Apolinario in the province of Tayabas and the insurrection of the Tayabas regiment [we will come to this in a later chapter — Ed.] have in a little more than one year placed these possessions [the Philippine Islands] on the verge of a terrible civil war and have compromised great interests."[25]

A historian for his part says that although the Puli revolt "is generally treated as a curiosity in Philippine histories, it led to an aftermath which even non-Spanish foreigners took note of, discussed and reported to their home governments. The colonial regime itself was jolted."[26]

Without meaning to downgrade or slight other great heroic movements, we say it is difficult to find rebellions that could equal Hermano Puli's in terms of the estimated danger that the Spaniards said it threatened to unleash on them.

Other uprisings exploded from personal grievances and torments, like Lakandula's. Even in the greater ones from Sumuroy to Maniago to Malong to Dagohoy and Diego Silang and the Tagalog agrarian pandemoniums in the 1740s and — mark this — to the glorious Katipunan itself, rebellion involved a mixture of motives that involved mainly a secular liberation.

The Ilocano Basi revolt in 1807 exploded not because of the desire to do away with the tribute and forced labor, or to challenge friar rule and the vicious *guadia civil*, or to protest long, grueling work in the Cavite shipyards. It broke out because of the desire to continue brewing and drinking *basi*, the wondrous alcoholic drink, which the Spaniards had cruelly banned.

Of course, who knows to what extent of outrage and revolution the people of Southern Tagalog would have resorted to if the ecstasies of *lambanog*, or the people of the Visayas and Mindanao would have reverberated with if the joys of *tuba*, were embargoed?

Why, they would have gone berserk.

Truly, Puli's movement was essentially, purely and exclusively conceived as a determined striving for religious freedom. Because he knew that some reforms were needed which would have been rejected by the Spaniards, he kept his organization secret at first.

Gregorio Zaide describes it as "the first major religious revolt in the Philippines."[27] The safety valve in this statement is the word "major," for Bankaw and Tapar and the Igorots and others before had waged a war precipitated by religious angst.

Some wanted to return to the old pre-Spanish *anito* worship of their forebears, others to indulge in syncretic pirouettes that mixed Catholic beliefs with native rituals and adumbrations.

But we must remember this fact: that from Hermano Puli's elimination in 1841 up to this day, there has been no "major" religious revolt. So his was the only "major" religious revolt in the Philippines.

Parenthetically, it was not similar to the Philippine Independent Church which has had its own glory and greatness. The Aglipayan Church pioneers, whose love of country and religious worship were just as intense as that of any bolo-wielding Katipunero or *cofradia* member, did not as a whole arm themselves and engage in violent struggle.

But the Spanish historian Sinibaldo de Mas, who lived during Puli's time, said that Puli's movement gave "the first hint of a National Church."[28]

The Spanish despots saw that his drive for religious freedom, if allowed to continue, threatened the very existence of Spanish rule. The supremacy of the colonial system depended mainly on the municipal friars and their stranglehold on the Filipino psyche, and it stood to reason that a powerful blow on this state of things could ultimately be fatal to the colonial regime.

This was particularly dangerous because the *cofradia* was not trying to wrench itself out of the dominant mainstream Catholic religion in order to subvert it. It asked for ecclesiastical recognition and could have succeeded in riding on Catholic institutional strength.

Of course, if it is true that, like some subsequent groups, the *cofradia* engaged in superstitious practices and believed in supernatural fantasies, then it had no hope for becoming a mainstream power.

Ileto declares that "the most intense form of resistance [against Spanish rule] was the formation of an alternative church."[29] He was specifically referring, in positive and laudatory terms, to the Puli movement.

The question is: Was Hermano Puli establishing an alternative? Of course not, because he filed petition after petition to have his *cofradia* officially recognized by both the Spanish secular and ecclessiastical authorities, a move that the Aglipayans would never have done under Spain.

And was not the Catholic Church so ingrained in the Filipino psyche that the great alternative that came later, the Philippine Independent Church, failed to dislodge Catholicism?

Was Puli's movement more dangerous — from the Spanish point of view — if it was not an alternative church but one with the desired imprimatur that he sought?

It would be hazardous to compare, or even to relate, it to the present El Shaddai movement which is able to draw millions of followers because, among other reasons, it is recognized by the Catholic Church. El Shaddai and the Cofradia de San Jose are different cases.

In any case, whether recognized or unrecognized by the Church, the *cofradia*'s continued existence from the Spanish viewpoint contained a potential for mischief that was too great to be tolerated or even just ignored. It had to be stopped at all cost before it was too late — if need be, across rivers of blood and fire.

And it was stopped. But in an overkill that shocked the Indios and some Spaniards themselves. The stark fact that stared everyone in the eye was that many women and children were killed.

The incident became a cause célèbre in Manila. It was publicly discussed and the brutality of the deed became a heavy issue even in that bloody era of the Spanish police state where massacres were not uncommon.

The Audiencia, which was a collegial body, blamed Governor Oraa for not making consultations with it first, and for his order to give no mercy or quarter. Oraa, of course, tried to hide his bloodstained hands by heaping the blame fully on the bloodthirsty butcher, Huet, who he said "exceeded his instructions."[30]

Leaflets circulated in Manila castigating the government and proclaiming the Hermano innocent of the charge of sedition and, therefore, he and his people were victims of mass assassination.

Then came a Spanish written account with "a tendency to conceal the facts and to emphasize the worst and to present Apolinario as a monster of vice."[31] For example, it said:

"He lived by himself guarded by top men of his confidence, in all comfort and pleasure, surrounded by beautiful young single women who came in rotation to satisfy his needs. It was also said that he died without any sign of repentance."

A good friar, who was shocked by the blatant fabrications, said that before his execution, "the Hermano was confessed by Fr. Esteban Mena, parish priest of Atimonan."[32] Imagine him confessing to his old foe, Lucban *cura* Fr. Manuel.

A serious flaw in the Filipinos' character is the lack of initiative to put down in writing their knowledge or view of historical events. So without eyewitness Filipino versions or an account by survivors, what are we to make of these Spaniard-told stories: that Hermano Puli convinced his people that during the [Alitao] battle a great lake would open and entrap the Spaniards; that a princess from heaven would materialize and become Puli's wife; that like those Galilean loaves and fishes he could produce from a handful of rice several cavans,[33] or at least several *panegas*?

With such awesome and exhilarating wonders, it is not surprising that his followers called him "King of the Tagalogs." What did the Hermano himself have to do with this?

What was true, according to Ileto, was that in the *cofradia* chapel, "one of the paintings was of this 'King of Tagalogs,'" but it was not as a king of the secular world for "it was done in the style of the saints."[34]

So there. It was either a deliberate plot to smear him or just a misunderstanding.

The story given by the government was that Lt. Col. Huet, the butcher, gave the *cofradia* three days to surrender before he attacked; this proclamation was known as "*bando.*"

But Sinibaldo de Mas, a pure Spaniard and historian who was a friend of Governor-General Oraa himself and was a well-known figure in high Spanish circles, says in a written commentary:

"This merely repels us, because as historians we know that they were not given three days but only a few hours. It seemed as if there was a great hurry to do away with those unfortunate [*cofradia* people]. The point was to punish, rather than to solve, a deep-seated problem that years later would come up again."[35]

Sinibaldo also denies that the *cofradia*'s untrained, ill-armed men immediately ran away at the mere sight of Huet's forces.

In fact, he says, there was enough time for paid government infiltrators to go to the *cofradia* ranks and distribute "the circular of the government and the pastoral letter which the archbishop of Manila had printed for the purpose. But the rebels would not give up, becoming more and more stubborn."

And he makes the stupendous claim that it was the Indios, not Huet, who first attacked, in which case it may not really have been an unprovoked massacre — although it may be said that the appearance of the Spanish troops was the true and original provocation:

"[The rebels] finally decided to come out of the barricades and attacked the troops, who also decided to advance … But the bravest among [the rebels] only got to about 15 or 20 steps from the troops, for as soon as they saw dead and wounded persons about they turned around and escaped."

It was then that the government *cavalry* charged and became a *calvary* for the rebels, "destroying everything that opposed their advance."

After brief comments on the very real danger that the incident had posed, Sinibaldo concludes:

"It is almost beyond the pale of doubt that if the parish priests were Indios [and not Spaniards], there would not have been the slightest suspicion [of the existence of the *cofradia*] until it had been so firmly and generally organized that our [Spaniards'] ruin would have been the work of a week."

A week! No Spaniard, and not even Bonifacio himself, would have thought that the Katipunan could demolish Spain in seven days' time.

That Hermano Puli was correct in trusting only pure Filipino natives who were poor, not Spaniards, Chinese and their mestizos, as well as the rich, was borne out by what Sinibaldo recalled, which confirmed that these people, or at least most of them, had no real sympathy for the lowly Indio:

When the first news of [Puli's] insurrection arrived [in Manila], I was at a gathering of several Spanish officials. They all believed, or at least suspected, that the whites [in Tayabas] had compromised themselves.

I maintained that the Spanish officials were mistaken, since however disloyal and intemperate one may fancy the Spaniards, it was impossible that it would ever enter their heads to arouse and arm the natives.

And now for the clincher: Sinibaldo added that when it was known that the *cofradia* was purely a native insurrection, it was not only Spaniards but the other Europeans in Manila who were reassured and breathed a sigh of relief.

Arrests continued. In February 1842, three months after the Alitao bloodbath, the long-sought Francisco San Juan alias "Purgatorio" was captured in Pagbilao with important papers and was sent to *impiyerno*. Others prominent in the movement also fell.[37]

But Hermano Puli and his Cofradia de San Jose remained in memory. Indeed a little more than a year after his death, in January of 1843, there exploded an Alitao-inspired event that turned Manila itself into a raging battlefield — the mutiny of the Tayabas Regiment, with which this chapter will continue later. The Indios, because of Hermano Puli, were now to bring their gruesome struggle right to the heart of Spanish suzerainty.

We have said that the Hermano was shot and then beheaded in Tayabas town. Present was the Lucban *cura*, good old Padre Manuel Sancho, who took the considerable trouble of riding on horseback from Lucban to Tayabas to witness with steady curiosity the death and final humiliation of his archfoe. Now triumphant, Padre Manuel had the easy tendency to be magnanimous — or truthful? — about the great man. He said that Hermano Puli "died serenely and showed unusual greatness of spirit."[38]

One year and some three months later, on January 20, 1843, came the Tayabas Regiment mutiny.

In Spanish times, the backbone of the army was the rank-and-file Indio troops. Each unit of the military was composed of men from the same province. One example of this was the well-known Pampango Brigade, which the Spaniards often used to quell rebellious natives in other provinces.

The soldiers according to unit were assigned to places not their own home provinces to prevent fraternizing with the population against the colonial government — a policy that was adopted at one time by the Marcos martial law administration as a precaution against home-based resistance.

The Tayabas Regiment's noncommissioned officers and men were from Quezon province, as its name explied. They were assigned to the Manila area, quartered in the Malate barracks.

In that long house beside their rifles and muskets, their ammunition and their gunpowder, their minds and hearts could not be kept from the memory of their relatives who had perished in the bloody massacre in Alitao.

They mourned and tore their hair with their hands over the gruesome fate of their loved ones amid suppressed lamentations which only the dead can hear.

In the dark, lonely rooms of their Malate barracks, they wept and wailed and raged against the foreign oppressors lording it over in their military drills and in the merciless quelling of their own kind.

As soldiers they could stand the violence, the gore, the ferocity of battlefield encounters — but not the massacre of their women and children. As the long shadow of Hermano Puli hovered above them, they traversed the secret and forbidden realm of mutiny, successfully enlisting the future help of a few other Tayabas soldiers in other army units.

The mutiny was one proof that many women and children were indeed butchered in Alitao. Otherwise, why would soldiers mutiny over a fair and gentlemanly battle?

In the evening of January 20, 1843 — a little more than a year from the Hermano's grim extermination, within which their consuming sorrow had not at all subsided — the surging Tayabasin quickly and quietly slithered across the distance between Malate and Intramuros.

In those pre-Edisonian days when there was not a single incandescent lamp in Ermita and the Luneta, under cover of night when both prostitute and foreigner were not on the streets but in their homes, nobody but themselves knew of any impending upheaval.

With only the slightest sounds from their urgent footsteps, they reached the old city's walls and slammed on the closed Sta. Lucia gate. It was opened by some who had scaled the walls and slit the throats of the surprised Spanish officers of the guards. The mutineers, in a moment of communal affinity, did not touch the nervous guards who were fellow native Indios.

They swarmed on to Fort Santiago, whose gates were unlocked by their coconspirators whom they knew were on guard duty. For the first time in the long centuries since Rajah Soliman, Filipinos were sovereign in that tiny territory which the Spaniards had made the seat of their archipelagic suzerainty.

Governor-General Oraa was then in Malacañang wallowing in the effete prerogatives of colonial viceroyship. The next morning, upon hearing the ghastly news of the mutiny, this old ruthless despot, who had ordered the annihilation of the *cofradia*, now ordered the annihilation of the Tayabas Regiment.

But his troops were repulsed by the well-entrenched Tayabasin.

Alas, a little while later, Indio soldiers loyal to Spain were able to open some gates, and numerous government troops poured in like a herd of Masbate cattle on the beleaguered Tayabasin, who with their shortage in numbers fought with a surplus in valor.

The spectacular battle lasted for several hours. Hoping that the government soldiers who were Indios may trade their stupidity for love of their own kind, the Tayabasin kept on shouting to them, while fighting like maddened cobras, to join in the effort to liberate their common homeland.

Thus did a Frenchman named Fabre, a young consul who was an *usisero*, or an eyewitness to the bestial fighting, immortalize himself in Filipino textbooks when, after the memorable tumult, he wrote his foreign minister in Paris:

"The rebels were heard to cry out to their countrymen to rise in arms and fight for independence. This was the first time that the word 'independence' had been said in the Philippines as a rallying cry. It is a milestone, your Excellency, on the road to freedom."[39]

As it has been said, the first Filipino Declaration of Independence did not happen in Balintawak or Pugadlawin, in Kawit or elsewhere, but in Fort Santiago itself.

And unlike the Kawit declaration which was long-winded and tortuous, or in the words of frustrated literary writer-turned-textbook historian Teodoro A. Agoncillo, "sesquipedalian," [40] the Tayabas declaration in Intramuros was, verily, extempore.

In spite, or because, of the odds, the freedom fighters gave so great an account of themselves that it was one of the most ferocious battles ever. No matter that they eventually lost and sustained many casualties, and the 82 of them who survived the carnage were all shot on the same day at the Luneta.

Leading the doomed men were one Sergeant Samaniego and his assistant, Sergeant Neri. Historian O. D. Corpuz notes that "this was the first important execution of Filipinos on this site."[41]

Of course, they were disposed of with dispatch. Those captured alive were herded to the brink of a newly dug pit. Like many victims of the Nazis during World War II, they were shot dead from behind, at the back of their cerebellum, and kicked into their one big common grave, "over which a mound was raised to commemorate the occasion."[42]

It appears that years later the mound was forgotten, leveled by the elements, and no one has since bothered to locate it for meditation today.

As we end this chapter, let us take a brief glimpse at another mutiny that happened 20 years earlier. The Tayabasin, being rank-and-file soldiers, must have been young when they mutinied, but they may have heard of this previous conspiracy in 1823.

Unlike the Tayabas uprising which was purely native, this mutiny was led by Spaniards called creoles, or those white men born not in Spain but in its colonies like Mexico and the Philippines, and were discriminated against or pushed around by the Spain-born Spaniards.

Among these discontented creoles was Captain Andres Novales — note that he was only a captain because, although Spaniard, he was only a creole. He and the other creoles started underground meetings, but the city was crawling with spies and their conspiracy was reported to the government.

The governor-general assigned — meaning exiled — the energetic Novales to Misamis in Mindanao where he could fight the Moros, just like army elements today who are sometimes kicked in that direction to fight today's secessionist rebels.

In that month of June, he sadly boarded the ship to take him to the south, but due to a storm its voyage was postponed. Novales disembarked with a burgeoning proclivity for rebellion.

At night of that very same day that he left his ship, he gathered an impressive rondalla of some 800 officers and men who shared his bitterness and outrage. Just before midnight, they pounced on the homes of Spain-born authorities in the city and clapped them in jail with obvious glee.

The governor-general at that time was, as in the case of the Tayabas mutiny, also in Malacañang. Novales' friend, fellow creole Lieutenant Ruiz, rushed to the house of the previously retired governor-general and asked him to hand over some keys to city gates. When the latter refused, Ruiz assassinated him.

The mutineers could not take Fort Santiago because its officers and men remained loyal to Spain and had dug themselves in. Their commander, it turned out, was the most loyal — and ironically he was Novales' brother!

Novales and his charges easily seized the governor's palace, the city hall, the Manila Cathedral, and all the rest, routing the defenders. Within three hours they were victorious, having started their assault at 11 p.m. of June 1 and mopped up the enemy at 2 a.m. of June 2.

Except for Fort Santiago which they could not take but which they could starve out anyway, they held the entire city. In their mutually intoxicating euphoria, Novales proposed to be proclaimed, and his soldiers by ringing acclamation agreed, as "Emperor of the Philippines." Nick Joaquin writes that "Manila was jolted awake by cries of...'Vive el Emperador Novales!' "[43] — as if they had not already been rudely roused from their sleep by the three-hour midnight commotion.

The incumbent governor-general, upon hearing the bad news in Malacañang in the morning, immediately sent a superior force of which the Pampango Brigade was a part, again, and which had an artillery corps. The one-sided balance — or imbalance — of forces persuaded some, and then later many, of Novales' men to disperse.

The government troops triumphed without much effort. Here is an eyewitness account, by one Proust de la Gironere, also a Frenchman:

Novales, who took his stand in the town hall with one artillery piece and three or four hundred men, found himself almost completely deserted by his followers who set refuge in small groups either in the Cathedral or private houses.

Broken in spirit, he tried to escape with an escort of half-a-dozen men. He found the royal gate shut, but managed by means of some planking to clamber down to the ditch. There, however, he came up against some of the garrison troops, and the sergeant pointing his musket at him said, "Give yourself up or I fire."

He allowed himself to be taken. Brought before a court-martial, he firmly maintained that he had no accomplices; that he alone was guilty and that he had deceived the troops. In the afternoon of the same day he…fell before a firing squad. He died calmly, without any sign of fear.[44]

It was later said of the headstrong Novales, "At midnight he was outlawed; at two o'clock in the morning he was proclaimed emperor and at five in the evening shot."[45] Was it the shortest imperial rule in history?

Joaquin is sympathetic to the short-time emperor. He writes:

"But that long day could have been the last of the [Spanish] empire in the Philippines, if Fort Santiago had only yielded. It was noticed during the uprising that the public cheered and waved from windows as the rebel troops marched past."[46]

The governor-general ordered the execution not only of Novales but of his officers. His friend Ruiz and 15 others were shot at the Luneta. The rest were pardoned.

"Incredibly, the governor-general ordered the immediate execution of Novales' brother, whose loyalty had saved the government. At the last minute, however, the govenor-general was forced by public fury to snatch him from the firing squad and release him. The poor brother went mad from the ordeal."

The family that did not stay together did not rule together.

6. The Ultimate in Intrigue: The Extirpation of Burgos

FR. MARIANO Gomez of Gomburza was a very rich priest. He was born of an exceedingly wealthy couple of Filipino-Chinese blood who knew their business very well.

Because of his unusual stature as a brilliant, talented, respected native priest, the friars could not push him around. The Manila archbishop could, but did not, do so. In spite of the demands of the religious orders, Gomez obstinately refused to vacate his position as curate of one of the richest parishes in the country — Bacoor.

Not that he was greedy. Perhaps he did not want Bacoor's considerable *collecta* to fall into the hands of misfits, while in his hands it served a most useful purpose, as we shall see.

He had stayed there as parish priest for an awesome total of 47 years until he was executed along with Frs. Jose Burgos and Jacinto Zamora.

Before he was hastily executed, he just as hastily executed a document bequeathing the stupendous sum of 200,000 pesos to his son, who was now also a priest. Having thus revealed his behind-closed-doors founding of a priestly dynasty, he was careful to state that he had sired him before he became a priest.

The amount belonged to him personally and not to the Church, we may presume, otherwise the archbishop would not have allowed it. It appears he had plenty of other funds which belonged to the parish and its people which, presumably again, he spent for them.

In any case, secular priests — meaning those who are under the supervision of bishops as distinguished from regular priests or "religious," as they are called, who are members of the religous orders like the Franciscans, Jesuits, Dominicans, Recollets, etc. — then and now are not bound by a vow of poverty.

Of course, in the old days, when the laity had no business sniffing on Church funds — unlike today when laymen may audit parish income — the line between what was personal and what was ecclesiastical fund was hazy.

Fr. Gomez was rich enough to financially assist other rich Filipinos like *ilustrados* and *principalia* who were in desperate need and who later could not refuse him in his requests.

He put up a bank that lent out money without requiring collaterals and interest! This astoundingly far-ahead-of-the-times practice benefitted the nearby salt makers. He was therefore a pioneer in livelihoodism and in propoor banking, which is now established in Bangladesh with the recently-conceived Grameen banks.

Most impressive of all, he persuaded the big landowners — some of whom were not as wealthy as he was and who owed him favors — to avoid troublesome litigation by granting their tenants small parcels of land. He was the first successful agrarian reformer since Dagohoy, who defied the Spanish dispensation by giving out some of Bohol's lands to Indio families.

In Gomez's time, Southern Tagalog was seething in agrarian unrest. Some 3,000 *inquilinos* supported an armed rebellion whose leader, who first laughed at his feelers, he persuaded to surrender. He brought the man and his angry followers to Malacañang where, with him as a beaming witness, an agreement was signed with the governor-general himself for them to return to peaceful life.

The condition was that the land rent would not be raised and no tenant would be evicted for failure to pay it. A good compromise which latter-day agrarian problem solvers overlooked.

Gomez was a nationalist who raised substantial sums of money which he sent to propagandists in Spain — many years before Lopez Jaena and Marcelo del Pilar ever dreamed of setting foot in Europe. At one time, he and two lawyers who sympathized with the cause of the native clergy sent the substantial sum of 20,000 pesos, without demanding postaudit.

When he was younger, he was a dynamic busybody. He initiated a road-building project where, to inspire his workers, he himself worked, sweating it out under the blistering heat of the sun. The circumferential road passed through 12 barrios. The Spanish Cavite governor brought his town mayors to Bacoor to let them see and emulate the phenomenon.

As bright as he was wealthy, he got the highest mark as a young priest in the competitive examinations to choose the curate of another wealthy and much-craved parish, Ermita.

As a defender of his fellow natives, he did not think his participation was limited to simply throwing money at the problems and perils of the nationalist cause in order to solve them. This man of action was also a man of thought — and a compelling orator and writer. He founded a newspaper, *La Verdad*, or "The Truth," where the brightest names in the native clergy gave vent to their sentiments — and helped doom him.

In the fearsome aftermath of the Cavite Mutiny where suspects were arrested and summarily shot, Bacoor folk heard that a small unit of government soldiers was on the way to arrest the well-loved padre, whose only crime was his support for the nationalist cause and his refusal to hand over his parish to the friars.

Parenthetically, it must be noted that he would have been immediately evicted in spite of his protestations if his superior, the archbishop, only agreed or yielded to the friars' demands.

About 1,000 townsfolk, armed with bolos, some coming from remote barrios, surrounded the soldiers to stop them from carrying out their mission. He asked them to desist from violence and go home peacefully, which they did.

Before we proceed, it should be noted that the above facts and those that follow have mainly been derived from a book about Gomburza written by journalist-turned-biographer Sol Gwekoh.

This writer — meaning Gwekoh — spanned the period from the pre-World War II years and the postwar era, and his work was in turn based on sources which his proximity and his leisure afforded him to consult, as it may be verified in its references.[1]

While Gomez was the most respected of Gomburza, Zamora was known widely in the capital. Because he was also brilliant, he was named cocurate of the Manila Cathedral itself with Burgos.

He was also made coexaminer of the archdiocese, again with Burgos, who by virtue of these posts was in a way the most powerful prelate, administrationwise, in the See after none other than the archbishop himself.

It may be conjectured that, with these solid if sensational qualifications, some enemies of Zamora and Burgos, while seeing the two native allies against Spanish priests rise in their careers, must have conceded at least that they deserved their high station by virtue of a dangerous superiority of merit.

Zamora was a Tagalog from Pandacan. He was a university scholar who had engaged in student demonstrations like his also scholarly friend Burgos, who was two years younger. Gomez belonged to the previous generation, being 38 years older than Burgos.

The two brilliant young priests were brazen enough to openly and noisily oppose the ecclesiastical policy of assigning Spanish regular priests to key positions in Manila's parishes.

One of their acts that provoked the gut hatred of the Spanish friars was that as coexaminers, Burgos and Zamora had jurisdiction over the Spaniards, and as such they declared — even if their superior, the archbishop, disagreed and ruled it out — that Manila's parishes properly belonged to Filipino secular priests.

To add to the unpardonable, they proposed the unthinkable — Spanish priests should now serve as coadjutors or assistants of Filipino priests, a monumental reversal of what had been obtaining for centuries. The archbishop, who could not be other than Spanish, promptly quashed the insolent suggestion down.

Burgos also suggested to use rice, or *bibingka*, for the Eucharist — antedating by more than 100 years the Filipino activist priests in the 1960s who proposed the same thing. What an incalculable sacrilege, his Spanish adversaries may have screamed.

Zamora for his part vociferously bridled at the practice of young Spaniards, newly arrived from Spain, who served as acolytes of white-skinned friars for six months, and who were allowed to take the examination for parish priest, while native aspirants had to undergo years and years of study and training before they could even be considered.

As coexaminer, the stunning Zamora refused to receive the Spaniards' applications!

He also denied burial on sacred cemetery ground of a Spaniard who had committed suicide. The friars were outraged, but he simply pointed to the regulation. Fortunately for Zamora, the dead Spaniard had no brother like Dagohoy.[2]

And he dared to sing the High Mass — which only Spaniards were allowed to do with two other Filipino priests. His easy, unconvincing and infuriating pretext: the Spanish priests were late.

Zamora was a friendly card gambler and cockfight afficionado who was sentenced to death for conspiracy to commit rebellion on the basis of a letter he received inviting him to a gambling session. It talked of "bullets" and "gunpowder" which actually meant gambling funds.

It has been said by Nick Joaquin that we have had accidental heroes, and that Zamora was the most accidental. "Even the warrant for his arrest was a joker; it was made out for a Jose Zamora, said to be an energetic foe of authority. But who got picked up was poor, innocent, fun-loving Padre Jacinto Zamora."[3]

This conclusion may not be correct. Zamora was a prominent, highly placed prelate. Those responsible for his frame-up must have known their man. It is said that when the arresting officer, while confronting Zamora, discovered that the name on the warrant was for a "Jose" Zamora, he simply crossed it and changed it to "Jacinto."

The officer would not have done that if he was not sure of the person he was to arrest. It is possible that it was the fellow who wrote out the warrant who committed the mistake by writing "Jose."

In another sense, Burgos was an accidental hero, too, it is said, because he was innocent of the charge of rebellion, or involvement in the Cavite Mutiny. His death, which is the fate of mortals but which made him immortal not only in heaven but here on earth, was therefore not heroic.

But it must be conceded that his struggles and ideas throughout his life were not accidental, but deliberate and willed, and as such he could not be dismissed as a fortuitous hero.

A commitment is not an accident. It is thought out. The final denouement may be fortuitous, but not the heroism itself. He did not have to be involved in the ludicrous Cavite Mutiny to be a hero; in life he already was one.

In any case it is wisely said that a hero, after committing himself to high ideals, sometimes cannot choose the field of battle; the gods do that for him. It was not by accident but by choice and by fidelity to the Filipino imperative that he led the movement to Filipinize the parishes.

Burgos' total shock when brought before the garrote is understandable, not just because, by his brilliance and personality, he was the most promising and the best situated among all Filipinos, lay and cleric alike, or because he was too young to die. It was because, as Mabini said, Burgos did not know it would cost him his life when he started his Filipinization fight with the friars.[4] He underestimated the power, and the evil, of his adversaries.

He was accused in court of conspiring to make himself king, and this blatant falsehood could be invented and foisted upon him for one or all of three reasons: because his stature and qualities were not way below the qualifications of a founding king; or because they tried to concoct the crime of aspiring to kingship in a land that already had a king, which was of course so monstrous an offense it deserved no less than death; or because his Mephistophelian foes wished to fatally taunt him about his supposed ambitions.

Physically, he radiated a handsome and reassuring presence. One Javier Gomez de la Serna later gave a recollection of Burgos:

A Spanish family had just lost one of their children whose dead body the mother, almost driven to madness, held tightly in her arms. I saw a young and serene priest entering the house. With marvelous eloquence, with a human warmth that only noble souls know how to express, he captured the souls of those parents.

With paternal tenderness, he took the cadaver in his arms and laid it on the bed. And when at dawn he departed, behind he left the scene of a resigned Christian home. The man gave the impression of a saint.[5]

The friars so hated him not only because of his Filipinization movement but also because of his withering denunciations in his powerful and influential prose, particularly those published in Spain.

Some works were concocted and falsely attributed to him to put him on the spot. One article he truly wrote and circulated abroad — and that gained for him another formidable foe — told of an influential friar who had robbed the Antipolo shrine of cash and jewelry.

His nationalist articles stand as irrefutable evidence against accusations that he fought only for the parishes, or only for his class interests as a native clergyman out to win privileges and perks for himself and his allies — and not really for the Filipino natives as a whole.

And now we finally come to the top-level conspiracy against him, Gomez and Zamora, and others whom the Spaniards hated because they fought for the Filipino natives' dignity and endangered their rule and privileges.

Burgos was once accused face-to-face of politicking by the head of the Jesuit order in the Philippines, whose words were breathtakingly prophetic. He told Burgos to desist from his Filipinization movement because the issue was "purely canonical and ecclesiastical."[6]

The Jesuit big boss added ominously that Burgos should refrain from "giving it a political color because you may not be able to prevent a doubly criminal hand from writing your name on a banner branded by the seditious."

In other words, the chief Jesuit was warning Burgos that he may become the victim of a conspiracy showing him to be not only antifriar but subversive, anti-Spanish and anti-king of Spain, in which case he may be severely punished.

Could it be that this Jesuit already had an inkling of what certain sectors, long threatened and outraged by the advocacies of Burgos — and of Gomez, Zamora and the others — were already exploring in their minds, and would later successfully implement?

Subsequent facts of history impel a "yes" answer to this question.

What is known forever as the Cavite Mutiny was immediately caused by the lifting of the exemption of soldiers in the Cavite arsenal from paying certain taxes — and other grievances. It had nothing to do with priestly quarrels or priestly kickboxing.

It broke out on the night of January 20, 1872. It took three days to suppress it. And yet, only some 20 hours after it started — meaning in the early evening of January 21 — the first arrests in Manila occurred, as if the mutineers were shouting out the names of their accomplices even as they battled in defense of the fort they had captured in faraway Cavite.

Incarcerated with Gomburza were nine other priests, six lawyers, six businessmen and former government officials. Another wave of arrests followed later, then another.

Spanish colonial rule, now approaching the sepulchral portals of its dying, writhing era, inflicted one of its most violent spasms.

Some 50 rebel soldiers who had surrendered after being promised leniency were executed on January 28 at the Luneta. More followed. Many civilians who were implicated were exiled to the Marianas — priests, businessmen, professionals.

Governor-General Izquierdo's cruel government worked nonstop day and night getting alleged witnesses and taking their confessions — now exposed in history as blatant fabrications.

Gomburza were tried behind closed doors, separated from all the other suspects — but friars, who had no business being there, were there.

Gomburza as accused were not given a chance to defend themselves. Burgos' own assigned defense lawyer, in an unexampled act of terrestrial demonism, declared that Burgos had confessed his guilt. Burgos jumped up and said this was false, he was denying the charges.

The chief judge commanded him to shut up, saying he would be given his turn to speak, which never came. It was a well-organized conspiracy of judicial murder.

The court convened behind closed doors for the first — and only! — time at four in the *afternoon* of February 15. Then the accused were admitted into the hall five hours later, at nine in the *evening!* That was clearly as fast as the Sanhedrin proceedings against Jesus. It was within this period that they cooked up the sentence.

All members of the kangaroo court promptly signed the death verdict by garrote. The extemporaneous decision that same night was sent to the impatient Governor-General Izquierdo — suspiciously impatient because only minutes ago he had sent a messenger hurrying to the court to get its decision!

And the court indeed hurried.

The bloodthirsty, tyrannical Izquierdo stamped the execution order first hour in the morning, eight o'clock. The official records of the trial were never released. On the last two nights of Gomburza on earth, they were incommunicado in spite of their repeated requests to see their families and friends.

Gomez was calm and resigned; at 73, he had lived not only a full life, but as a servant of the Lord. Who wouldn't be at peace with that?

Burgos was quite nervous and pressed for an audience with the governor-general, not suspecting that Izquierdo was part of the plot. He also wanted to insist on their innocence before his archbishop, but was denied.

Poor fun-loving Padre Zamora, knowing he would lose his life, first lost his mind. He wore a blank stare that never deserted him up to his extinction.

Before execution day, Izquierdo asked the archbishop for the canonical degradation of Gomburza — meaning they should not be wearing their priestly clothes when garroted. The prelate, in spite of past verbal tussles with Burgos because of the latter's militancy on Filipinization, to his credit refused.

But it was an easy thing to refuse, since it was a balm to conscience; besides, the condemned men were HIS priests. The archbishop wrote Izquierdo asking for clemency but was ignored.

He wrote again, and this time the despot, probably irritated by his *kakulitan*, told him that the execution must be carried out "to serve as a salutary lesson in the future to those who intend to rebel against the integrity of Spanish territory."[7]

All the minimalist pen-pal-seeking archbishop could do now was to order the tolling of a mournful requiem by the bells of all the churches of Manila on the hour that Gomburza were being garroted. Again, an easy thing to do, being only acoustic. Again, a balm to conscience.

What he did not know, or knew but did not reveal and condemn but only refused the priests' degradation precisely because of such knowledge — was that, according to later allegations which went the rounds, Izquierdo had received an astronomical bribe, amounting to 40,000 pesos, from a group of high-ranking friars, and consequently agreed to execute the three priests.

Any archbishop in those days presumably knew everything, or at least knew more than anyone, including the governor-general himself. If he believed they were guilty, why did he refuse their degradation? Moreover, he would have been the first to raise an outcry against Gomburza if he had the slightest knowledge that the three priests were traitors. But he kept quiet.

On the other hand Izquierdo was so enthusiastic in giving judgment because he was so enthusiastic about the 40,000 pesos.

Some 25 years later there was an amazing turn of events:

In 1897, as the Katipunan Revolution raged, Aguinaldo's men captured two Cavite friars who talked about a shadowy priest who had gone to the arsenal before the mutiny. He said he was Fr. Burgos [which he was not], and encouraged the discontented soldiers to rebel. He even gave money and promises of support."[8]

Was this fabrication conveniently used as evidence in the closed-door trial?

But how could the friars stage-manage this scenario before the mutiny? It may be because they had expected the soldiers in the arsenal sooner or later to make — not necessarily a mutiny — but some kind of trouble, for it was not difficult to know they had been restive for days and even weeks.

It was therefore not difficult to preplot the complicity of Burgos in any kind of trouble there, not necessarily in an outright mutiny. But when mutiny did occur, they jumped at it. And they also clearly used it to implicate other nationalists/Filipinists.

The so-called charges included the story that the Cavite mutineers were waiting for a signal to start hostilities from their Manila cohorts — meaning Burgos et al. — in the form of fireworks.

But the friars, especially, must have known that there was a religious fiesta celebration involving a lot of fireworks that very same evening of January 20 when the mutiny exploded.

One of the friars captured by Aguinaldo's forces said there had been a conference of Augustinian, Recollet, Dominican and Franciscan provincials on a petition for Filipinization, naturally believed to be the handiwork of Burgos.

If that friar knew it, why not the archbishop?

The scheme, as it was claimed, was to destroy Burgos by making him appear anti-Spanish. Note that the Jesuit provincial who had warned Burgos of a possible plot to implicate him in an anti-Spanish subversive movement was not mentioned as present in or as part of the conspiratorial meeting.

It has been noted by some that the hero in Rizal's *Noli*, which was written some ten years after the Gomburza execution, was a young man who defies the friars with his liberal ideas. The friars destroy him by paying a group to use his name as a rallying cry in an uprising.

Was Rizal, who was only 11 years old during the Gomburza garroting, in fact referring in his fiction to what he may have heard as a similar, real plot against Gomburza?

Did Rizal not say, explicitly, in his introduction to the *Noli* that there was nothing in his novel that did not happen in real life, that his fiction was based on fact?

Just as the Spanish friars were curiously present in the trial of Gomburza, they were also just as curiously present during their execution. It would not be too uncivil to say today that they antedated Adolf Hitler, who enjoyed film clips showing the hanging of his fellow German enemies who had attempted to assassinate him in July 1944. Good old Hitler reportedly twisted in uncontrollable euphoria as his would-be assassins wiggled and writhed their last.

The difference was that the German assassins were guilty, albeit heroically, of the charge of attempted assassination. Gomburza were not guilty of the accusation of conspiracy against them. They were the victims, not the perpetrators, of a conspiracy.

Of course, the association of the names of Burgos and Rizal is striking. Both were exceedingly brilliant. Both wrote luminously — and voluminously — for the cause. Both took on the same foe, the friars.

Both are now described by some as accidental heroes. Either can be called "the First Filipino," depending on one's premises. Both died at the same young age of 35.

Wild rumors flew in 1896 that the body of Rizal was first thrown into the same grave in Paco Cemetery where Burgos' remains had first been buried. In secrecy, too, for both were feared for the power of their memory — and history shows that this fear was hardly exaggerated.

February 17, 1872, is an immortal date in our history. Like other such moments, it is better narrated than explained. In this we depend on Antonio Ma. Regidor, who wrote an eyewitness account.[9] It is a detailed — and very partisan — account.

As early as four o'clock in the morning a huge crowd started to gather at the Luneta. Big groups of Filipino native soldiers enlisted in the Spanish army came from various Manila garrisons and were posted at strategic places, with Spanish troops manning artillery pieces in combat positions.

It appears there was much more security during the Gomburza execution than during Rizal's, although in the former the Revolution had not yet exploded and there was no Katipunan at all!

The death stage was surrounded by battle-ready troops under the command of a lieutenant. At exactly seven o'clock a column of soldiers in gala uniform marched in and formed a square on the ground in front of the garrote, as if their colorful sight could remove the barbarity of the event — or its presence exactly was to stress the Spaniards' joy and celebration over such barbarity.

In fact, just as in Rizal's execution more than two decades later, Spaniards gathered on the death site in a cheerful, celebratory mood, with full champagne glasses in hand.

The Gomburza death procession appeared on the dot from the ancient walls of Intramuros. Lines of soldiers escorted the four doomed men, each of whom was accompanied by friars on the left and right sides.

Four? The first candidate for the afterlife was 23-year-old Francisco Zaldua, but he was not going to the same eternal place as Gomburza. He was the traitor who had sympathized with the Cavite mutineers but later turned state witness, presumably in exchange for clemency — and a consideration dangled by the friars just as Judas had been titillated with it.

Zaldua the young fool was smiling during the procession. Alas, instead of an on-the-spot release, he was quickly garroted, but not before "he broke down and cried that he was induced to implicate falsely the condemned prisoners."

Either this account was an invention by the nationalist Regidor or only a few heard Zaldua and these did not bother to tell then, or later. In any case he was not taken seriously. Others say Zaldua was not able to make even a whimper and carried the vile secret of the friar conspiracy in which he had become the last accessory — and his stupidity — to his grave.

Zamora, supported by two Jesuits, "had to be dragged as he did not care to walk." Thus was he rubbed out.

Then the dignified Gomez appeared, flanked by soldiers and by an Augustinian and a Recollet — the religious orders seemed to have divided equally their serene participation in the deadly ceremonies.

Gomez was superplacid. He blessed with his hand the multitude of Filipinos gathered, "who took off their hats to salute him and had fallen on their knees as he passed by."

While ascending the "stairway to heaven," as Neil Sedaka would croon later, Gomez saw the trial judge advocate, one Major Boscasa, who had prosecuted them with horrendous lies. Boscasa "was hiding on one side under the stairs, and Gomez said to him, 'God pardon you, as we are forgiving you.'"

And as the iron collar painfully squeezed out his life, he was heard to commend his spirit to God.

More than halfway of the procession earlier, whose tail-end was composed of soldiers, walked two Jesuits with Burgos, apparently chosen to be the last victim because killing him first would have made the execution of the others anticlimactic and less enjoyable.

The masterminds of his downfall, almost certainly in the crowd of Spaniards seated around the garrote stage and surrounded with protective soldiers, must have wished to have their pleasure enhanced by ocular prerogative.

Regidor says grimly that Burgos "was not reconciled to his fate." When he reached the stage and was asked to go up, he paused and made a final protest. "But for what? I am innocent. This is an iniquity."

When a career Spanish officer, trying to score more points in accumulated subservience to his superiors, tried to push Burgos to go up, he told him, *"Noli me tangere."*

On the scaffold, seeing the thousands upon thousands of mournful and silent Filipino faces, he cried out once more in a loud voice, "My God, I am innocent!"

One of the eyewitness friars responded loudly, "So was Jesus Christ." That impertinent friar was one Fr. Benito Corominas of the University of Sto. Tomas, who was a professorial colleague of Burgos. Regidor does not indicate if the yelling friar said it in sympathy or in mockery.

Burgos, who was good at repartee, was not in his usual polemical mood to give one at the moment. He could have retorted, "And who, this time, is Judas, Pilate, Caiaphas and Annas?"

Or if that Corominas was comparing the case of Burgos and that of Christ by saying Burgos was innocent like Christ, then Burgos in referring to his own innocence may as well have repeated what Christ said in his own trial in Jerusalem, "It is by your own lips that you say so," or, "Thou hast said it."

There were parallels in the killing of Christ and Burgos, and let us touch on them even if any adduced similarity with the case of the Nazarene is usually regarded with disdain, since Jesus is incomparable. But it can help us in our reflection on Burgos.

Both were priests. Both were unjustly condemned through the machinations of the priestly class; the friars were the Sanhedrin, although Burgos was under the jurisdiction of the archbishop. Both were thrown to the mercy of the temporal authority, the colonizer, under whose power they were sentenced to death.

The concocted charge in both cases was under the general category of, for want of a better word, sedition. And both Christ and Burgos were sarcastically touted as kings.

Izquierdo was more stupid than Pilate — instead of washing his hands, he stained himself forever by welcoming, even craving, the task of signing the death warrant. Of course, Pilate was not an accomplice in the initial stage of the conspiracy to murder Jesus, while Izquierdo was involved all throughout the plot up to its fulfillment.

Zaldua also committed suicide like Judas, but in a way that was more or less roundabout, some kind of involuntary euthanasia which he caused the masterminds of the conspiracy to apply to himself.

The executioner of Burgos had roughly the same attitude as the centurion, who was not bloodthirsty like his fellow Roman crucifiers. He asked Burgos for forgiveness, in crisp words that could have been curtly said in the script of a Mexican western cowboy movie: "Father, forgive me for what I am going to do. I will kill you."

Of course, Burgos granted his request, and the *berdugo* knew for sure that the dying priest would, hence his plea. Nobody can imagine Burgos saying, "No, you cannot be forgiven, you are part of the conspiracy to kill me."

What Burgos said was this: "I forgive you, my son. I know you are only complying with your duty. Proceed then and do the work assigned to you."

He then extended his hand, blessing the people who were still on their knees, many intoning the sad litany of the dying, words that Burgos as priest only knew too well from Catholic liturgy and had said countless times on the occasion of other people's death.

Like Gomez, he commended his spirit to God. Before the litany ended, he was dead, the garrote being an instrument of torture and death that disposed of its victims in less than a minute of breaking the neckbone. And then something happened. Regidor writes:

Soon after the execution of Burgos, a sunbeam suddenly appeared through the overcast skies and illuminated brightly the platform where lay [the bodies of] the condemned priests. Immediately a wild stampede took place while the spectators fell on their knees and wept as they prayed loudly, invoking divine help for the eternal repose of the souls of the three martyred priests.

[The phenomenon] frightened the filthy friars....They were stampeded down.

The Filipino crowd now looked sinister to them. [The Filipinos'] haste, their look, their voices, alarmed the European elements who in turn became frantic and ran, seeking protection among the troops that were deployed in the field of Bagumbayan.

The commanders of the troops that surrounded the gallows gave the order, "Prepare and face the enemy." The friars sought shelter under the platform with Major Boscasa and his various prosecuting aides who drew their swords.

The commanders of the regiments shouted to their men to prepare for battle; the gunboats maneuvered for combat; and there, atop the wall of the prison's bastion, were Governor-General Izquierdo and his staff firing through the artillery embrasures. [Then they] ran precipitately to seek shelter behind the parapets.

Only the Filipinos, especially the women with heroic valor, remained where they were, looking with disdain at that shameful episode.

Before his murder, the eminently promising Burgos must have looked forward to a long and successful life. Now, at his execution, the incredible was happening, and he was on the receiving end.

But as one who had willfully chosen to be a priest, he must have been well-acquainted with scriptural passages that "he who loses his life will gain it"; that a mustard seed may be the smallest but it "can grow into a large bush in whose branches the birds of the sky can come and dwell."

Note that on the scaffold, he lost his composure but regained it upon Corominas' mention of Christ's name, and then faced the garrote with courage and grace.

There was fire on the scaffold that morning, and that fire was never to be snuffed out. On the contrary, it became an ever-growing conflagration, like a forest blaze at high noon during a Kalimantan summer. Burgos' death multiplied its radiance in the souls of his countrymen who, in the next generation, became the nation that, consciously or unconsciously, he had prefigured.

7. Bonifacio Extinguished

[handwritten annotation: Rivalry b/w Aguinaldo & Bonifacio]

AMONG THE most diabolical plots in Philippine history is the presentation of Bonifacio as a craven coward.

A moment before being executed, so it is said, the Supremo pleaded for mercy, wept and knelt and embraced with his arms the two legs of his standing executioner. Not immediately getting mercy, he ran away like crazy in a desperate but obviously vain effort to evade certain death.

He was shot dead beside a river within a minute or so of fleeing.

This story is well-known. It was told by the officer who led Bonifacio's execution-ers—Lazaro Macapagal of the Magdalo group, the mortal enemies of Bonifacio.

But the ones most responsible for spreading this canard around were some historians, who published its details in their popular college textbook in the 1960s. Curiously, in later editions of the book, this story was quietly expunged.

But the damage had been done.

In our own day, as late as 1999, a glamorous radio broadcaster, perhaps unaware that this story had a fractured credibility, opined to her millions of listeners that while Rizal died a brave and noble death, Bonifacio lost his nerve and behaved like a despi-cable coward.

More damage to poor Bonifacio.

It was not the broadcaster's fault that she was misinformed. Even some historians themselves, in their professional advantage but intellectual indigence, did not know that there were other versions of Bonifacio's death.

In the first edition of the mammoth book, *The Tragedy of the Revolution*, by Adrian Cristobal, the stories about the execution are not complete.

The best-known version, of course, is the story above. It gained unrivalled currency because it was popularized in schools by some University of the Philippines historians, who enjoyed preeminence in the academe — at least in those days before complaints about their inaccuracies and motive arose. In other words, some UP people can be anomalous — and vicious.

Another version says that the unsuspecting Bonifacio was suddenly and treacher-ously hacked with bolos by his escorts from behind, and had no chance to make any plea or any attempt to escape.

This story was told allegedly by some peasants who had by chance witnessed from afar the execution at Mt. Buntis. They quickly fled in terror for their own lives. It was only later that they knew it was Bonifacio being killed.

What is not widely known even today is another version that Lazaro Macapagal himself had also told, one that differed from his "exposé" of Bonifacio's "cowardice."

This version is narrated in the little-known memoirs of Katipunan General Santiago Alvarez. After decades of oblivion, this autobiography was finally published by the Ateneo de Manila Press recently, in 1992. It was translated into English from its original Tagalog by Paula Carolina S. Malay.

In his book, General Alvarez tells the story of Bonifacio's execution as narrated to him by Macapagal himself. Alvarez does not seem aware that Macapagal had told two stories, or would later tell a different one, as he makes his narration without the slightest sign that he knew of another version.

On page 118, Alvarez quotes directly from Macapagal the following:

> After I had read the order to the prisoners, Procopio wept, embraced Andres and asked, "*Kuya*, what are we to do?" Andres did not say a word. He bowed his head and sobbed while tears welled in his eyes and rolled down his cheeks. Not able to bear it, I turned my back, and when I faced them again, the deed was done. My men had fired the shots and the poor Bonifacio brothers were prostrate and dead.

Why picture Bonifacio as a coward

Since Macapagal told two different stories—and there is no way to reconcile them—the question is: why?

It may be convenient or easy to argue that he told the craven-coward story because he was of the Magdalo faction, who were bitter enemies of Bonifacio. They were the ones who ordered him killed, and therefore had to accumulate all sorts of justifications for it.

But this cannot be used as a decisive explanation, for even if Macapagal was one of the Supremo's mortal foes, why did he give his other version, probably the earlier one, where Bonifacio was not pictured as a coward?

We can only speculate. And in this book we dare surmise that the reason why Macapagal changed his version, with or without the order of high authority, is that the matter of Bonifacio's personality and character had become a historical issue in his confrontation with the Magdalos — and impugning his character was a logical resort to help them face the hard verdict of history.

But the bigger question is: which of Macapagal's versions is the truth?

Noriel

It is not enough to reason out that Bonifacio all his life showed that he was undoubtedly courageous, and therefore the craven-coward story is not credible. For a man may have been courageous all his life, but he could lose his nerve at the moment when death is certain. Unlikely, but possible.

At any rate there is one angle in the version of Macapagal showing Bonifacio was not a coward, as quoted above —which should persuade us to believe that this nonslanderous version is the truth.

Note that Bonifacio's brothers and sisters, being orphans, all depended on him in life. In earlier days he had acted as their father and breadwinner. And he was the leader of the family all throughout, even taking his two brothers into the bloody waters of the Revolution to serve as his own aides.

So while death faced them in the eye, Procopio's last act of turning to his older brother, who had always been their family's chief, is not only believable, it was practically inevitable, or instinctive. In the original Tagalog Procopio's desperate words were, *"Kuya, paano tayo?"*

If this was the case, we can only shudder in the realization of how dastardly and abominable Bonifacio's Magdalo enemies were in fabricating the craven-coward story.

Equally dastardly and abominable have been those latter-day historians who served their obnoxious purpose of character assassination by spreading the tale around.

Spreading the story decades after the event — deliberately, cold-bloodedly, without the excuse of enmity or passion — these historians committed a crime worse than killing Bonifacio's body. It was a horrendous attempt to kill his soul and legacy —in order to mitigate the stern judgment of history.

And they should be called to account for it.

There is another aspect to this tragedy. Macapagal was a trusted subordinate of General Mariano Noriel, head of the military tribunal that condemned Bonifacio to death. Everybody knows that it was Noriel, along with General Pio del Pilar, who had urgently persuaded Aguinaldo to change his decision from merely exiling Bonifacio to executing him.

Noriel was the one who gave the sealed letter to Macapagal ordering the execution of Bonifacio. And he gave it under dubious circumstances.

The Spaniards were about to overwhelm the Naic *poblacion* which General Noriel, as commander in the absence of Aguinaldo, was defending, and where the Bonifacio brothers were being detained by their own compatriots.

The Spaniards' cannonade and bullets were already bursting and whizzing all around, and for the revolutionaries to keep body and soul together, however tenuous that connection already was, there was no time to lose.

Noriel decided to retreat, or escape. But before doing so he made sure of one thing—Bonifacio must be killed. Thus, it was while the rampaging Spaniards were about to raze, in a few minutes, his sphere of defense that he gave the fatal order to Macapagal.

In other words, the heavens may fall flat on the Revolution, everything in their struggle may come to naught and an ocean of blood may drown Cavite, but Bonifacio, the greatest conspirator of the Malayan race, Leader of the Katipunan, Founder of the Revolution, splendid author of "Aling Pag-ibig Pa ang Hihigit Kaya," who had sought the freedom of his country more than any man, already wounded and subjected to subhuman treatment by his fellow Indio captors, and who would have been tortured and killed anyway by the Spaniards themselves if they found him there in that improvised jail, must first die —by the Magdalos' own hand.

As for the craven-coward story, let this be said: If public relations spin doctors today were hired by partisan elements to concoct a story to doom Bonifacio's character in history, it could not have done better than Macapagal's account.

And who were Macapagal's clients?

This brings us to still another aspect. Macapagal's craven-coward story reeks of too much malice. No man of honor would ever have the gall to publicly ventilate such a story about an oppressed and defeated dead man, even if true, for it was just too horrible. Don't Filipinos have a tradition of respect for the dead?

An intelligent reader would see that any man who is capable of spreading that vile story about one who is dead and could not defend himself must have a gross character and should not be believed.

Curiously, that Macapagal actually put the craven-coward story down in his own handwriting for posterity's sake — as if the stakes in having it taken in history as factual were more important than the fact of the execution itself—is suspicious. It appears he—or his superiors who had power over him—had a deliberate purpose in having it committed into writing.

Parenthetically, there is a historical vignette which occurred during the presidential elections in 1965 between Ferdinand Marcos and Diosdado Macapagal. The propagandists of Marcos spread throughout the archipelago a leaflet titled, "The Three Macapagals in Philippine History."

The first Macapagal, it said, was the one who betrayed an 18th-century Pangasinan revolt by conspiring with the Spaniards based in Pampanga.

The second Macapagal was, of course, Bonifacio's executioner. The third, it said, was poor Dadong Macapagal, who ignored the ridiculous black propaganda, which unfortunately may have negatively influenced some unthinking voters.

But unwittingly, it was a declaration, even though it was only a gimmick, further confirming by implication that the execution of Bonifacio was a shame and horror to the Filipino people.

The death of the Supremo must have stunned Katipuneros everywhere, especially those outside Cavite where his name was still more potent than Aguinaldo's. These Bonifacio admirers were in Caloocan, San Mateo, Marikina, Balara, in Batangas and Laguna, even in faraway places like Panay where two of his best friends were successfully organizing a Katipunan army.

His men may have felt like shedding blood from their parched eyes, gnashing their teeth, protesting to heaven, crying out in vain before the nameless horror, and swallowing red-hot coals of sorrow.

His great wife Oryang was drained of life and the brother-patriot Emilio Jacinto grieved as if for all eternity as old Manila's sunset turned to crimson red. And from that hour of dread the abject nation walked into the future with an ugly limp, head bowed in grief and shoulders stooped, as the noble soul of Andres Bonifacio, like a drop of rain falling upon the ocean, became as boundless as the everlasting waters, just as in earthly life his giant heart was larger that his people's little dreams.

But life—and the struggle—had to go on.

The Philippine Revolution was a grievous and gnarled era, not only riven by hazards and pummeled by odds, but also fraught with conspiracies and saturated with plots.

There were the Magdiwang-versus-Magdalo plots that reached their climax in Tejeros, the personal plots of Bonifacio and Aguinaldo against each other, the Tirona plot, the Naic plot, the Bonzon plot, the Biak-na-Bato plot, the Hong Kong Junta plots, the Paterno-Buencamino plot, the National Loan plot, the autonomy plot, etc., until the fatal plot against the Super-General Antonio Luna—after which, with the total defeat of the Revolution only a matter a time, the major plots disappeared for there was nothing worth plotting about or against anymore.

We shall not discuss and belabor all these plots in this short book.

However, we shall not content ourselves with the shortfall in thought that Bonifacio was executed as a matter of political policy—that is, to save the Revolution from mortal division and immortal ruin. The fact was that Bonifacio and Aguinaldo had learned to personally despise each other's guts to the extreme. It was not *trabaho lang*, it was intensely *personalan*.

The personal conflict had become so deep-rooted and deadly. If Aguinaldo had failed in obliterating Bonifacio, would it be tenable to say that Bonifacio would have obliterated Aguinaldo? Probably.

To understand the hurts and hatreds that had developed between the two, each of whom had had personal flaws, let us consider the following:

1. Before the Revolution exploded in Balintawak or Pugadlawin, Bonifacio had plotted to assassinate Fr. Mariano Gil, already notorious to the Filipinos even before the grim apparition of the traitor Teodoro Patino. He was restrained by Pio Valenzuela who said that the assassination might lead to widespread arrests and investigations and to the premature discovery of the Katipunan.

This means Bonifacio was not incapable of committing assassination. Of course, assassinating a vicious Spaniard was not the same as killing a fellow Filipino, something that Bonifacio never did. Besides, wasn't it the eventual mandate of the Katipunan to kill oppressive Spaniards?

2. Aguinaldo in his autobiography, *Mga Gunita ng Himagsikan*, says that Bonifacio and his men recklessly tried and executed three captive friars in spite of Aguinaldo's written appeal.[1]

He adds, "*Saka sinabi ng Supremo na ang sino mang Frayleng mahulog sa kamay niya'y hindi na makatitikim pa ng grabansos.*" Is there some bit of hostility, rather humor or admiration, in that?

On the other hand, some historians are disturbed about Bonifacio's extirpatory attitude when it came to the friars, for whom it appears he harbored no mercy.

In Bonifacio's behalf, it is true that mortal hostility against friars who were oppressive—as distinguished from those friars who were good and respected by Filipinos—was a dominant, rampaging mood during those revolutionary times. Many were summarily killed, others tortured then shot without a word. It was a time when the whole scene was exploding in fire and brimstone, blood exploding left and right in fearsome volumes of sight, smell and wetness.

There was nothing special about the horrors. The case of the two friars ordered executed by Bonifacio, considering the nature and tumult of the times, was no big deal. In fact it came to be known in history only recently, based on a Katipunero's unpublished memoirs.

Assuming this story was true, it may be noted that there was a trial, and a deliberate decision. Bonifacio's critics today should be reminded that, in addition, he never killed a single Filipino, he was the one killed by Filipinos. He is not known to have humiliated any Katipunero. He was the victim, not the oppressor.

More than a year later, after the friars' execution, in an interview in Biak-na-Bato with a European correspondent of the Madrid newspaper *El Imparcial*, President Aguinaldo said, "Andres Bonifacio [was] a cruel man whom I ordered shot."[2]

[handwritten: Bon. Saved fom himself]

Was this always his opinion of Bonifacio, and a sign that even with the Supremo dead, Aguinaldo was not through with him?

It is the privilege of any reader to have his own interpretation of the implications of Aguinaldo's last words about Bonifacio in the chapter in his memoirs talking about the Supremo's death. These words were in connection with the charges of treason and sedition, which included a supposed attempt to have Aguinaldo assassinated:

"Makikitang maliwanag na kung hinatulan ng Pamahalaan ng himagsikan na barilin si G. Andres Bonifacio, ay pinatutohanan ng pangyayari na nailigtas siya sa malaking krimen na tinangka niya at siya'y naging dakilang Apostol at bayani pa ng ating lahi."

In other words, Bonifacio was saved from Bonifacio, his execution saved him from his own ignominy. Was that revolutionary euthanasia?

In Aguinaldo's reckoning above, Bonifacio was a *bayani* and *Apostol* —apostle of freedom? However, when he delivered his historical inaugural address before the Malolos Congress on September 15, 1898, he excluded the Founder of the Revolution to whom all Filipinos are indebted hugely:

Illustrious spirit of Rizal, of Lopez Jaena, of Marcelo Hilario del Pilar! August shades of Burgos, Pelaez and Panganiban! Warlike geniuses of [Crispulo] Aguinaldo and [Candido] Tirona and [Mamerto] Natividad and [Edilberto] Evangelista! Arise a moment from your unknown graves! See how history has passed by right of heredity from your hands to ours, see how it has been mul-tiplied and increased to an immense size to infinity by the gigantic strength of our arms, and more than by arms, by the eternal divine suggestion of liberty which burns like a holy flame in the Filipino soul![3]

[handwritten: Alvarez — caw across B&A arguing]

3. In January 1897, Cavite towns were besieged by the Spanish counterattack, what with the dreaded *cazadores* recently arrived as reinforcements from Spain. During a lull in the bloody battles one moonlit night, in the open air along a narrow town alley, General Alvarez by chance came upon four men arguing heatedly.

No, they were not an incendiary mixture of Spaniards and Filipinos who acciden-tally crossed paths and wanted to cut one another's throats. They were Aguinaldo who had with him Mariano Trias, and Bonifacio who was accompanied by his brother Procopio. All were armed.

In the heat of their argument, Alvarez in his memoirs recalls, "the two parties aimed their guns at each other."[4] He successfully pleaded with them to settle things amicably in the presence of the new parish priest, who presumably was a native and sympathetic to the Revolution, for all the friars at that time had either fled or were already taken prisoner.

But it may be said that both the Bonifacio and Aguinaldo sides were not sincere, that their mutual hate continued to fester without the slightest diminution.

4. Aguinaldo was strongly against the outbreak of the Revolution without arms, thus presumably putting him foursquare against the fiery Bonifacio. The Kawit Katipunan municipal council of which Aguinaldo was the controlling president said so in a little-known written resolution.

Previously Aguinaldo had expressed such opposition in that early Pasig meeting on May 9, 1896—four months before the Cry of Balintawak or Pugadlawin—called by Bonifacio to decide whether it was time to resort to open rebellion.

It was in this same Pasig meeting where Aguinaldo successfully suggested that Rizal be consulted in Dapitan, knowing full well that this would take many weeks. Was he stalling in the face of Bonifacio's perceived impatience?

At the same time Aguinaldo also suggested, successfully again, that as cover Dr. Pio Valenzuela should bring with him an eye patient, who turned out to be one whose family name was, appropriately, Mata, and who also turned out to be Aguinaldo's man.

Was this Mata of the eye problem also supposed to be Aguinaldo's mole in the Rizal-Valenzuela meeting?

Parenthetically, after telling Mata eye-to-eye that his case was hopeless, and putting him in a patient's room in his humble but functional nipa "hospital," Rizal invited Valenzuela to the beach where they could talk alone without anybody hearing them.

5. Bonifacio on August 24, 1896, informed Aguinaldo of the planned attack on Manila, with the shutting off of the lights at the Luneta as the signal for the start of the general uprising. In his autobiography, Aguinaldo bitterly says this "astounded" him because "we were not yet ready."[5]

When the lights remained on did Aguinaldo—who had watched the whole night from the Kawit Bridge with his Katipuneros armed only with daggers but presumably ready to jackknife into the unclear waters of revolution if Bonifacio could indeed handle Manila—form a low opinion of the Supremo's leadership?

And, worse, when the Revolution indeed broke out later, he must have thought that he and his fellow Caviteños were *napasubo*, or *isinubo*, by Bonifacio.

Didn't the Caviteños successfully revolt in Cavite while Bonifacio was supposed to take care of the capital? And since Bonifacio failed, the Caviteños would now be in mortal danger from the Spaniards in spite of their having done their local job well.

Besides, months before the Revolution broke out, Bonifacio and Jacinto led Caviteño Katipunan leaders to a ship in the Manila Bay where a Japanese naval officer, one Admiral Kanimura, courteously entertained their call and spoke in behalf of no less than the emperor himself. The Caviteños were led to expect some decisive help in arms from the Japanese.

When no arms came they may have thought Bonifacio had deceived them. Because of this, days before the Tejeros Convention, Daniel Tirona charged Bonifacio of trying to entice them to a premature revolution because he was a spy for the Spaniards!

Evangelista meets Bonifacio in Cavite

6. When Bonifacio arrived in Cavite, the first official sent by Aguinaldo to meet him was General Edilberto Evangelista, who must have irritated the Supremo by proposing a new constitution for the rebel movement to replace the Katipunan.

Bonifacio contemptuously dismissed the proposal, which in turn could have irritated Aguinaldo. It was an unfortunate, but maybe not unintended, compendium of mutual irritations.

Battle of Salitran

7. In the gruesome battle of Salitran, Aguinaldo's brother, Crispulo, perished valiantly and the meetings among the Katipuneros were postponed to give Crispulo a hero's funeral. Before one meeting dispersed, the following transpired:

General Mojica proposed a resolution of condolence and prayers for patriots who had died heroically, like Lt. Gen. Crispulo Aguinaldo. The Supremo Bonifacio [*who was apparently presiding – Ed.*] thought this was superfluous and objected to such a resolution.

"True love of country," the Supremo tactlessly argued, "and service to the cause of freedom for the Motherland are the most noble attributes that would ensure one's place in heaven. Lt. Gen. Crispulo Aguinaldo and the comrades who died before him are truly blessed in their respective places in the heavenly kingdom."[6]

If the grieving Aguinaldo took this as a most cruel insult rather than a most breathtaking compliment, no one could blame him.

8. For his part, Aguinaldo did nothing to stop or discourage other Cavite leaders like Tirona from assassinating Bonifacio's character. Titfortat.

9. Aguinaldo in his memoirs says that the Magdiwangs proclaimed Bonifacio "king,"[7] and Bonifacio accepted it. Not exactly. This referred to the Supremo's supposed new title of Haring Bayan, which semantically does not mean king of the people, otherwise it would have been spelled *Hari ng Bayan*.

The term *Haring Bayan,* clearly means "the sovereign people," as distinguished from *Hari ng Bayan,* or "king of the people." As a native Tagalog Aguinaldo should have known that.

In the English translation of Aguinaldo's autobiography, Bonifacio is inescapably designated by Aguinaldo's translator, apparently with sarcasm, as "king," and Magdiwang Chief Mariano Alvarez as "vice king." Never in human history has there ever been a title of "vice king." "*Only in da Pilipins.*" Aguinaldo had a lugubrious sense of humor.

In this book, we have previously noted such rebel leaders who were proclaimed "King of Ilocos," "King of Pangasinan" and "King of Tagalogs." Note that three major Filipino figures were executed after being falsely accused, among other crimes, of plotting to make themselves king—Burgos, Rizal and Antonio Luna.

10. When General Ricarte wrote Bonifacio to leave problematic Balara and come to triumphant, celebrating Cavite, the latter refused at first, and could not resist the following dig:

"It is not proper that all the leading Katipunan chiefs should be in the same district or province, intoxicated with the joys of triumph and the pleasures of the moment with their families."[8]

A quaint, if tactless and unprovoked, reply? Was something rankling in Bonifacio in the face of his embarrassing military defeats and the Caviteños' military victories? The Supremo was referring to continued fiesta celebrations in liberated Cavite in spite of the continuous bombardment coming from Spanish ships in Manila Bay.

Did Bonifacio say those words with an eye on his own forlorn troops who may be getting demoralized because while Caviteños stayed in their homes and drank *tuba* and gin with plenty of *puto-dinuguan* and *kambing-papaitan* for *pulutan*, there they were in Balara and elsewhere, moving about as hunted men and unable to visit their families in Tondo, Caloocan and nearby areas?

11. The worst hurt on Aguinaldo, which led to his great consuming anger, came on February 15, 1897. The numerous reinforcements from Spain arrived and some 40,000 *cazadores,* according to his intelligence, were on the verge of attacking his Magdalo turf in Cavite.

Aguinaldo in his memoirs says he swallowed his pride and went to Bonifacio for help:

Aking isinamo sa kanya, na yayamang kaming lahat na manghihimagsik ay iisa lamang ang layon at adhikain, na dili iba't ang katubusan ng Inang Bayan, hiniling ko sa Haring Bayan [note the sarcastic term – Ed.] Andres Bonifacio *na ako'y padamayan niya sa kanilang mga kawal ...*

Nguni't sinagot ako ng Supremo ng ganito:

"Dinaramdam ko Capitan Don Emilio, *na tanggihan ang inyong kahilingan, sapagka't may panganib naman kami dito, na ang mga kastila'y lumunsad sa dalampasigan o baybaying dagat at kami'y haharapin dito."*

Aguinaldo says that what Bonifacio claimed—that he and the Magdiwangs, too, were in danger — was false. This was because in the four months that the insurrection had been going on, the Spaniards never attacked from the sea — and that on land, before the horrible battles against the fearsome *cazadores* could reach Bonifacio and the Magdiwangs, the Spaniards must first pass Magdalo defenses.

A look at the map seems to support Aguinaldo's aggrieved point. Besides, the Spaniards may not have had enough boats to ferry thousands upon thousands of troops for a concentrated amphibious assault that could withstand a Cavite home defense on the shoreline. Hence, Aguinaldo on land was exposed first.

Later, forced to retreat with enormous losses from the mighty juggernaut of *cazadores* attacks, Aguinaldo says that even while he was prostrate in bed, defeated, feverish and delirious from pestilential malaria tremors, his aides said he was unconsciously babbling like a silly child about this incident, often spewing out the words *Bonifacio* and *Silang*.

If true, his hate for Bonifacio, justified or not, must have exacerbated at this stage, irreparable and beyond forgetting — or forgiving.

12. Aguinaldo also talks about a joint general meeting of both Magdiwangs and Magdalos called by Magdalo to iron out differences. When Bonifacio arrived, the Supremo and his men quickly took the seats in the presidential table.

Bonifacio without batting an eyelash proceeded to open the meeting and presided, according to Aguinaldo, *"kahit na ang nagpaanyaya noon ay ang* Pangulong Baldomero Aguinaldo *ng* Magdalo."

Of course, the Magdalos had previously charged that not only did Bonifacio proclaim himself king, he also behaved like a king.

13. Bonifacio and Aguinaldo started as good friends, of course. Before the Revolution, the former went to Cavite to inaugurate, secretly of course, new Katipunan cells. At one time the Supremo enthusiastically embraced Aguinaldo, so says Aguinaldo in his memoirs, because of the speedy increase of the Katipunan's membership in Cavite.

But in those early days, when Aguinaldo was mistreated by a Spanish guard at Manila's port, Bonifacio insisted that Aguinaldo challenge the Spaniard to a duel.

Aguinaldo did not wish to do so and wanted to forget the incident, but the Supremo insisted.

In those memorable, beautiful, precious early days, when there was still no Revolution and they could walk unhindered in Manila, and they had no ill will yet toward each other, Aguinaldo obeyed the Supremo and sent the challenge to the Spaniard.

Alvarez, who was with Aguinaldo in that trip, while they were about to spend the night in Bonifacio's Tondo home—that was how close they were, and that fact could bring us Filipinos today to sentimental tears—teased Aguinaldo about the impending duel.

Aguinaldo was annoyed. Shut up and go to sleep, Emilio snapped at his good friend Santiago Alvarez, who was his sponsor for Katipunan membership. Of course, Emilio and Santiago had a falling out years later in the heat of the Revolution.

To go back to the duel, the Spaniard luckily refused the challenge, and even apologized. But note that if the duel went through, Aguinaldo could have been killed. If Aguinaldo was irritated by Bonifacio's provocative insistence—after all, it was his and not Bonifacio's life that would be at stake—he did not show it.

But it could have started right then and there that historic enmity between the nation's greatest conspirator and its greatest revolutionary leader.

In the second volume of his memoirs, *A Second Look at America*, written in original English with Vicente Albano Pacis, Aguinaldo stresses most strongly again that the Revolution was premature, as if to say that he was indeed *napasubo*.

Bonifacio's great fault?

We noted that General Mariano Noriel and Pio del Pilar led the group who grimly persuaded Aguinaldo to execute Bonifacio. After all, the original sentence of the tribunal was death, which Aguinaldo, probably awed by the unfamiliar prospect of executing no less than the Founder of the Revolution, had commuted to banishment—but which at the insistence of Noriel and Del Pilar and others he restored to death.

In fact, poor imprisoned Bonifacio was shown the written commutation order, which he, wounded and pus-ridden and hungry in detention and cruelly left half-naked with only a blanket to wrap himself with, signed in receipt—relieved by Aguinaldo's decision, we may presume.

But Aguinaldo's later order restoring the death penalty was kept secret from Bonifacio by Macapagal. Whether this was a kind or cruel expedient is anybody's guess.

Why, even doctors today hesitate to tell patients they have AIDS because that's tantamount to a death sentence, besides being a revelation of a past libidinal depravity.

death to Bonifacio

Bonifacio was of course lulled in his hammock into having false hopes. But it would be the depth of poetic injustice to imply today that Bonifacio's tormentors, in his hour of affliction, wanted to nourish him with the milk of human kindness.

Thus, when he was being brought to his execution site, carried in said hammock, he was so curious about the sealed order and asked insistently that it be opened immediately, which Macapagal on Mt. Buntis did and quickly implemented.

Bonifacio's death, strictly speaking, was an "execution." But earlier he was the object of what we may term as an "assassination" attempt, although it started with a skirmish, and some may insist it was a simple case of battlefield wounding.

But how could that be when the Supremo, when shot and stabbed, was not in the act of fighting but was in fact nonviolently approaching, not an enemy, but his fellow Revolutionarios? Let us quote the words of an eyewitness:

Very early in the morning of the next day, April 28, 1897, the Supremo's troops assigned to guard the fort of Limbon were surprised by the sudden assault of the detachment under Colonel Bonzon and Insik Pawa.

Caught unprepared, the guards fell into disarray. As a consequence, Ciriaco Bonifacio, elder brother of the Supremo, was killed at once, and the troops with him were captured and their arms confiscated.

When he heard the gunshots the Supremo quickly came down from his temporary residence inside the fort to investigate ... He was about to approach Colonel Bonzon and Pawa when Bonzon rushed headlong and shot him with a revolver. Wounded on the left arm, the Supremo was easy prey for Insik Pawa, who then stabbed him on the right side of the neck with a dagger.

Blood spurted out and made the Supremo dizzy. When Pawa made another move to attack the piteous Father of the Revolution, Mr. Alejandro Santiago rushed forward and pleaded that they take his life instead.

He was ignored.

The captors...laid the weakened Supremo on a hammock. They bound Ciriaco, the Supremo's brother, rounded up the others and brought all of them to Indang. From Indang they proceeded to Naic, where they locked up the Bonifacio brothers in a narrow, dark room under the stairs of the friar estate house. The thick wooden doors were barricaded with stones and strictly guarded by loyal troops.

Capture & Rescue

The two prisoners were not allowed any visitors and were prohibited from talking to anyone. In the three days that they were detained, they were fed only twice with food that had better not be mentioned at all.[9]

There is a story told of Agueda Esteban, a heroine who later conducted covert intelligence operations for the Revolution. She sometimes journeyed from Cavite to Manila to buy saltpeter, copper, lead and other materials needed to make ammunition, and acted as a courier between General Ricarte and the revolutionary agents in Manila.

In a book series published by the National Historical Institute, it is written about her earlier times:

One day, while Agueda Esteban was selling, she saw a hammock being carried past her stall. Wanting to know who was inside, she ran towards it and lifted the linen that covered the man being conveyed to the tribunal. She saw the Supremo curled up and covered with blood.

Desirous of knowing what had happened to Bonifacio, she approached a soldier whom she knew and softly asked him about the incident. The soldier was surprised and, apparently frightened, ran away. A few minutes later he returned and told her secretly that anyone mentioning the name of the Supremo would be meted the *pena de la muerte* [death penalty].[10]

Such was the fate of the great man in the hands of pygmies.

We shall not venture to guess what crossed the imprisoned Bonifacio's spirited mind as the world turned on its axis and brought darkness to the strange land of Cavitismo. Like Rizal and the other patriots, he had seen his people abused and debased. To Bonifacio it must have seemed decades ago when the idea of forming the Katipunan came to him, so many things had happened in so short a time.

In more peaceful days, as he read history, he gazed upon ten thousand Indio homes, devoured by the vile Kastila; in his ears resounded the cries of maidens raped by masters of three centuries; he felt the eerie silence of the villages, left by menfolk sent to wars and shipyards; and down his skin from cheeks to shoulders and arms and bosom flowed the muted tears of the exiles being torn away for all eternity from their immortal roots, as if he bathed himself in a cold embrace that had never known sanctuary except in the novel strength and honor of his soul.

He vowed to fight and free his people at all cost. Only nine months ago, he had raised the fateful cry: To arms! And the Revolution was on.

Except for the corrupt and bloodthirsty Governor-General Izquierdo and a few others, we may say that those colonial officials and friar bosses, who had presided with hellish satisfaction over the barbarous repression during and after the Gomburza murder, were still around when Bonifacio's Revolution exploded. The two historic events were only 24 years apart.

Why, even today, when the rhythm of history pulsates and careens much faster, elective politicians manage to stay in power for longer periods, as not-so-subtle punishment wrought on those who had elected them and who, as an inescapable example of human stupidity, will elect them again.

The arrogance of colonial power led the Spaniards to think that the Katipuneros, like the Indios of Burgos' time, would again be easily cowed into submission and routed, arrested, shot, jailed or exiled. Indeed, the Spaniards' grim determination and outrage during the 1896 conflagration surpassed in angst and wickedness the previous 1872 pogrom.

And the oppressors' expectation of renewed success was only logical under all considerations, for Spanish tyranny and grandeur had held the islands in iron grip and the Indios were utterly powerless, like a medical patient who was not only paralyzed but senile.

But they failed to reckon with the unexpected existence of a most extraordinary man and his most extraordinary movement.

Their confidence and later shock were understandable because his conspiratorial and organizational achievement was practically impossible to foresee. Nor did any Iberian psychic behold that it would survive its initial reverses and the Revolution it spearheaded would finally cast down to the dust Spanish valor and Spanish arms.

If someone in those days whispered to his friends a plan to organize a secret movement to eventually topple the European colonizer by force of arms even when there was no prospect of getting arms; and if that someone was speaking in detail about secret recruitment and oaths and cells and coded messages as for a fringe group; and if, further, he was not a wealthy person, not a lawyer or even a grade school graduate or a *guardia civil* member who had at least some bit of military experience, but a clerk who lived in a small house and could not afford to buy a pistol, maybe only a pop gun, and could not even spend for a campaign for barrio *teniente*, they would have rightly dismissed him as a drunk or yahoo who had lost his marbles, assuming he had any.

Indeed, both Rizal and Luna received the news of the Katipunan's existence with unmanageable disdain.

And yet the passion and power of this man changed the course of history in a way and to an extent no Filipino could match, much less surpass. It overtook no less than

Jose Rizal, confounded the caution of Aguinaldo, stunned and confused the calculations of Luna, overshadowed the labors of Marcelo del Pilar and Graciano Lopez Jaena, discombobulated the expectations of the cynical, infuriated the colonial army and officials, astonished the university dons of grammar and canon law and rudely interrupted their campus wet dreams, and unleashed torrents of energy and daring that smashed the historical floodgates through which the nation's celebrated heroes, from the Evangelistas, the Ricartes, the Tandang Soras, the Trinidad Tecsons, the Llaneras and Tinios, the Agueda Kahabagans, the Malvars to the tens of thousands of Filipino freedom fighters, only followed his lead and marched resoundingly forward to the fields of battle and to the pantheon of our national glory.

What a pity that some today take for granted, or even demean, that man's achievement that was as immeasurable as it was magnificent.

It is no accident or inanity that the monuments of Rizal are static and serene, while those of Bonifacio are dynamic and surging. The representation is apt in both cases. Rizal stood for peace, Bonifacio for war; the former was for vertical elevation in character, the latter for onrushing forward movements to freedom.

And where one was cerebral and sublime, the other was robust and elemental.

Together they provide an example of how the fine Xrays of philosophy differ from the muscular emanations of poetry, of how thought and action can be contained in the hearts of different heroes in different existential volumes and ratios, with Rizal being philosophy in-depth and Bonifacio poetry incarnate.

One was ruminatory, governed by the mind; the other was sanguine, driven by impulse, and yet also full of thought.

Moreover, Rizal believed in the power of collective virtue, Bonifacio in the virtue of collective power. Both perished, for death is the leveler of the seekers of life.

Life during the colonial times was described with heartbreaking pathos by Apolinario Mabini. Cesar Adib Majul quotes him: "Feeling pain, the Indios became aware that they lived and then reflected on how they lived. To wake up was painful and to work to live was more so. But it was necessary to live." [11]

The Supremo taught the opposite : that in slavery it may be necessary to die—to die fighting for freedom.

Bonifacio as the solution to tyranny in the form of poetry in motion and commotion is not an original idea of this book; this has been said by other Filipino writers. Besides, foreign authors today have claimed that the only solution for example, to the question of human suffering—why we have to suffer for various reasons and even for no reason at all—is neither ideology, nor science, nor philosophy, nor religion, nor stoicism, nor ideas of the transcendent, nor the amazing but bland science fiction of the future, but poetry.

Whatever they meant, or pretended to mean, or said but really meant nothing, is better illustrated by Bonifacio instead of it illustrating Bonifacio.

A bias against Bonifacio has existed then and now in some sectors—among our former conquerors, because he led his people's grand attempt to be free from them; among certain of the upper classes who cannot accept leadership from below in times past or even as an idea; and among individuals of various stripes who are above him in various aspects of existence but way below him in patriotism, achievement, intelligence and valor.

But such is the greatness of Bonifacio that his stature remains unvitiated or undiminished in spite of their academic duress. To strike at him for his faults is for rats to nibble at fallen logs at the foot of the great mountain named Bonifacio.

They can never make a molehill out of that mountain.

The Revolution had led to his own undoing, prompting some present-day observers to say that it devoured its own father. Worse than being devoured by its own mother — Mother Spain?

The courage of his life can neither be denied nor obscured. Like a fist rising from the quagmire, he had seized greatness by the throat, and from his tightened fingers the scum of history squeezed out like tiny streams of seamy waste, leaving in his grasp nothing but the timeless love and gratitude of his people.

He held infinity in the palm of his hand; not only did he finally belong to the ages, the ages now belonged to him.

8. Noriel Devastated, Pio del Pilar Execrated

ACCORDING TO Aguinaldo in his memoirs, two of his favorite generals, Mariano Noriel and Pio del Pilar, joined Bonifacio in conspiring to organize their own government that had been elected in Tejeros with Aguinaldo as president. Bonifacio wanted to replace him as president.

This, of course, was treason from the viewpoint of the Tejeros government. The fight between Bonifacio and Aguinaldo had become deadly.

The well-known story goes that one night, in a big dimly lit hacienda house in Naic, Bonifacio, who was defeated by Aguinaldo in the elections, was with Noriel and Del Pilar, along with General Ricarte, the Alvarez brothers and many others discussing their next moves, one of which was the appointment of Del Pilar as overall commander of their armies.

Aguinaldo, who was looking for some of his soldiers, came into the house and surprised the conspirators. Bonifacio and his two brothers—Aguinaldo also had two brothers, brothers being serviceable during the Revolution—and the others promptly left the house due to Aguinaldo's unexpected and unnerving appearance. But not without first having a gentlemanly but strained exchange of amenities with Aguinaldo.

Noriel and Del Pilar remained and both apologized to Aguinaldo, saying they had been taken in through false promises and claims by the Supremo.

One of these claims was that Aguinaldo had sold out the Revolution by negotiating peace with the Spaniards through an emissary, a Spanish friar with the quaint family name of "Pi," otherwise a mathematical configuration involving circles.

Aguinaldo forgave the two and accepted their apology, keeping them in his highest graces and even appointing Noriel chairman of the military commission set up to try Bonifacio for sedition and other crimes.

This was not difficult to do, for those were dangerous times of conspiracy and intrigue, and it was better to be deliberate and accommodating than castigating and truculent. Revolution, like politics, is addition.

Besides, they were really HIS generals from the beginning. In terms of loyalty they were, like respectable women, sort of chaste, except that with Bonifacio they were momentarily aroused.

Noriel's appointment as tribunal chairman to try Bonifacio was a very inappropriate—and ominous—appointment, considering that with his protestations of loyalty to Aguinaldo, was he not expected now to be biased against Bonifacio to prove such loyalty?

But then, wasn't Aguinaldo himself, as president, the ultimate authority who would judge Bonifacio? Who could be more biased against Bonifacio than Aguinaldo?

It may be noted that almost 80 years later, Ninoy Aquino said that although President Marcos had already declared him guilty even before the start of his trial by the military tribunal, it was still Marcos in the end who as commander in chief was empowered by law to review and issue the final decision.

In effect, said Ninoy, Marcos was his investigator, prosecutor, judge and executioner rolled into one.

Aguinaldo told the story above of the Naic conspiracy starting with his suspicious first peep from the outside into the dining room where the conspirators were intensely in conference, ending his narrative of the incident in his memoirs again with a dig at Bonifacio:

> *Subali't gaanong pagkamangha ko na nasa kanan ng* Supremo *ang dalawa kong general na minamahal, sina* Heneral Del Pilar *at* Heneral Noriel... *at marami pang iba....*
>
> *[Pagkatapos na kami'y nagbatian, saglit akong umalis para hanapin ang aking mga tauhan] ay may patakbong dumating sa akin at ibinalitang ang* Supremo *at ang lahat ng mga kasamahang nagpupulong ay nagpanakbuhang manaog sa hagdanan.*
>
> *Mabuti na lang daw at nahawakan agad ni* Heneral Ricarte *ang* Supremo *kung kaya hindi napasubasob sa pagmamadalian at pag-aagawan ng pagpanaog.*[1]

But who were Generals Mariano Noriel and Pio del Pilar, and what were the subsequent events in their lives?

Orlino A. Ochosa, a careful and reliable historian who is our main source in the latter half of this chapter, collects in a biography descriptions of Pio del Pilar from various sources, some of which are:

> *Antipatico*...womanizer... sports a villainous-looking moustache and a sharp sinister look...sly...cattle thief...hinted at as Aguinaldo's hatchetman to assassinate Nakpil and other Bonifacists after the Bonifacio killing...rather unsavory...distinguished himself with immorality and misdeeds whom the

[Malolos] government wanted to discipline by threats of dismissal…denounced for his harsh methods…[3]

Immediately after the Pact of Biak-na-Bato, this great Revolutionary General Pio del Pilar joined the Spanish militia. *Aba!*

And then later, having joined the Revolution again against Spain when Aguinaldo returned from Hong Kong with American support, and after the Revolution when Aguinaldo had been captured, he was suspected of being partly responsible for the fatal disappearance of another Filipino general—and suspected also of becoming, rather most unbecomingly, a paid informer of the Americans. *Aba!*

He contributed a document—said later to be forged, by himself?—that helped in the conviction and execution of the last of the top-level patriots. This was none other than General Macario Sakay, under whom he, good old Pio, was operating as a guerilla officer, and whom he was praising to high heavens!

He had his good side, of course—patriot nonetheless, a courageous and brilliant battle tactician, admired and praised by no less than Antonio Luna, fearless and could defy Aguinaldo himself as on the latter's order to give way to the Americans just before the Mock Battle of Manila, etc., as we shall see.

Was he a cattle thief—or only a cattle trader? He sold meat to the Jesuits and others. He helped no less than the great Emilio Jacinto put up a sort of business by having the three thousand carnivorous men of the famous Pio del Pilar Brigade buy Jacinto's meat —and he refused to accept a single centavo as commission!

We shall deal with this problematic Pio later. Our first subject in this chapter is Mariano Noriel.

Pio del Pilar's not-so-flattering picture on the cover of Ochosa's book may lead the suspicious reader to imagine he, Del Pilar, was some village toughie, maybe not without a tendency for sexual harassment, who had blundered into the Revolution's officer corps. Meanwhile, the pictures of Noriel, like that one in Aguinaldo's biography,[4] show Noriel to be pleasant-looking, with a mien that was obviously acceptable among Christians and not unqualified to perform the duties of a *sacristan mayor*.

Noriel was a dyed-in-the-wool Caviteño from Bacoor and was therefore Cavitistic. He was born in 1864 and was therefore five years older than Aguinaldo.

Unlike Pio who left an autobiography, albeit only of monograph proportions, Noriel apparently was bio-shy, and the National Historical Institute[5] claims nothing is known today about his education.

But his appointment as chairman of the deadly commission to try Bonifacio may indicate he may have had some legal background or at least some high education which made him qualified or tenable for such a high-voltage post.

From the start of the Revolution Noriel almost immediately became a brigadier general, and later lieutenant general. He distinguished himself in many battles—like those in Cavite which he fought alongside Generals Pio and Ricarte Vibora and others including, at one time, Bonifacio himself and his troops from Manila and its environs.

It was Teodoro Agoncillo who gave Noriel great national renown among college students, for it was he who talked in his textbook about the latter's role when the Filipino Revolutionary forces had totally encircled the Spaniards in Intramuros.

In that situation, the Spaniards were on the verge of starvation in the Walled City, eating horseflesh and rats and drinking coliform-infested water, fetched from the Pasig River when the Revolutionaries were not looking, beyond hope of aid from the outside.

The ragtag Filipino armies had dug in along a formidable line of trenches surrounding Intramuros in a huge semicircle that extended for more than seven miles from vital Pasay in the south, where Noriel was commander, to the east up to the north in Malabon.

Filipino troops were also in full control of Binondo, Tondo, Sta. Cruz, Quiapo, Sampaloc, San Miguel, Ermita. The only escape route for the Spaniards was through the sea, but they had no ships and, moreover, Dewey and his fleet were in Manila Bay without liquor to affect the accuracy of their artillery marksmanship that had routed Admiral Montojo.

Unknown to the Filipinos, who were the allies at that point of the Americans, the latter were determined to capture Intramuros for themselves and, as events later showed, they were under instructions from Washington that they should be the ones to capture Manila, to the exclusion of the Filipinos! And that joint Fil-Am occupation later was out of the question for obvious political and diplomatic reasons.

When the Americans decided it was time for their troops to attack Manila, they had to do it by land, along the Parañaque-Pasay shore occupied by who else but the fearless Noriel and his entrenched forces.

So the American commander now faced a dilemma because Aguinaldo's forces fully occupied their chosen lines of attack. According to Teodoro Agoncillo, the American commander General Green "concocted a plausible excuse, namely, that the old 6-inch columbiad [artillery] which Noriel had in his trench was already obsolete and very ineffectual against Spanish artillery.

"Green suggested that if Noriel would evacuate his trenches to about 400 yards from the shore [and let the Americans occupy the vacated area] he would give the

Filipino rebels 'fine pieces of artillery.' Either because Noriel was naïve or sincerely believed in the good intentions of the Americans, he considered the idea...."[6]

But Noriel, who was no less than the Revolutionary armies' formally designated chief of Manila operations, chose to let Aguinaldo make the decision and Aguinaldo, headquartered in Cavite, ordered him to give the territory and its hard-dug trenches to the Americans. But only if the American commander, Aguinaldo stressed, would make his request in writing—a vital and clever piece of machination on the part of the Mabini-advised Aguinaldo in those critical moments of suspicion and of the need for determining who had primacy in the struggle.

General Green promised he would and—after he had occupied Noriel's trenches —never did. Cleverness could never win over treachery, for even Houdini could not have defended himself if a friend swung and buried an axe in his back, not having eyes there.

While giving way to the Americans, so the well-known bit of history goes, Noriel finally saw their own folly and wept openly before his nonplussed troops.

Parenthetically, days before this happened Noriel showed his amazing sense of enterprise. He discovered—through his spies?—that the American officers "were preparing charts of the area from Pasay to Pasig,"[7] which bolstered their suspicions that the Americans had arrived from across the seas with the most shameless and evil intentions.

Then, even as the Filipinos held the rest of the trenches without malice aforethought, the Philippine-American War broke out on the night of February 4, 1899, when an American soldier shot a Filipino trooper walking on a bridge, and the latter's comrades shot back.

Key Filipino generals at the time were not in their posts, like Ricarte and others who were in Malolos, having been summoned on other matters by Aguinaldo. Meanwhile, Luna, in the midst of the historic turmoils, was in San Fernando, Pampanga, admirably having secretly sneaked out at night from battle-threatened Caloocan to visit a sick sister for a few moments, with the fulfilled intention to rush back to the company of his troops before daybreak in order not to demoralize them with his absence.

Which showed that the Americans, not the Filipinos, had provoked and planned the outbreak, to stampede successfully the American Senate—amid self-righteous courage in the Hearst yellow press—into ratifying the Treaty of Paris that ceded the islands from Spain to the United States.

Neither was the then 35-year-old Noriel with his troops on that day of infamy and peril. Showing once again his amazing sense of enterprise, he was in Parañaque—getting married![8]

Since war had broken out, he had to leave immediately the marital explosions to attend to the martial explosions. Such was the measure of his true patriotism, an extreme personal sacrifice unknown to Mark Anthony.

The Americans attacked Noriel's forces on land and at the same time bombarded him from the sea. He had to maneuver out of the impending disaster at great cost. After a few weeks more American reinforcements in men and weapons continued to come in horrendous numbers, and for the Revolution thereafter it was continuous retreat.

Three years of attrition later they treacherously captured Aguinaldo, and the mainstream Revolution ended. But the Revolution, having demonstrated unmatched Filipino courage, had declared independence, put up the first constitution and republic in Asia, and proved to be a successful flop.

Noriel did not surrender even as the captured Aguinaldo, saying, "Enough blood," had called on all Filipino generals from his detention quarters in Malacañang to lay down their arms. He waged guerilla warfare in Cavite, but human endurance and courage could only go so far.

One full year after Aguinaldo's perfidious arrest, and only one month before General Miguel Malvar, supposed to be the mainstream Revolution's last general to surrender, gave up, Noriel brought himself in.

In those days, some revolutionary guerillas fighting a lost war all over Luzon were merciless in their assaults on fellow Filipinos who were collaborating with the American dispensation. But Noriel was a kind man who was never known to have committed an outrage against his own population.

Noriel then lived in peace in his hometown of Bacoor. Unfortunately, he had a most energetic rebel cousin known to historical records only as Felizardo, whom the American colonial government called a bandit, and whom it could not catch.

In those days, revolutionaries who continued the struggle to the embarrassment of the Americans were called bandits and were most ferociously tracked down. Not that a bandit was necessarily a revolutionary, but a revolutionary was necessarily a bandit.

Felizardo became the most hated prey of the colonial government in Cavite, particularly of the American-led constabulary. Even if no one could choose or un-choose his relatives, they implicated Noriel with Felizardo's depredations. Three times they charged Noriel in court of *bandolerismo*, and each time he was acquitted for lack of evidence, naturally.

It was already a sign that they may have wanted to frame Noriel, even after Felizardo had already been killed during a constabulary operation.

Such consistent exoneration from consistent accusations must have multiplied the American constabulary officers' hatred of Noriel. They may have never forgotten he was their great Revolutionary foe who never kowtowed to them like some other brown natives.

Then Noriel was charged with a murder committed in 1909. In 1914 he was convicted, and on January 27 of the following year he was hanged.

The case was about a man who, in Noriel's hometown of Bacoor, was killed in his bedroom just after midnight while sleeping beside his wife. A bayonet or long double-bladed weapon had been pushed rudely and deeply through his neck. His painful death gasp or gargle, probably not unlike that of Commodus from Maximus' thrust, awakened his wife, who saw the killer jump out of the window but did not recognize him because it was dark.

Three men were charged with the crime. One of them, the supposed mastermind, was the rival of the murdered man for the affections of a local lady, whom we may presume was irresistible. Hell knows no fury like a man outwitted?

Curiously, the prosecution witnesses recanted their testimony and the judge had no choice but to acquit the three. Later, the provincial fiscal filed another complaint over the same murder with an apparent bias for numerology, charging another three of the crime—Mariano Noriel as the mastermind, the incumbent mayor of Bacoor as an accomplice and another as the executioner.

More curiously, the witnesses against them were the same persons in the previous case over the same murder who had by their own admission committed perjury. The judge who had acquitted them most properly inhibited himself in the second case. The special judge appointed to try the case convicted Noriel and the others and sentenced them to death by hanging. The verdict was affirmed by the Philippine Supreme Court.

Most curiously, the very same witnesses again retracted, and the task of the Noriel defense was now to overthrow the death sentence—all the way to the United States Supreme Court if necessary.

It was the most sensational criminal case during the American regime, and it involved the era's biggest names—including US President Woodrow Wilson.

Mrs. Mariano Noriel was doing everything she could to save her husband. The living legend of the Revolution, Emilio Aguinaldo, who during that period had vanished from public view, rose in familiar crew-cut apparition and moved to express his determined support. The newspapers in Manila "unanimously maintained Noriel's innocence."[9]

Noriel's lawyer was no less than the great first diplomat of the nation, Aguinaldista Felipe Agoncillo, who had jousted with the foes of Philippine independence from Washington to Chicago to Paris and Madrid. Later, another lawyer, American Amzi B. Kelly, took up the case after sentencing, saying that his fellow Americans did not understand the Filipino psyche on a certain matter.

He was referring to the fact that instead of trying to reopen the case, Noriel's lawyers appealed for clemency. Here is Kelly's point, a cry in the wilderness that was elaborated in a book.

In the Philippines in those days, there were judges who were shamelessly corrupt, exchanging their vows for a mess of pottage. With this in mind, innocent clients who were convicted and had no chance of being vindicated by the same corrupt system—sounds familiar today in an era of hoodlums in robes—would willingly go to jail with the understanding that three or four years later they would easily be pardoned. Lawyer Kelly says he found this out in his years of practice in the Philippines. He stresses in his book:

> Mrs. Noriel, an estimable woman, insisted on an appeal to the US Supreme Court. But the [Revolutionary?] leaders, imbibed with [the above] line of thought, and delighted and overjoyed at Governor-General Harrison's [pro-Filipino] public utterances on the Luneta on arrival [in Manila], told her, "That is un- necessary. We now have a governor-general friendly to the Filipinos, and he will pardon General Noriel and the malicious scheme will lose out."
>
> They tried to get Harrison to pardon General Noriel—not a complete par- don but the commutation to life imprisonment, expecting later, as he was inno- cent, to obtain complete liberty.[10]

In other words, says Kelly, instead of understanding the Filipino's psyche and sys- tem, some Americans took the plea for clemency as admission of guilt. Worse, as Agoncillo said, American governors-general had the tendency to believe their fellow American subordinates and constabulary officers as infallible and completely reliable as against the Indio testimony, implying unmistakably that Harrison had been unjustly influenced by his insular countrymen.

In fact, it was noted that "the secretary of [the previous governor-general] Forbes, a Mr. Minturn, drove the assistant solicitor general who prosecuted the case in his car to Cavite on nearly every morning of the trial." [11]

It was noted that the accused in the previous case, one Gregorio de Guia, was acquitted largely because he was a Philippine Scout whose commanding officer, Ameri- can Captain Small, in his oversized influence, "appeared as a witness in court to testify [in favor of De Guia] on a point so trivial that one can only conclude that his main purpose was to impress the court with the fact that De Guia could count on [his] support." [12]

Indeed, no Filipino in those days understandably could win against Americans or those with American support because that was one of the premises and effects of colonialism—until young lawyer Manuel Quezon caused the conviction of an American, a powerful publisher and lawyer at that, and, partly on the basis of this singular triumph, became a sensational political possibility acclaimed in the nation's capital.

Another amazing development unfolded when, after the death sentence had been pronounced against Noriel et al., and affirmed by the Philippine Supreme Court, the same witnesses, who had recanted in the first case and then redirected their forbidding finger of accusation to Noriel in the second case, again retracted!

As it was said further in Kelly's book, "We have here a case where the [same] witnesses against Noriel first say black, then white, then black again, then white again. With such a case it is not possible in conscience to convict." But the general was convicted.

Contrary to the expectation of the defense, Harrison—who incidentally had thrilled Filipinos and offended his fellow Americans with his stunning anticolonial slogan, 'The Philippines for the Filipinos'—refused to intervene in Noriel's favor.

At that stage entered the dragon—Manuel L. Quezon, then the country's resident commissioner to the United States.

Quezon had also been a *revolutionario* and therefore Noriel's comrade-in-arms, a minor officer with a slightly more-than-respectable record of battlefield heroism under Tomas Mascardo, a Caviteño and also an original general of the Revolution who had fought in as many battles and intrigues as Noriel or anyone, including an aborted shootout with General Antonio Luna over the petty anatomical dispute of who between them had the bigger balls.

Quezon, with his bewitching powers of persuasion, mesmerized President Wilson, who consequently cabled Harrison to reinvestigate the Noriel case! In effect this could mean, optimistically, the shelving aside of the death sentence.

Harrison, one of Quezon's best friends and, of course, a political protégé of Wilson who had appointed him governor-general of the Philippines, unexpectedly was outraged. He said his president should not intervene, otherwise he would resign!

Unexpectedly, too, Wilson forgot Quezon's importunings and withdrew his instruction to reinvestigate.

Then the bells began to toll, and it tolled for Noriel and his coaccused. His hanging was scheduled for high noon on January 17, 1915. Two days before this black date, Aguinaldo again tried to save his general.

With Kelly, he made a call before the aging Chief Justice, the renowned pro-American Cayetano Arellano, who granted a hearing on the case and scheduled it at nine o'clock on the same day that Noriel was to be executed only three hours later!

But, as later described by Kelly, who being a lawyer had a professional craving for unbridled verbosity, "Secretly, surreptitiously, contemptibly and un-Americanly, the time of execution was changed from 12 noon to 6:30 in the morning, after [the prison authorities concerned] had been notified of the hearing granted for nine a.m."[13]

Noriel was hanged before Arellano could, or would, cry uncle.

Kelly said he believed Governor-General Harrison, whether he ordered the advanced hanging or not, knew of the change in schedule because later he did not remove the prison officials responsible for the deed. And Cayetano—no relation to a very legal senator today—and his court did not bother to look into the matter.

Such was the pervasiveness and persuasiveness of opinion in favor of Noriel's innocence that as late as 1987, or only 13 years ago with Cory Aquino as president, the Historical Conservation Society published a book detailing the whole course of the celebrated trial, in an effort to show through its proceedings and transcripts how unbelievable was the conviction of Noriel and how justice was miscarried under the solemn auspices of American rule—or misrule.

Noriel's last words were that he was innocent; that, he said, if Christ suffered for the sins of others, who was he, a poor creature, to complain about being unjustly sentenced; that his death was "an expiation of a crime I did not commit….Do not mourn for me."[14]

He was only 50 years old.

Pio del Pilar's father was surnamed Isidro. But it is said that he changed it to Del Pilar to avoid being suspected as a *filibustero*. Does this mean that Del Pilar's father, or his father before him, was profreedom, in one way or another, and that the name Isidro had already become suspect?

Ochosa expresses surprise at the choice of that dangerous name of Del Pilar, and surmises that Pio's father was an admirer of Marcelo del Pilar. But at that time—remember we are talking of Pio's father and not of Pio—Marcelo del Pilar and his nephew Gregorio were neither well-known nor accursed. This is because Pio's father was much older than Marcelo, and Gregorio was only a toddler. Therefore, no Del Pilar was yet in the Spaniards' hit list; the name Del Pilar was not yet dangerous.

Pio was born in 1865, one year younger than Noriel. He must have shown some neighborhood leadership qualities. In his early 20s he got elected barrio *teniente* of Culi-Culi, Makati. He started small-time.

Although he was not wealthy, he was somewhat *principalia*. The *guardia civil* for some reason arrested him and, under third-degree torture, unsuccessfully tried to make him confess he was a *filibustero,* which truly he was not.

That he was arrested and tortured at all shows he was not exactly pro-Spanish either. Or that they sensed, correctly, in his temperament or in that sinister face with those sinister eyes, some glimmering proclivity for the hidden and dangerous elements of insurrection.

Four months before the outbreak of the Revolution, presumably still smarting from the agonies inflicted on him, he obliged his *guardia civil* tormentors by joining the Katipunan.

Two weeks later the Culi-Culi chapter was formed with the Supremo himself inducting the members, whose secretary was Pio. It appears that he was unimpressed by Bonifacio.

When the Revolution broke out, Bonifacio gave him orders to join the first grand attack in San Juan, but Pio with his Makati squadron found himself trekking towards the victorious Aguinaldo in Cavite.

In no time he proved himself as a battlefield commander. Aguinaldo quickly promoted him, calling Pio his "beloved General." [15] His case was different and special because, while he was not a Caviteño, he came in early in the struggle. And he was an unmitigated plus in Aguinaldo's war effort, striding into the scene like an Oriental mini-Patton in the bloodiest and most important battles.

When they lost Cavite to the Spaniards, Aguinaldo moved to Biak-na-Bato. In that most perilous journey where they feared Aguinaldo could be assassinated or ambushed by either the Spaniards or the Bonifacists, Pio the Makati hardball wonder was the only non-Caviteño of the five generals who served as extracareful escorts.

As most trusted top-level henchman of no less than the president of the Republic, who was also a legendary general with the supernatural powers of Cavite's Nardong Putik's *anting-anting,* he had gone a long way from Culi-Culi, which in the 1960s was to gain distinction as the place to get libidinal pleasures the short way.

With the Pact of Biak-na-Bato, Pio was among the revolutionaries who remained in the country while Aguinaldo sailed to the conspiratorial exile in Hong Kong.

Ochosa writes that the rebels who remained at home were given passes by the Spanish government to enable them to return quickly and unmolested to their hometowns, with "the sole exception of Pio who, on account of his animals—horses and carabaos—met with difficulty in securing a pass. Where did all those animals come from?"

Sole exception. Horses and carabaos, wherever they may have come from, from cattle rustling by his men or not. Really enterprising, this Pio.

Ochosa, our authority on the Pio story, also notes from reliable sources that Pio had been selling cows at 200 pesos each in the city although "in peacetime cattle cost between 20 and 30 pesos each." Pio had now become a businessman, he says. And, on that basis, clearly a ruthless one.

Pio also was reported to control, not to say intimidate, gambling joints in Malibay, Makati and Pasay. Not surprising for a general, since today military and police officers are sometimes implicated in the same trade. Was good old Pio then a pioneer gambling lord?

In this lucrative endeavor he had the cooperation of a woman, probably voluptuous, whom Apolinario Mabini described as "Pio's ever-pretty mistress, Monica." For a woman to have stimulated, without even trying, a perpetually seated man who was a paralytic from the waist down, why, she must really have been devastating.

She may have been the only one who could soften Pio's famed sinister look—or exacerbate it.

Pio was also reported to Aguinaldo by other commanders as allegedly having received bribes and tolerated his men's abuses like rape, thievery, plain hooliganism and maltreatment of prisoners of war. At first, Aguinaldo did nothing, for Pio was his semicrony and besides, in battle, the mini-Patton often carved up more than reassuring notches in the military totem pole.

To add to his calculated or disciplined notoriety, did Pio later become a mercenary and bounty hunter, too, who would deliver his fellow revolutionaries to the Spaniards at a price? There were more than suspicions and specifics.

In those complicated, perfidious times after the Biak-na-Bato Pact, when even Vibora himself and other generals were working for Spain in the Spanish volunteers' militia, and wavering whether to rejoin the newly returned Aguinaldo, no less than Mariano Trias was reported to have turned traitor.

Trias, we may recall, was a trusted Caviteño/Magdalo who was Aguinaldo's own elected vice president in Tejeros and Biak-na-Bato. He was rumored to have "promised to bring Aguinaldo's head to the Spanish governor-general for 100,000 pesos." [17]

Of course, it is difficult to take this rumor seriously, since it was probably floated by the enemy to sow distrust and dissension in the Revolution's officer corps.

The amount concerned of 100,000 pesos was huge—until it shrank later to mere crumbs when another rumor came about saying Pio was offering Aguinaldo and his entire Cabinet, alive, to the Americans for one million pesos!

The source of the story? None other than General Elwell Otis, said to be the most cruel and ruthless of American governors in the Philippines, whom Ricarte later planned to assassinate; he was saved when the parade he was to attend changed its route at the last minute.

The truth was that within days of Aguinaldo's arrival from Hong Kong, Pio presumably having made a practical—and possibly self-serving?—assessment of the situation, wrote Aguinaldo that he was rejoining the Revolution with his 500 men then based in Makati, and that he was waiting for the latter's orders.

Aguinaldo, acting as a solicitous employer, wrote a reply to his "Beloved General" on the same day he received the latter's application, profusely welcoming him back into the death-defying fold.

Then was born the celebrated Pio del Pilar Brigade, with Pio in command of Zone 2, or Segunda Zona, of the formidable Revolutionary forces that had encircled the Spaniards in Intramuros—a ring not exactly of steel, but of muscle, now with rifles besides bolos and spears. He had some 2,700 troops covering Paco, Pandacan, Sta. Ana, Guadalupe, Pasig, Pateros and Taguig.

There were four zones in all blockading Intramuros, with Noriel in command of Zone 1 consisting of Pasay and adjacent areas, as we have said. Zone 3 and Zone 4 extended from Pio's right flank going all the way to what is now Quezon City in the east, and Caloocan and Malabon in the north under other generals. Zone 4 later was commanded by the great General Antonio Luna in the war against the Americans.

Pio's troops were loyal to him first of all, in every sense of the word, and were consequently called Pioistas. They would follow him and no other.

When phosphorescent Spanish mestizos and Creoles defected from the tottering Spanish army to fight the invading American forces, they were also affected by the same strange, black charisma, and chose to join under Pio's jurisdiction—which with the fanaticism of his troops may well be called sovereignty — reflecting their high opinion of the general with the sinister look.

The Americans tricked the Filipinos — and made a deal with the Spaniards through a Mock Battle of Manila wherein the latter surrendered to the US forces after an ostensible, or mainly acoustic, struggle. Tension now increased between the American interlopers and Aguinaldo's forces as Filipino soldiers were kept out of Intramuros.

Outside the Walled City, the Filipino soldiers were allowed to languish in American-controlled areas only if they had passes — a bitter humiliation.

Among the most outraged of the Filipino generals over the American perfidy was, not surprisingly, Pio. In violation of the so-called "territorial regulations" between the Filipino command and US forces, both of whom continued to pretend they were allies even if the Castilaloy enemy had already been crushed, he went promenading with his fully armed men in that portion of Pasay near the beach which was held by the Americans.

Of course, the US sentinels arrogantly blocked him.

This tit he met with a tat by holding up navigation by a group of Americans on an engineering mission in his jurisdiction in the Pasig River—in spite of their passes signed by Aguinaldo. "Del Pilar's guards then arrested the American officer they found on board, who turned out to be none other than General Thomas Anderson, the division commander himself." [18]

So when war broke out, "those Yanquis opposing Del Pilar's men always made it a point not to take prisoners alive and wanted to wipe out the Pio del Pilar Brigade to the last man if possible."

The day after the opening of hostilities, the Americans made Pio the target of a special operation. The soldiers from Idaho and California, with heavy weapons, succeeded in surrounding the Brigade in Sta. Ana. The Pioistas, overwhelmed by artillery fire, ran away in all directions, many toward the river. A massacre ensued.

An American writer describes the carnage on Pio's men.

"The marksmanship of the [Americans] was so accurate that not a single rebel body was seen to reach the opposite bank of the river. It is estimated that some 700 insurgents were killed, captured, wounded or drowned in this quick bloody attack." [19]

Pio escaped. Within days he showed up in far Antipolo, having hiked uphill, presumably swearing a comeback in between gasps. In two weeks the Pio del Pilar Brigade, with astonishing Darwinian powers of survival, resurrected with additional recruits and logistics, and then continued to play a significant role in the gruesome war for many weeks more.

Complaints against the Pioistas for misconduct continued to flow copiously into the Republic's headquarters. But Pio and his men had staying power in the esteem of Aguinaldo and his military high command, based on an open secret expressed in the statement, "They were not notorious but they were victorious." [20]

Still, the Malolos government must have realized the advisability of heeding the mounting complaints against Pio. In an apparent effort to keep him out of the military field, Aguinaldo appointed him delegate to the Malolos Congress representing Negros Oriental, which had failed to send a representative. As such he became a signatory to the Malolos Constitution.

Since his old notoriety was now no longer being deodorized by new victories, Aguinaldo's government "exiled" Pio and his Brigade from the tense confrontations in Manila to the rustic terrain of La Union. Then as the Revolution sustained more defeats

defeats in the hands of the Americans, it decided to wage a guerilla struggle. Pio was assigned by Aguinaldo to Bulacan — and promptly, outside their authorized sphere, his troops suffered a debilitating defeat in San Isidro in Nueva Ecija while foraging for food.

From then on the Pioistas "made no raids, wrecked no bridges, derailed no trains—not a single fracas emanated from their side to even momentarily disrupt the Americans" and their drive to capture the retreating Aguinaldo. They were now considered a failure, and Pio was eclipsed and replaced as Aguinaldo's Beloved General by the young Gregorio del Pilar, who events would show later was Pio's superior in courage and patriotism.

Then the final blow came. Pio without warning or explanation or notice was dropped from the list of the Revolution's commanding generals. He and his Pioistas were now unofficial. They lumbered on to Morong where the official guerilla commander was Bonifacio's lead killer, Lazaro Macapagal, now a general, who ordered them chased, arrested or shot.

The Pioistas in turn captured a major in Macapagal's forces. Pio himself was no longer in the field; he was shamefully in hiding in the environs of Manila giving long-distance orders to his loyal men in Morong or elsewhere.

To his loyalists in Taguig he cruelly ordered to bury a man alive in what else but most logically the town cemetery, and arbitrarily ordered another Macapagal henchman executed.

The two men—Pio and Macapagal—who both critically figured in Bonifacio's extinction, were now uncommon enemies hating each other more that they hated their common enemy, the Americans.

In June 1900, Pio was captured ignominiously in Guadalupe, helplessly without his personally fanatical army. But the embarrassment happened during an amnesty period, and he grabbed the opportunity without delay or rumination. This meant he took an oath of allegiance to the United States—for in those days, as during martial law under Ferdinand Marcos, no one could be released from captivity without signing that oath.

Of course Pio was only one among the many captured generals who did so. Ochosa writes:

"General Tirona, Montenegro, Makabulos and others joined the growing number of patriots-turned-Americanistas banding together into the Federal Party. Had Pio fraternized with this group, he could have been a free man. But they were so *antipatico* to him as he was abominable to them." [21]

It appears that this striking language—*antipatico*, abominable—was not an exaggeration.

When the next round of arrests came about, owing to what the nervous Americans regarded as the Filipinos' incorrigibility in revolutionary sentiment, the submissive, collaborative Federalistas were of course untouched, and Pio was again incarcerated even without having exhibited any intention or motion of recalcitrance—with the Revolution's greats like Mabini, Ricarte, Llanera, Hizon, Ocampo, etc.

In lonely exile in Guam they formed what can only be described as some kind of a captive neighborhood association, and chose their officers by balloting.

This time, unlike in Tejeros, they were all friendly with one another. There was no obnoxious Danilo Tirona, no one whipped out a pistol for they had none, or questioned their election of officers, where Pio trounced for president no less than his historical and personal superiors Mabini and Ricarte!

Pio admirably refused the meaningless but historic honor, saying that as a humble Tagalog he did not know either Spanish or English, a disclaimer that Bonifacio would not have possibly resorted to in Tejeros. Mabini, who was presiding, said Pio would have the benefit of interpretation services.

President Theodore Roosevelt declared an amnesty on July 4, 1902. Pio went back to his homeland, but the rest of his life went downhill. He was now suspected as an informer for the colonial government. Possibly a paid one, as it appears he had no visible means of support—for him and his provocative mistress?

In 1904 Ricarte tried to recruit the ostensibly harmless but still potentially powerful Pio to help resuscitate the Revolution from its lingering death throes. According to a Watson document, Pio "listened [to Vibora] attentively and gave the impression he was willing, but at the close of the interview he dispatched an agent of his to the provincial governor of Rizal to report what had occurred."

In spite of this betrayal, which was known to the Americans but apparently unknown at that time to his compatriots, Pio was appointed "division general" of General Sakay's Revolutionary forces a short time later.

He pledged "to support, obey and carry out [the true patriot Sakay's] orders for the sake of our country and people ... and accept whatever punishment will be given by the highest command to anyone who will disobey....".[23]

Worse than his Ricarte gambit, a document materialized during the treacherously captured Sakay's trial where the latter instructed Pio to take the town of Teresa and make arrests and punish some people by cutting their Achilles' heel and crushing their fingers and feet. "Should the town offer resistance, [Pio] must burn all the houses without showing mercy."

With such evidence, how could the shocked Sakay have escaped the gallows?

The document was dated 1904, at about the same time when Pio supposedly betrayed Ricarte as shown above. Who produced the document and gave it to the government or prosecutor? Pio? If it was forged, who did so and concocted the details? Pio?

As we end this chapter, historian Orlino A. Ochosa may wish to answer this question: Although your book, reliable as it is, is full of alleged infamies and misdeeds of Pio del Pilar, why do you regard him still as your major Filipino hero?

Maybe you have already given your answer right in the same book. In the last chapter, you quote Pio's written words, translated from Tagalog:

"Sakay may have been a bandit in the eyes of the Americans. That is why they sentenced him to the gallows. But before God, Country and Truth, he was a true *makabayan* who deserves to live in the minds of all countrymen for all times."

And then you end with your own words about Pio: "In those days, anyone good enough to recognize and brave enough to call Sakay a hero must also be, at heart, a hero."

What is the implication of the words, "at heart, a hero?" Could this imply that he was a hero only at heart but not in deeds?

How many Filipinos have caused injury and misery to their countrymen by being heroes "at heart" but villains in deeds? How many people can render lip service to true heroes, just as the devil can quote scripture?

Moreover, are we not all heroes, if only at heart? Did we not all start as heroes at heart, when we were young? Good or bad, beautiful or ugly, violent or meek, etc., aren't we all heroes in desire, in intention, in sentiment, in dreams?

Don't we all wish what is good for our country—except for the difference that our own frailties, or our circumstances, or our choices, make us villains, or nonheroes, or men who did or undid nothing, for there is always a price to pay?

In a movie house, everybody is against the villain, and for the hero. All cheer for the latter. We have yet to see a man who, while watching a film and crushing his popcorn, roots for the villain. That's because we are all heroes at heart. That is why all movies end in triumph of the hero and defeat of the villain; otherwise, if the villain wins, we feel very bad.

But that does not mean all of us are heroes. Most are not, but at heart all are. Even Judas Iscariot, in modern exegesis, was a hero and patriot at heart who wanted to force Christ's hand into liberating Israel.

The difference lies in our deeds. So, saying that Pio del Pilar was a hero at heart, after showing his gross misdeeds, may not be saying anything at all that is much favorable to him.

Maybe Ochosa's book, unintentionally, has made so great and formidable a case for proving that Pio del Pilar was not really a hero. To rescue him from this unintended judgment, he is therefore called "a hero at heart" *na lang*.

Pio del Pilar died of natural causes in 1931, aged 66. May God and history bless him, anyway, if only for fighting his people's oppressors.

9. How They Liquidated Luna

PRESIDENT Aguinaldo and his government were in continuous retreat from the battle-field attacks of the American armies. At one time Aguinaldo established his headquarters in Cabanatuan, Nueva Ecjia.

At the same time General Antonio Luna, director of war and overall Central Luzon commander, was in Bayambang, Pangasinan. He was covering Aguinaldo's retreat by setting up the Revolution's troop formations, trenches and fortifications in preparation for more hideous assaults by the Americans.

Luna received a telegram, purportedly signed by Aguinaldo, ordering him to proceed to Cabanatuan. No one knows exactly what that telegram contained, but it is said that it made Luna believe there was to be a change of government, meaning a Cabinet revamp, and that he was to be appointed premier or head of the Cabinet. What a come-on.

Just like the deposed premier Apolinario Mabini, the incumbent premier Pedro Paterno was precariously tottering from office. Aguinaldo himself encouraged in some way the hopes of succession by Luna, who even carried around a tentative list of his prospective Cabinet secretaries.

Luna at the time of the telegram had already been outraged by the behavior of some members of Aguinaldo's Cabinet who were negotiating for peace and autonomy with the enemy. He called them cowards and traitors.

He even arrested and jailed several of them, like Premier Paterno himself and Foreign Affairs Secretary Felipe Buencamino! Then he delivered them to Aguinaldo. When Luna left, Aguinaldo released them.

Poor Aguinaldo was caught in a balancing act in the middle of the political crossfire between the Paterno-Buencamino clique of autonomists, on one hand, and the rampaging Luna, who also had his faction in Congress. Parenthetically, did Aguinaldo, like Mabini, feel that although Luna was only fighting the autonomists as a matter of principle, he was the troublemaker?

Luna was therefore elated by the telegram he now received, since as premier he could reorganize and reenergize the government and pursue the war with the Americans with utmost vigor, free from hindrance by the opportunistic and wavering Paterno-Buencamino elements.

He sent back a telegram informing Aguinaldo he was arriving immediately.

The assassination of Luna is well-known, but not many of its details. Historians have diligently dug up the different, sometimes conflicting, records, and from various sources Vivencio Jose has presented the most finished and the most careful account, which appears to be fair to all. Let us base our story on his book, *The Rise and Fall of Antonio Luna.*[1]

Parenthetically, through his whole book, Vivencio Jose has done to Luna what Cesar Adib Majul did for Mabini and what Leon Ma. Guerrero did for Rizal — write the defining biography. Hence, our choice of Jose, a University of the Philippines dean like Majul, as our authority on Luna.

He says that Luna in his trip to Cabanatuan brought along some of his staff officers led by Col. Francisco Roman and his cavalry escort of 17. It must have been quite a sight, for Luna's escort was reputedly mounted on the best horses of the Revolution.

Near Cabanatuan, Luna for some unclear reason instructed his cavalry to stop and remain where they were, while he, Roman and another officer continued the journey in a *carromata*.

Leaving behind his cavalry escort was a fateful move, although the very numerous and fully prepared assassins of Luna in Cabanatuan would still have succeeded in killing him and whoever his companions would be, anyway. From Filipino folk superstition, should we say it was Luna's time?

The unsuspecting Luna's *carromata* halted in front of the convent which Aguinaldo had converted into his headquarters. At this time, Aguinaldo's Kawit soldiers, too many of them, who were deployed to kill Luna, may have experienced strong feelings, including nervousness, for Luna was such a powerful and dominant personality with a sensational battle record of ferocity and fearlessness — and with a volcanic if abusive temper that could erupt and produce a cataclysm anytime, anywhere, on anybody.

The best thing we could do at this juncture is to quote at length Jose's account:

Luna entered the convent door [leaving his two companions outside]. The guard, upon seeing him, got so unnerved that he did not know what to do. Luna, apparently peeved, turned to him and asked whether he knew what he was doing. The soldier got more bewildered and was unable to answer. Luna, vexed at this unexpected reaction from a soldier, slapped him on the face.

Not far off, Luna saw another soldier, an officer, whom he remembered was disarmed at Kalumpit. "Don't you remember that I disarmed you because of your cowardice?" The officer, Captain Pedro Janolino, could not answer.

He stood there, stiffly, before Luna who was now beside himself with anger. "And you still have the courage to face me?" Luna asked, adding, "Who reinstated you?"

"The officers up there were the ones, sir, who did."

"Well," Luna said, "I will settle you all presently."

Then he hurriedly proceeded upstairs. Up there in the convent, whom should he see but the autonomist whom he hated very much, Felipe Buencamino, now obviously free. To add more to his consternation, Luna learned further that President Aguinaldo had earlier left and was on the way to Tarlac, apparently not complying with the appointment.

"Why didn't they tell me that they were going away?" Luna said, further angered .... In no moment at all, hot words were exchanged between him and Buencamino. And soon they were quarreling while below the presidential guards kept coming and going, whispering tensely among themelves.

Then, as if in preconcerted signal, a rifle shot tore through the blazing afternoon. Hearing the gun report, Luna disengaged from his verbal duel with Buencamino. He went hurriedly rushing down the stairs, where he met Janolino and some soldiers.

Luna shouted, "Who among you fired? Now I am more convinced than ever that you don't know how to handle a gun." Luna was indeed seething with uncontrollable rage. Janolino, thinking that Luna would attack him, whipped out his bolo and hacked the general, hitting him on the temple above the ear.

The Kawit soldiers then joined the fray, firing and stabbing at the hapless general. In spite of his wounds, the surprised Luna managed to pull out his revolver and, withdrawing to the streets, tried to press the trigger. Pain and loss of blood were slowly blurring his vision and he missed when he fired.[2]

Roman and the other Luna officer, Captain Eduardo Rusca, ran to help their chief, whom they saw "staggering towards them, chased and attacked by the Kawit soldiers." The presidential guards fired repeatedly also at Roman who was hit, fatally. Rusca sustained a wound on the leg and fell on his knees, and while crawling got hit again and fell unconscious, and survived to tell his story.

While Janolino and his companions were butchering Luna with a mixed brew of bullets and blades, many other soldiers were ready behind concrete walls. Luna now reached the plaza, his fist clenched, trying to return the fire of his assassins as copious blood gushed out from his many wounds.

A bit later it was seen that his intestines were already out. He suffered at least 40 wounds. Each of some 30 of the wounds was said to be fatal. The horror of it all. Never in the course of human assassination was so much wrought by so many on one fellow.

Luna, in one last great effort, showed the will to fight .... to the bitter end, as he muttered audibly, bravely, "Co...wards! Assa...ssins!" Then, strength leaving his body and will weakened to its last gasp of life, Luna slumped to the ground, face upward, his fist still clenched, as if challenging his murderers, his teeth gritting in rage.

Before expiring, he instinctively turned on his right side. So great must have been the soldiers' fear of Luna that, when they thought that he would stand up in that last gasp for breath, those in the front line hastily stepped backward, pushing those behind them who fell down!

Three things worthy of note are said to have happened:

First, Buencamino emerged and asked a soldier to examine Luna's body and get all the papers there. "If there's a telegram, get it. Don't be afraid for we will take care of you," he said. Was the telegram allegedly signed by Aguinaldo — Ambeth Ocampo calls it "a notice of execution"[3] and O. D. Corpuz "a death warrant"[4]— one of those papers? Another was an unsent letter Antonio had written his mother.

Second, an old woman from the window said in a loud voice, "Why did you kill the general? Don't you recognize him? You are all bad men!"[5] It was said by others that the woman instead asked, "Well, does he still move?"

She was Aguinaldo's mother.

Third, Luna's dead body lying at the center of the plaza remained unattended for one hour.

Then, for no apparent reason, the soldiers returned and began hacking Luna's body again in sadistic glee [just like Diego Silang's corpse — Ed]. Some took off the uniform and among themselves divided the loot of money and jewels.

After this dastardly act, they wrapped the body in an old and tattered mat and brought it to the ruined church .... There, when darkness crept and settled down the earth, only the bats and other night birds remained the [two] dead men's sole companions.[6]

Luna and Roman were buried the next morning with honors, with brass band and funeral march, attended by Gregorio Aglipay, and officials of the government led by Luna's foe, Buencamino.

The soldiers who had committed the deed were presumably there. Even if they were identified, they were not accosted or arrested or investigated. The place may have been occupied almost wholly by anti-Luna partisans.

In the meantime, Aguinaldo was in Bamban, Tarlac, with General Gregorio del Pilar. The president proceeded to consolidate his position against a possible mutiny by Luna loyalists, starting with an on-the-spot inquisition by Aguinaldo himself of Venancio Concepcion, a high-ranking general identified with Luna.

Del Pilar at the same time secured Concepcion's headquarters and its surroundings with his own soldiers, having quietly shunted aside the previous guards.

General Concepcion was gradually eased from his post, and he resigned. Aguinaldo rejected his resignation, but reassigned him to another post where he could easily be watched.

Aguinaldo also replaced other known Luna officers and disarmed some of the latter's companies, none of whom resisted. In the purge, two officers — the Bernal brothers who were in Luna's headquarters in Bayambang — were executed without explanation or ceremony. They were the only casualties in the upheaval.

Of Luna's angry friends, only General Maximino Hizon in Dagupan organized his troops and sent them to Cabanatuan to arrest the Cabinet members whom he suspected of masterminding the deed and the soldiers who committed it, intending to try them by a military court.

But Hizon's act came more than a week later and when his soldiers arrived in Cabanatuan they found no one to arrest, since Aguinaldo's headquarters had been transferred.

This was the exact opposite of the situation just after the murder when practically all officers and soldiers in Cabanatuan were Aguinaldo's men, like the Kawit companies, among whom were the murderers. So there was no arrest or investigation, even when Aguinaldo arrived in six days.

But there was widespread resentment and demoralization in the Revolutionary army, like what obtained after the execution of Bonifacio. According to Vivencio Jose, many abandoned the struggle because of this — but many more remained.

That the greater majority continued the fight for freedom even under such disconcerting circumstances proved once more that Aguinaldo had enough stature and following — more than anyone or any group.

Gradually, Luna's men, like General Jose Alejandrino, came over to Aguinaldo's side and served him faithfully, thus remaining in the Revolutionary mainstream.

Those whose loyalty were doubtful or unclear were strictly watched and monitored. A few days later, Interior Secretary Severino de las Alas, with the help of Buencamino, wired all the Republic's provincial officials their version of Luna's death.

It was a long telegram, saying Luna started the trouble and was killed by guards. It claimed that Luna "desired the Supreme Power of the Nation [with the purpose of] usurping the power of our Honorable President."[7]

No historian has ever come out with the slightest evidence that Luna was guilty of this charge. Even his closest friend and constant companion, General Jose Alejandrino, told Aguinaldo frankly Luna never plotted against him.

But Luna had tried to campaign for popular support among the Revolutionaries in his fight against the autonomists led by Paterno and Buencamino. It is easy to speculate that the autonomists used this, among other things, to poison Aguinaldo's mind that Luna was planning a coup to replace him as president.

Luna was a fast-rising general who could ultimately be a rival to Aguinaldo. The former, six years older than the latter, should have been extracareful and should have made clear signs of deference to the president. But he did not seem to be very respectful, since even in the presence of Aguinaldo Luna broke up a Cabinet meeting with a temperamental outburst.

Aguinaldo was a living legend grown out of his immensely successful first Cavite campaign against the Spaniards. He easily surpassed in popularity and power Bonifacio, who could not acquire a military stature because he had been disgraced by his battlefield defeats, and could offer no strong leadership rivalry to Aguinaldo.

But here was Luna, well-trained in military science, whose main reputation also was as a field commander, like Aguinaldo, and who was proving his reputation as the one who could whip up the Revolutionary army into a great fighting machine.

It was not as if Saul had slain his thousands, and David his ten thousands, for Luna, like Bonifacio, had not won a single great, decisive battle either. But Luna's military capabilities were rightfully unquestioned. And the potential for mischief and rivalry was there, abetted by what was perceived by Luna's enemies as his unmitigated arrogance — and ironically, by Aguinaldo's promoting him to higher posts!

De las Alas in his announcement also said an investigation will be made. It was not, and the assassins, led by the easily identifiable Pedro Janolino, were never punished.

On June 12, a week after Luna's murder, on the first anniversary of the Declaration of Independence, the brothers of Luna — Joaquin and Jose — who were Revolutionary officers, were with Aguinaldo, Del Pilar, Makabulos, Concepcion, Mascardo and others at the presidential banquet table.

Vivencio Jose cites a source noting that Jose and Joaquin, from their conversation, "were completely ignorant of the causes and details of the death of their brother."[8]

They must have been told another story and misled, but of course they would have known the truth later.

Defending himself from accusations that he was involved in the plot, Aguinaldo asked why he would have Luna killed in his own headquarters. He could have had him shot at the back during a battle, said Aguinaldo.

But some replied this was difficult to do, because Luna in action was well-guarded and well-watched by his many aides — a counterclaim that was also difficult to accept because Luna in his recklessness and courage sometimes rode alone on his horse and traversed the field as if he were born in Krypton.

Buencamino, the man whom Luna had once slapped during a formal Cabinet meeting presided over by Aguinaldo and who fell down on the floor from the blow, was also suspect. Many years after the Revolution he asked Aguinaldo through Gregorio Aglipay to make an announcement that he, Buencamino, was innocent. Aguinaldo promised he would do so but never did.

This request by Buencamino is curious. Why should he count on Aguinaldo's testimony when Aguinaldo himself was suspect and not believed by many on the matter? The interested reader should go to the evidence gathered by Vivencio Jose on the different aspects of the assassination.

Buencamino was widely suspected of being the mastermind because he was there on the assassination scene, and he had had many bitter personal quarrels with Luna. His courageous son Joaquin volunteered to fight on the frontlines because Luna had unjustly called him a coward. Joaquin died a hero's death, fighting. Was this another case of Luna's vicious tongue and temper getting loose again, this time because of his personal animosity towards Buencamino?

Shortly before he died, Buencamino left his written account of the whole story of Luna's assassination, which is in Jose's book. He swore "before God and the ashes of my father" that he had no involvement in the killing, direct or indirect.

As in the case of the Aquino assassination where people wondered if anyone would slay Ninoy without clearance from Malacañang, we may also wonder if the one who managed or masterminded the killing would have done so without clearance from Aguinaldo.

For readers today who would like to wade into the gripping circumstances and facts, the certainties and imponderables, the suspicions and accusations surrounding this most infamous killing, they may turn to Vivencio Jose's level-headed book.

They should go to chapter 16, "Death in the Afternoon"; chapter 17, "Epilogue to Disaster"; chapter 18, "Luna on Judgment Day: A Perspective," with sections A, "The Character of the Internal Problems of the Republic," B, "Facts Before Luna's Assassination," C, "The Question of the Telegram" and D, "The Facts After the Murder."

Almost a century later, in the 1980s, Senate President Blas Ople said he noticed in private conversations that the late Ferdinand Marcos had been cool to the memory of Aguinaldo — and Gregorio del Pilar, Ople's Bulakeño provincemate. This was because the murdered Luna was Marcos' fellow Ilocano. It was Diosdado Macapagal who was an advocate for Aguinaldo and transferred the country's Independence Day celebration from the Americans' July 4 to Aguinaldo's June 12.

As we shall see in the next chapter about the attempt to kill President Quezon, Aguinaldo did not bother to campaign in Ilocoslandia when he ran for president against Quezon in 1935, presumably because of the lingering animosities over Luna's horrible death.

The parents of Antonio Luna were from Ilocos Sur and La Union where three of their children were born. They later migrated to Binondo in Manila, where they thrived as merchants, and where four more offsprings came for a total of seven — with Antonio as the youngest.

The Luna children were sensationally talented, like Juan Luna, the first-rate painter, of course; Manuel, the first-rate musician; Jose, the first-rate doctor; and finally Antonio the first-rate chemist and first-rate general — and first-rate face slapper. They were educated in Europe.

Why do we include the words first-rate face slapper?

When future president Manuel L. Quezon was still a kid he had a peculiar predilection for slapping other kids on the face, and slap them often he did. His father scolded him about it, telling him not to do so because a slap on the face is the worst insult one can give.

But he still went about his slapping sprees, presumably because slapping other people's faces was the best pleausre. This habit later vanished because, when he once told a lie, his father slapped him. The positions had been reversed and he got the point.

Quezon's temperamental outbursts were legend. Once, it was said, he nearly struck a newspaperman with his horsewhip, and another time he suddenly barged into the editorial room of the newspaper, *La Democracia*, and physically assaulted an editor.

Quezon's violence

But his temper tantrums were mere child's play compared with Luna's gotterdamerung explosions, which included slapping people on the face. General Alejandrino in his autobiography talks of one officer who quavered and sweated on short notice because he thought an enraged Luna would eat him alive. As we have seen above, moments before Luna was killed, he was at least able to slap someone.

Antonio Luna graduated with very high honors from the Ateneo, won first prize in a big chemistry essay contest in Manila, and won again in another contest with his biography of prominent Filipinos.

He was athletic and could fence very well. Once he joined a grand exhibition contest in Manila where he was pitted with the finest professional fencer of the day, and he scored an impressive tie.

He was also a first-rate polemicist and journalist at the *La Solidaridad*, and same thing as publisher of *La Independencia*, perhaps the most swashbuckling newspaper ever to blaze across the Philippine scene.

From Vivencio Jose's well-chosen quotations from Luna's written works, it appears that had Luna concentrated on writing instead of his scientific and other academic studies — like producing a tract on bacteriology, titled "El Hematozoario Paludismo," which gained prominence among European scientists — he could have produced major works of stunning literary quality.

Even as a child, Luna was already physically formidable. One time, it was said, he engaged in a fight, and he "whirled a boy up into the air and threw him down on the grass below. Many playmates remembered that incident and, henceforth, anyone who incurred unnecessarily the ire of Antonio evaded him with reason, fearful of his strength and temper. For he was undoubtedly strong; he hit hard with his fists. Besides, he was never daunted by anybody."[9] Moreover:

"At 16, Antonio studied fencing, the handling of swords, and military tactics .... He became very adept at shooting so that it is said he could 'put out the flame of a lighted candle at a considerable distance with one shot and could discharge his pistol before any opponent could draw.'" Whew!

Legends grew about him and his brothers, and because of their personal bravery they "were held by their contemporaries with admiration mixed with fear."

For the reader's entertainment, here is a passage about Luna's fellow Ilocano, Ferdinand Marcos, in the latter's controversial political campaign biography, *For Every Tear a Victory*, which critics have roundly criticized:

One *juramentado,* having killed seven men with his kris, headed for Mariano Marcos and his son. [Note the use of the number seven; was someone really able to count and remember seven, or was it Marcos' own mystical bent on that number that was again speaking, although the author of the book was someone else, the American Hartzell Spence?]

The father warned Ferdinand, "Don't move," and let the enraged killer approach to within three steps before, sure now that he could not miss, he felled the assassin with a revolver shot. As expert as Ferdinand became with a rifle, both his father and his brother were more adept with the pistol.

The father could knock the ace from a playing card at 15 feet, and brother Pacifico could shear the bonds of hanging coconuts tall in a palm and bring the fruit down without damage. But it was Ferdinand who, with a rifle, unerringly sniped moving targets at 300 yards.[10]

Truly?

Unlike Luna, Marcos was never assassinated, even though there were many attempts on him, while Luna was the object of only one.

In the first years after the declaration of martial law, Marcos did not very often venture out of Malacañang because of the perceived assassination plots. But when he did, a well-equipped, most modern ambulance was among the many security vehicles that followed him — a precaution that would have astonished the brave but careless Luna.

Luna's bad temper largely helped in his own most untimely undoing. If even a slight temper could rub people the wrong way, how much more a terrible one like Luna's?

It must be said that his savage temper diminished him as a man — as it diminishes anyone who has it. It reduced him in both stature and substance. If the extent of his temper was inversely proportional to his stature, then it may be said that it had shrunk him decisively in the esteem both of his contemporaries and of history.

But he was so great a man that since his stature was, say, ten feet tall, and it suffered because of his temper, he had been reduced by three feet to seven feet tall, meaning to say that in spite of the great diminution he still ended up a giant.

Rizal himself would have been greatly diminished if he were violently temperamental. He was not — like Aguinaldo, one of whose great qualities as a leader was that he was deliberate, always polite, calm and self-possessed. Aguinaldo never lost his temper, not once!

Probably one reason why the Caviteños — we are not referring to Caviteño officers and troops but to the common Cavite folk — couldn't care less about Bonifacio when he was wounded, arrested, tried and executed was that he lost his temper in a most unfortunate way.

Bonifacio loses his temper

Bonifacio at the top of his angry Tondo voice screamed an order — which proved to be unintended, it was only a momentary temperamental outburst, after all — to burn to ashes the town of Indang, from whose population he was asking food for his hungry troops but was rejected.

Many were within hearing distance and the Caviteño folk later came to know about the horrible order, which was not implemented by his understanding soldiers. But the Caviteño townspeople were of course turned off by the same Supremo whom they had earlier welcomed in Cavite with festivities fit only for a conquering hero — even if he had never conquered a single inch of territory from the Spaniards.

Compounding Luna's temper problem was that he never had a comeuppance — no one ever stood up to him in a violent physical encounter or shocked him with a slap on the face in return. Luna never met his match.

Of course, any Filipino would welcome rather than rue that incident where he spat on the face of one Spaniard in Barcelona named Mir Deas, who had insulted Indios in a newspaper article.

Barcelona spillovery

Parenthetically, when Luna slapped the high-ranking Buencamino, the latter, like Mir, did not fight back but only muttered something to the effect that Luna would later be sorry for what he did. An ominous threat?

Why didn't Buencamino then challenge Luna to a duel? That was the ordinary course of events in those days when someone was slapped. But tough luck, Luna, as we said above, was such a good shot.

Vivencio Jose notes that when General Luna personally disarmed Aguinaldo's Kawit soldiers — what recklessness, disgracing Aguinaldo's own longtime personal troops! — for their disobedience and cowardice, they could have resisted, what with their numbers and guns, and the fact that they were seasoned veterans on the battlefield who had fought much earlier than Luna and had killed so many Spaniards.

They could have killed him, easily, right then and there. But they meekly submitted because he was imposing and fearsome, not to say energetic and very angry — and most of all because they had no time to make a plot, which they did for days in Cabanatuan.

We cannot blame Luna wholly for his apocalyptic fits of supernatural rage. That pestilential flaw appears to have been genetic; his DNA was unfair to him.

More important, he did not totally allow it free reign, or indulged in it with malice, or gloated over it. Most assuredly he was not a man who on the basis of his temper could be termed an evil man. On the contrary, from all other indications he was what is ordinarily regarded as a great and good man, and he had a huge job to do, a sworn duty to his country and the Revolution, and his outbursts were related to these. But did that make his violent loss of temper excusable?

Once while drunk, and apparently jealous over Nelly Boustead [busted by Boustead, pun intended] he challenged Rizal to a duel, which the latter bravely accepted — bravely because, although Rizal was himself a dead shot, Luna was no doubt much more deadly.

Luckily the matter was settled at the initiative of their own seconds. But according to Luna's elder brother Juan, the great painter, Antonio was extremely sorry for his behavior, saying "I would rather be killed than hurt Rizal whom I respect and esteem highly."[11]

So why did he challenge him to a duel in the first place? Loss of temper.

Juan added that Antonio gave people "permission to tie him up if he got drunk again." For Luna having to go to such an unfamiliar act of ridiculous self-immolation shows his temper problem must have been very serious indeed.

Bad temper ran in the Luna family. His elder brother Juan in a fit of rage shot to death his own wife and mother-in-law — a most evil deed. In 1988, Mita Pardo de Tavera, niece of Luna's wife, and welfare secretary of President Cory Aquino, said her family always thought Juan Luna was "abnormal." Juan also shot his wife's unarmed brother who nearly died.

Another brother of Luna's wife was later suspected of having hired an assassin to kill Juan in revenge. This deed was supposed to have been fulfilled in Hong Kong where the great painter died of a heart attack — brought about by criminal poisoning, it was said.

No one, however, has proved, or gathered any evidence, that poison it was. The official medical report did not bear it out. But if it was true, who would blame one for avenging the cruel and most unjust killing of his mother and sister, and nearly fatal wounding of a brother, all in the same incident, in what was almost a family massacre — committed by one hand wielding a pistol?

You, reader, may do the same, or worse, if you were in the same bitter situation. You may even draw your own Spoliarium which would show not two dead gladiators but two dead ladies being pulled out of the arena.

Antonio Luna did not join the Katipunan during Bonifacio's time because he believed it was stupid to rise up without arms. But along with his brother Juan and some friends, he was arrested and tortured by the Spaniards anyway. Antonio was undone brutally enough that he even had to invent some confessions to prove to the Spaniards he was not defiant or uncooperative.

A brave, temperamental, proud, high-handed man who was also a squealer?

Because of this some say he had turned traitor to his fellow Filipinos and may have caused the arrest, torture and even death of others. But nothing is certain about this, since he was against the Katipunan and knew almost nothing about it, so there was nothing to be treacherous or to squeal about.

What is clear is that he was sorry he caved in under torture. But wouldn't practically all of us do so too, especially over something we do not believe in, as Luna in those early days did not believe in the Katipunan? In any case he more than made up for it by his willingness — nay, eagerness — to fight for his country to the utmost and to the very end.

Luna was six years older than Aguinaldo. Did he regard the latter as some kid brother who did not deserve respect? He was 33 years old when the Kawit soldiers extirpated him. On the other hand, Aguinaldo was president — at only 28!

In his own time and in history, Luna is known to have been the best or ablest general of the Revolution. Both friend and foe, Filipino and American, attested to this in historical sources too numerous and too well-known for us to bother about here.

These admirers included Aguinaldo himself, who must get credit for the fact that when he read the military plans of Luna, who was then in Hong Kong and pleading to be taken into the Revolutionary armies, Aguinaldo accepted him in spite of his past record in prison.

Without hesitation Aguinaldo started him out with an appointment as brigadier-general! And from the record, Aguinaldo never personally slighted Luna. On the contrary, Luna once rebuffed Aguinaldo when the latter ordered a troop movement which, as Luna explained, was not advisable. Aguinaldo yielded to Luna, and did not show if he was offended.

From the very beginning Luna was an energetic superphenomenon who, in a few weeks of dogged exertion, was making a true army out of the untrained and undisciplined ragtags of the Revolution — to the consternation of observant American officers.

At the same time Luna knew, also from the very beginning, that the superbly armed and equipped American forces could not be beaten in positional warfare.

But he also analyzed and concluded, contrary to the claim of the autonomists and many others, that the Filipinos also could not be beaten if they would only hold on not just to their feeble arms but to their robust courage and wits — and most of all to their patriotism.

And so in the midst of the most horrendous debacles before the solid might of American steel, he conceived a grand design for guerilla warfare in the vast northern mountain ranges of Luzon — a formidable reboubt which would have exasperated and exhausted the Americans.

Had he lived to command its strategic retreat and steer its latent military vigor for years and years, with the Filipino masses' obvious and unwavering support, he would have made it impossible for the Revolution to be beaten — with enormous consequences, even without television, to America's perverse Philippine policy back home, just as America's Vietnam policy suffered from inescapable domestic outrage more than 50 years later.

In the heat of the unequal struggle, in the abyss of despair, treachery and cowardice, in the quagmires of gangrene, dysentery and slime, General Luna, like reverse sunshine gleaming from the caverns of the earth, would sometimes produce and assemble, seemingly out of nowhere, fit and well-motivated Indio troops to enrapture the Revolutionary cause and beguile even his own adjutants and aides.

His simple technique — he asked those able-bodied but unengaged Filipino men in far towns to join his forces, otherwise he would have them shot!

In addition, his sensational feats of personal courage were many, and Vivencio Jose points out that this was not because Luna was a great exhibitionist but because he wanted to motivate his troops.

Had he lived, Luna would have been the fulfillment of Bonifacio's dream, and possibly Philippine history's ultimate hero to eclipse Bonifacio, Rizal and Aguinaldo themselves, and stand in the same rank with Washington and Bolivar — or, to satisfy the leftists, with Giap/Castro/Che Guevara/Mao.

Of course, we cannot include in the list Jose Maria Sison, still in the Netherlands dining on nutritious Dutch hotdogs while his followers starve in Mt. Banahaw.

When the Philippine-American War broke out, Luna was assigned by Aguinaldo to lead the defense of Caloocan. Arriving in the area he immediately led not a defense but an attack — on American emplacements in La Loma from where the latter had been pummeling Caloocan with continuous artillery bombardment.

Luna's attack was repulsed, and they retreated. The brave Major Torres Bugallon was seriously wounded. Bleeding and moaning, he was carried by Luna personally many kilometers back to Caloocan. After a few hours Bugallon, certainly thrilled by Luna's heroism, nevertheless died of his wounds.

A day later, Luna's longtime best friend and fortifications engineer and later general, Jose Alejandrino, saw Luna "morally and physically crestfallen, these being the first words he uttered upon seeing me: 'Our enemies are too strong and superior in their means.'

"Later on I learned," Alejandrino continued, "that neither he nor his soldiers had had a morsel during the whole day. The troops were half-dead from hunger and fatigue after a whole day of fighting ....We could not even organize guards, such that in case of an attack we would have no alternative but to run away disbanded .... During the days that followed the American squadron bombarded almost without interruption our positions in Caloocan."[12]

Luna at least in that area saw the futility — Alejandrino used the word "impossibility" — of defending their hellhole and decided to withdraw. Continued Alejandrino:

"Luna was one of the last to retreat. He took a rifle and stationed himself in the town church, from which position he kept up an intense exchange of fire with the American forces. He withdrew only when his bullets ran out."

As we said, this was only two days after the outbreak of the Philippine-American War. In spite of the bitter one-sidedness of the initial bloodbath in favor of the Americans, Luna as Aguinaldo's director of war, and ever the aggressive warrior that would make even Patton blush, immediately plotted a grand counteroffensive less than three weeks later.

It was a daredevil do-or-die operation, the modest forerunner of General Giap's renowned Tet Offensive some 70 years later in Vietnam against the same interloping enemy.

It involved all the Filipino forces around Manila, with Luna attacking from the north, and with Ricarte, Noriel, Pio del Pilar and other generals attacking from other points, except from the sea in the west.

O. D. Corpuz writes that it was only Luna among the commanders who "could entertain the boldness and comprehend the complexity of the project."[13] Indeed, Aguinaldo himself did not understand it and at the last moment chickened out — he sent couriers to say he had disapproved the plan. Too late. The "project" had begun.

The Kawit soldiers, who were in position physically but not mentally, were the only ones who defied Luna and did not attack, their commanders saying they obeyed only Aguinaldo — although they were sent by Aguinaldo himself to fight under Luna! Luna thus suffered a situation unparalleled in military idiocy, and they did not expect him to complain?

The Kawiteños were there for the precise purpose of attacking as a diversionary force from the main assaults. Because of their disobedience the grand offensive sustained heavy casualties and wilted. In a real way, the Kawiteños caused the death of many of their comrades-in-arms.

Luna therefore had every right to slam and damn and disarm the Kawit companies and regard them with irreconcilable anger. In fact, the Kawiteños deserved not only to be disarmed but to be shot.

But since they were Aguinaldo's favorite troops — they were his personal/presidential guards — they were not punished; instead, they were the ones who punished, and they punished none other than Antonio Luna. With death.

The Luna grand offensive on Manila began on February 22, George Washington's birthday, with the initiative of swarms of the old Katipunan's bolomen stationed in

Sta. Cruz, Tondo and Binondo, who began the battle with arson and continued with mutilation, even as the simultaneous attacks from the outer rim of Manila ensued.

The electric Luna was able to penetrate with his troops as far as Sta. Cruz and Tondo, Noriel up to Ermita and Pio del Pilar up to Sampaloc and San Miguel! What a historic triumph it would have been, gaining for the Revolution no less that Manila itself, and consequently it could have led to the Filipinos' immediate independence and nationhood.

For almost two days they were triumphant in Manila's suburbs. Then the Americans counterattacked with blazing firepower that ruthlessly raked the Revolutionary troops, and all the Filipino columns were thrown back.

Damn those Kawiteños. And Luna, the great general, became the pearl who had to throw himself into the mud pit of the Kawit swine, if only to preserve the rule of discipline, which was vital to the Revolutionary armies. Like hogs they ate him up.

To Vivencio Jose, Luna was not only a patriot but a true and complete patriot. This was true even in the eye and ire, impersonal and implacable, of objective historical terms. This simply means Luna did not compromise in any way the struggle for national independence from foreign rule — regardless of his own experiences or feelings or fate.

An individual may compromise his personal freedom, say, obey his foreman for eight hours of grueling work a day in his place of employment. Fine, it is no cause for contempt, for such is the nature of livelihoodism.

A soldier may allow himself to be ordered around like a dolt by his military commander without feeling humiliated, and a general may foolishly forego the pleasures of peaceful life by undertaking the foulest burdens of battlefield command. That's all right for both of them, they are only doing their duty.

But personal freedom is different from national freedom.

The fight for national independence during colonial times could not be compromised by administrative concessions for, or political subordination to, or pious understandings with, the colonizer, even if mutually beneficial. For sovereignty cannot be compromised without being lost; an independence struggle cannot be diluted without being betrayed.

To Luna, the struggle against the colonizer in the days of the Revolution, considering the nature of both the national and international epochs, could only have one method, meaning armed struggle; and national freedom could only have one character, meaning whole.

In his struggle for the political liberty of his nation, in which he sacrificed the social liberty of his own person, Luna had no doubts or qualifications, no ifs or buts or whens, no provided this or on condition that, no autonomy clauses, no periodic or gradual stages of liberation, no strained constitutional syncretisms or strange political compounds or mixtures or mutants.

He only had one why and one how — one why, because his people must live in freedom to rid themselves of oppression and be dignified, happy and fulfilled; and one how, which was to fight, fighting being the only way to win it — and to deserve it.

Unlike the autonomists who were sometimes here, sometimes there, sometimes nowhere, sometimes in the latrine, Luna knew exactly where he was going, however difficult and unlikely or almost hopeless his progress would be. For it is better to know where to go and not know how, than know how to go and not know where.

In those days, not to fight was not to be free. Darwinism was still the rule, unlike in today's age of satellites and computers and welfarism when the law of survival of the fittest may sometimes be qualified or even eschewed.

For in today's society there are ramps for the handicapped to enable them to go to the movies or shop in malls — not to mention the looming geriatric age when even doddering old fools who could not have survived for a moment the ravages of the Bronze Age could continue writing newspaper columns for a fee.

To put Luna's distinction as a hero in another way, there are many patriots, all sorts of them, patriots to the left of us and patriots to the right of us, patriots in front and at the back, patriots above and below, young and old, male and female, devoted or part-time, rich or poor, military or civilian, brilliant or folksy, hypocritical or hypercritical, philosophic or visceral or just plain unflappable — but Luna was simply the correct and total patriot, in the context of his times.

In that correctness, he gave his all to his country — his courage, his sentiments, all his strength and all his life in his final days, everything he could do and everything that he had and everything that he was.

Unlike other heroes whose perceived level of greatness would not fluctuate whether they were right or wrong, like Rizal for example, Luna's value was tied up to the correctness of his vision, indeed to the correctness of his means — because he insisted on them with all his might, and risked everything for them, flowing on and on like a mighty river, irresistible, undeniable, inexorable, tempestuous....

He was unlike Rizal who was flexible. Upon realizing that his legal efforts to be free from execution had failed in spite of having renounced and denounced the Revolution, Rizal suddenly claimed in his "Last Farewell" same Revolution as his own, as Guerrero referred to this *bulaga*:

On the field of battle, 'mid the frenzy of fight,
Others have given their lives, without doubt or heed,

> The place matters not — cypress or laurel or lily white,
> Scaffold or open plain, combat or martyrdom's plight.

For Luna, patriotism in his own day was not only a question of ends — but of the nature of the means insofar as they impinged on the truth or quality of those ends. It was a question not only of meaning but of manner — insofar, again, as they were substantively related to the liberation of his homeland. If to MacLuhan the medium is the message, to Luna the manner was the meaning.

But here was a Greek or Shakespearean tragic hero because he had one big, hopeless, unscratchable flaw. The heat of his temper was neither tolerable nor understandable — nor honorable, in spite of the fact that it always had basis. And it gave his enemies the excuse to do with him as they pleased.

Vivencio Jose points out that Luna did not crave death or martyrdom, not because of cowardice or selfishness but because that would shorten the period of his service to the Motherland. If the ink of the scholar is more valuable than the blood of the martyr — or the saliva of the traitor for that matter — the sword of the liberator was by all means greater than the tomb of the hero or the altar of the sacrifice.

But his temper, although it destroyed him, did not invalidate him. It was in a way "only" a matter of method. And yet, ruthless and energetic display of authority, which was perhaps the correct method in those days of military indiscipline in the ranks, and of brooding self-indulgence in the high echelons of the Malolos Congress, not only determined but also hastened his physical undoing.

He was destroyed. But to the face of his enemies must be thrown the eternal, because they are transcendent, words of Hemingway — "Man can be destroyed, but not defeated."

He did not strive to preserve his life at any cost, or become a death-fearing wimp. Once wounded in battle, he fell from his horse and he found himself alone in the field, in danger of being captured alive. He drew out his pistol and pointed it to his temple, about to blow his own brains out because if captured alive his usefulness to the country would have been over anyway.

Luckily an aide came in the nick of time and prevented the horror.

But did it really matter? He was willing to destroy himself because, as Hemingway said, destruction is of no moment. What is important is the struggle, especially the correct struggle.

Here was a man in whose honor superlatives are not hagiographic, for he was heroic at the highest and most intense level conceivable within the context of his times and circumstances. He was pure concept embodied in pure struggle.

And he knew it not only because he was a writer, but because he was a true writer, and true because he had integrity. And who would understand him best but another writer enamored with the same truth, none other than Vivencio Jose. Jose writes, exquisitely, with an awesome combination of skillful precision and disciplined passion in his Luna book. Let us savor at least one passage which can be read only with great pleasure, accentuating that unsuspected, extreme human sensitivity which Jose alone accords the great general:

But in Luna, whether in the battlefront or in his personal sanctuary, there were private feelings as there were private dreams. In his years abroad the stage, with its attractive aura of illusion and violence, fascinated him deeply, for in that compulsive world were real people, both different and like ourselves, who acted and made believe as if they were feeling and struggling in real life.

One of those presentations he could never forget. About it he wrote skillfully and remembered so many years after. In his hectic schedule that summer day, in the fire of struggle and the din of war, did he remember — rarely? frequently? — on this side of the frontline, that nightmarish show, alas, which happened a long time ago?

"I went home to sleep and I dreamt — what things I dreamt of! I dreamt that in my room, converted into a stage, the two women were dancing furiously but a kind of infernal dance to the tune of the guitarist beating my head instead and I heard the voice of the singer — shrill, nasal, sharp, and a cry that was like one from the dead. Suddenly, the stage was lighted like a ball of fire. The dancers looked like witches, the guitars broke into pieces, the shout became more mournful .... I woke up frightened and turned on the light.

"There was nobody; a cat was meowing under my bed. I kicked it and immediately turned off the light."

It is difficult to recall a man in Philippine literature or historiography who has presented Antonio Luna in a major book as his major hero until Vivencio Jose came around. He has chosen his hero well, for Luna, in the age of our Revolution, was under certain compelling terms the greatest Revolutionary of them all, and even in other epochs of the future in other terms, we know we shall never see the likes of him again.

10. Mission Possible: Assassinate Quezon — and Mrs. Quezon

OF ALL Philippine presidents, Manuel L. Quezon, the greatest of them all, and his family suffered most from physical violence.

When he was studying law in Manila, his father and his brother were murdered on a lonely mountain trail in Baler. After a while Quezon himself, in the company of another brother, was nearly murdered also in the same mountain range, but his quick thinking saved him, as we shall see.

It was not only his beloved wife, Doña Aurora, who perished in an ambush in 1949 along the old Bongabong-Baler highway. Among the casualties in that dastardly massacre were his favorite daughter Baby and his son-in-law, and about a dozen others.

Their families — both Quezon and Aragon — suffered much during the Revolution, when Aurora's father was jailed and sent as a prisoner to Manila. When he died she and her sisters lived in poverty, tilling the soil with their bare hands in a vegetable farm that was not theirs.

It is said that with this experience Doña Aurora developed a most admirable social personality, treating everyone simply and respectfully and alike — rich or poor or whoever — even during her husband's most glorious days in Malacañang.

It was also during Quezon's term that the most violent and most cruel years in Philippine history occurred — World War II and the Japanese Occupation. More than 50 years before, Quezon himself was a young combatant who had seen the brutalities of war during the Revolution where he was an officer who fought with the Filipino armies against the Americans.

Of course, the materials about Quezon are endless and widely known, and here we shall make only short preliminaries before we go to our subject — the plot to assassinate him in 1935 in a dance hall.

Quezon was beyond doubt the most impressive statesman ever to appear in Philippine history. Douglas MacArthur paid him the ultimate tribute when he described Quezon as "one of the greatest statesmen of all men of all time."[1]

Ultranationalists, of course, condemn him for laying down his arms as a Revolutionary months after the capture of Aguinaldo, who had issued a call to the men of the Revolution to return to peace. But the war had been lost, and only Sakay and a few others without much impact continued the struggle.

Of course Filipinos still abhorred foreign rule and wished to drive out the Americans, but not as badly enough as to join Ricarte's, or any other's, call to revolt again. Revolution was becoming pretty tiresome, even to this race of heroic men.

Quezon proceeded to finish his law studies which had been interrupted by the Revolution, then became a practicing lawyer and governor and ... the rest is history.

The ultimate nationalists charge that Quezon as governor hounded in his province those bandits who were actually Revolutionaries. They have not done their homework. In some instances, the bandits were indeed former Revolutionaries, who were hunted down without mercy by the Americans, but were not many of them really nothing more than bandits?

Besides, these absolute nationalists, who are good in criticism but have themselves not done anything concrete for the country, and have read only one or two books about Quezon, know less than Quezon's own provincemates. The old prewar Atimonan historian Jesus C. Olega wrote:

"Ang Pangulong Quezon *(nuong siya'y batang abogado pa lamang) ay siya ring naging tagapagtanggol ng maraming taga-*Tayabas *na napagbintangang nanunulisan dahil sa hindi nila pagsuko kaagad sa mga* Amerikano. *Ang kaunaunahan niyang pagharap sa hukuman ay nang kanyang ipagtanggol ang 16 na manghihimagsik."*[2]

The trial was held in Manila before one Judge Sweeney. The accused were acquitted.

Incidentally, Quezon as a young lawyer did not charge fees from his poor clients, and for this he became known all over Tayabas. Often in the provincial capital, where supposed offenders from the towns were clapped in prison, Quezon proved many of them innocent. And so, as the black image of death approached to claim him, while lying down in his hospital bed ravaged by tuberculosis in the United States, this lovable egocentric gloated, justifiably, in his autobiography:

"I hope I may be forgiven if I proudly state that I won the liberty of every man whom I defended"[3] and "I served with as much interest and zeal as I did when working for money."[4] And how he charged rich clients!

In his young days he was provincial fiscal, whose concurrent function was to act as register of deeds. A prominent and arrogant American lawyer, who was also a Manila publisher and was therefore powerful, barged into his office to ask why he, Fiscal Quezon, had not processed papers about the lands which the American had earlier submitted for registration.

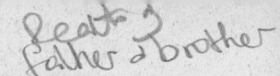

An argument ensued. An infuriated Quezon, with his Luna-like temper, drove the American out of his office by threatening to smash his face with an inkstand. The latter left hurling invectives and threats.

Quezon had indeed forgotten about the papers, so he hurriedly took a look at them. The staggering documents concerned several thousand hectares, 50,000 coconut trees and 300 work animals, which were being transferred by several Filipinos then in jail to the ownership of the American. Quezon grew suspicious.

He went to the provincial prison and found out that the lowly illiterate Filipinos signed the documents thinking that they were only pledging their small parcels to the American as lawyer's fees.

Quezon prosecuted, won and became a formidable political possibility because in those days no one dared to sue an American, and this time it was a lawyer and publisher at that, who later jumped bail by going to Hong Kong. Of course, the Filipinos in jail were freed, and got back their lands. What can today's excessive nationalists say about that? Was this not true nationalism rather than armchair nationalism?

As he started practicing law, the memory of his father and his brother who were murdered must have constantly rankled in him. He could have plotted revenge and murder. After all, there were suspects — wayward elements of the former Revolutionary units under the command of Novicio Luna (obviously related to General Antonio Luna), who was the first commander of Baler's anti-Spanish rebels and who, like Major Quezon before, was under the command of General Mascardo/Llanera.

Quezon, with another brother, decided to hunt down the murderers to bring them to justice. Most unfortunately, the same killers captured them in a hilly deserted place! It looked like a repeat of the previous two Quezon murders would most unfortunately ensue. How unlucky can a family get?

The bandits were hungry — most bandits, if not all, are — and Quezon had the quick wit to offer them the food he was carrying. The bandits wolfed it down like crazy, laying aside their arms in the meantime. Of course Quezon and his brother grabbed the guns and the situation was reversed. He delivered his captives to one Col. Calixto Villacorta.[5]

One more short story before we go to the assassination attempt.

By 1905 Quezon had become known as the champion of the common man and got elected to the provincial board. Then he ran for governor, who in those days was elected by the councilors from all towns. Candidates therefore had to spend a small fortune to transport their voters to Lucena, where the balloting was held, and later from Lucena back to their respective towns. Who says it was only recently that elections had become expensive?

suspect Luna relative

There were three candidates for governor, the other two being wealthy aristocrats, as historian Carlos Quirino stresses,[6] while Quezon only had his lawyer's provincial income to spend — and he had not much left, having been a free-spending bachelor. Quirino continues:

"Quezon's two opponents had their own ships and a fleet of *carromatas* to bring their supporters to the capital. Fortunately, Quezon was a good friend of the army quartermaster, Lt. Hunter Harris, who mobilized the US Army transport system in the province to help him bring his supporters to Lucena at no expense." *Caramba!*

But Quezon's problems had just started. The first balloting was indecisive. Another balloting — next day. His two rich opponents had a field day wining and dining the voters while Quezon ran out of wherewithal. Worse, they paid the storeowners not to give Quezon any credit, and laughed at him. *Puñeta!*

Then seemingly out of nowhere, his longtime *lavandera* materialized with food and fowl and sacks of rice to feed Quezon's voters. She was spending her life's savings for him, and thus paved the way for Quezon to remain in the running, and eventually win the first big fight of what was to become an astonishing political career. Still from Quirino:

> Many years afterwards, after he had become a national figure, he asked to see the humble *lavandera* during one of his visits to Tayabas. The sight of the little woman, bent, almost blind in her advanced age, who had never asked him for a favor or a reward for her generosity, made him burst into tears in front of an audience of several hundred people.

Who was this man Quezon? The answer is best provided by an American, one Col. Harbord, who was Quezon's friend when he was governor. When Quezon became president this Harbord was chairman of the Radio Corporation of America.

Harbord in his latter years wrote about an incident decades previously when he accompanied young Governor Quezon in his first homecoming to Baler:

> He came on board the cutter. As we landed through the surf, the narrow sandy beach was filled by a great crowd of Filipinos. The whole population of Baler was there.
>
> The village band played gay and patriotic airs all the way from the beach to the town. Old women who had known the governor from babyhood crowded to march in turn with arms around him, with many cries of "Manuelito!" And there was much joyous laughter and some weeping....

Wood contzwersy

We found the plaza crowded. The whole day was given to rejoicing. Speeches were made. Native games were played all afternoon and the whole day was gala day.

That evening there was a great banquet and much music and more dancing. The full moon of tropical night lighted us down to the beach when the feasting and dancing were over, and we went down accompanied by the whole village.

In my 12 years in the Philippines I saw many moving spectacles of joy and sorrow but that day at Baler remains in my memory as the most dramatic and touching.

I never saw my friend Governor Quezon again without a different feeling toward him than I have toward any other Filipino, and I have known the best and the brightest of his contemporaries. Nearly 40 years have passed and I am proud to say that our friendship is still the same.[6]

That Manuelito was the same man whom some Caviteños wanted to kill in 1935 after he trounced Aguinaldo in the election for Commonwealth president.

For a few years after the Revolution, Aguinaldo was content to live quietly in Cavite, occasionally going to Manila serving the Revolution's veterans association — as its president, what else.

Then the Wood controversy exploded and Aguinaldo took a position different from Quezon's and became the latter's political adversary, their conflict marked by bitter charges and countercharges in the newspapers. In 1935, the only one who could give Quezon a fight in the presidential election was Sergio Osmeña, but he decided to run as Quezon's vice president.

The situation now was that no one else had the stature to fight Quezon but Aguinaldo. Naturally, the Caviteños presumed that their revered generalissimo was certain of winning against Quezon, who was Aguinaldo's unknown and undistinguished subordinate during the Revolution and whom they regarded as nothing more than a slick, opportunistic run-of-the-mill *politico*.

Which Quezon probably was — slick and opportunistic, but hardly run-of-the-mill.

At one stage in their political kickboxing, Quezon denied he was a member of Aguinaldo's veterans club, whose leadership he had naturally belittled as inept. Aguinaldo caught him there, red-handed, by producing Quezon's membership records.

Mission Possible: Assassinate Quezon — and Mrs. Quezon

This was, of course, a peripheral issue. Aguinaldo charged that Quezon did not really want independence, a forbidding stance by the former because he was the great leader of the Revolution's struggle for independence.

Quezon for his part questioned Aguinaldo's personal financial loans in public institutions — not an exact parallel of those Caviteños of the revolutionary days who had previously tried to assail, in a most ridiculous way, Bonifacio's handling of Katipunan funds.

No matter, Quezon was the sure winner in the presidential contest. The Caviteños were out of touch with reality, of course, for Aguinaldo's age had passed, and the rest of the nation did not fully share their undiminished adoration and worship of the Founder of the First Philippine Republic and Father of the Filipino Nation.

It was also Aguinaldo's misfortune to bounce back to the national scene at a time when the dominant leader was so spellbinding a personality like Baler's Manuelito.

Another great leader who had remained nonpolitical since the Revolution now also reactivated himself, and announced he was running for president with the explicit but forlorn goal "to defeat Quezon."[8] His name: Bishop Gregorio Aglipay.

That both Aguinaldo and Aglipay were not viable candidates was clear from the fact that, like some present-day presidential aspirants whose ambitions exceed their worth, they could not get well-known runningmates.

Aguinaldo's bet for vice president was one Raymundo Melliza of Iloilo, a forgotten — if ever he had been remembered in the first place — former Supreme Court justice whose distinction no one seemed able to divine.

While in the Aglipay ticket was a firebreathing radical with the name of Norberto Nabong who was also not considered seriously.

A historian wrote a few months after the elections:

Aguinaldo stumped in Central Luzon and the Visayas, but avoided the Ilocos provinces because of his unpopularity there with the followers of General Antonio Luna. Bishop Aglipay proved to be the most colorful and sensational of the three candidates.

The white-haired bishop, who is nearing 70, spouted blood and thunder. He added salt and pepper to an election which would otherwise have been colorless because of the one-sidedness of the elections.[9]

Of course Quezon was more colorful than anyone ever, but he mounted a low-key campaign, already being sure of winning. The results:

For president:

Quezon................................. 695,332 or 67 percent

Aguinaldo............................ 179,349 or 17 percent

Aglipay........................... 148,010 or 14 percent

Racuyal............................... 157 or what percent?

For vice president:

Osmeña......................... 812,352 or 86 percent

Melliza............................ 70,899 or 7 percent

Nabong............................ 51,443 or 5 percent

It may be noted that Osmeña got many more votes than Quezon himself because his opponents were political midgets while Quezon's were legendary names. Quezon won in all provinces, with an awesome landslide in each one, except in Ilocos Norte and Nueva Vizcaya where Aglipay won, and in Cavite, of course, which was Aguinaldo's Magdalo territory forever.

In those days, Quezon's candidates usually lost in Manila, then often an opposition-ist city, but when he himself ran he won over Aguinaldo by a huge 15,000 upheaval. Wasn't Manila Bonifacio territory?

Parenthetically, in his conflict with Aguinaldo, Quezon the astute politician resur-rected Bonifacio's name. He encouraged the writing of articles honoring the Great Plebe-ian, and even ordered the construction of what is now the grand Katipunan monument in Caloocan, the most impressive in the country.

One day, government agents arrested a Pedrong Kastila who according to Quezon's aide, Captain Sergio R. Mistica, was "a revolutionary soldier and rabid follower of General Aguinaldo,"[10] and a few others and kept them in the Kawit jail. Quezon and Pedrong Kastila, in fact, knew each other as fellow soldiers during the Revolution.

In Pedrong Kastila's possession was found a revolver which was believed intended for use to kill Quezon. He was charged with illegal possession of firearm and with plotting to assassinate the president. Indeed he had quickly confessed to the assassination plot with-out implicating anybody.

Pedrong Kastila's lawyer, the garrulous and truculent Congressman Jose Topacio Nueno, in an article published more than a decade later, in 1948, recalled:

"The plot was to shoot Quezon at the Sta. Ana Cabaret on the night of his birth-day celebration (August 19). Somebody was to put out the lights. In the midst of the confusion, Quezon was to be shot. Consternation, panic and riot would follow and enable the killer to escape."[11]

to be killed on night of birthday

Quezon summoned lawyer Nueno from Cavite to see him in his famous Pasay residence.

"I prepared for the worst," said Nueno, thinking no doubt of Quezon's redoubtable personality and temper. "But to my surprise Quezon received and treated me so nicely. I felt embarrassed to be the lawyer of his would-be killer."

Quezon asked him what he would do as Pedrong Kastila's lawyer. Nueno replied that since the fellow had confessed, and was already old, he would ask for the minimum penalty.

Quezon then said with a smile, "If I pardon and set him free, you people of the opposition may shout again that I am afraid!"

Nueno replied, "Who in the world, Mr. President, would believe that you are ever afraid of anything? A pardon would be an unparalleled act of benevolence and greatness."

"Do you guarantee that he and his fellow conspirators will behave well, as law-abiding citizens?"

Nueno said he was speechless, but at last he managed to say, "I will be a conspirator myself against them if they reciprocate your kindness with ingratitude and treachery."

Quezon patted Nueno on the shoulder — good boy, good boy, must have been the shrewd Quezon's regard now towards Nueno — and said, "Go to Cavite right now. Tell the judge and the fiscal to drop all the cases against Pedrong Kastila and bring him here tonight. I want to talk to him. Make it secret. I trust you."

It was about seven at night when Nueno and the would-be assassin arrived in Quezon's Pasay home. Here was the conversation between Quezon and Pedrong Kastila, according to Quezon's aide Mistica:

"Hoy, Pedro, ako nga ba ay papatayin mo? O, naito ang revolver na ipapatay mo sa akin. Bakit, bakit mo ako papatayin?"

The rebel, visibly trembling, answered, *"G. Presidente, totoo nga pong papatayin ko kayo. Hinihingi ng bayan pagka't kayo ay ayaw ng kalayaan."*

" Nagkakamali kayo, Pedro. Sa bayang ito ay walang makatatawad sa aking pag-ibig sa kalayaan. Matagal tayong magkakasama sa bundok, sa pakikilaban sa Amerikano, hanggang sa ako ay nagkasakit ng malubha. Sa katunayan, Pedro, ay matagal nang sumuko [sic] si General Aguinaldo ay kami ni General Mascardo ay lumalaban pa....

"Pagkaraan ng sampung taon mula ngayon ay magkakaroon tayo ng lubos na pagsasarili, ayon sa Batas Tydings-McDuffie. Ano pang kalayaan ang gusto

ninyo? Ang isang bansang kaparis natin na magsasarili ay kailangang bago tumulak sa dagat ng pagsasarili ay dapat magkaruon muna ng sapat na panahon upang makapaghanda ng magiging tanggulan niya laban sa masasamang loob na katulad mo....

"Ukol naman sa balak mo sa akin, baka hindi mo nalalaman, Pedro, *na baka hindi ka man lamang makalapit sa akin upang isagawa ang banta mo. Maraming totoo ang pagmamalasakit sa akin. Ano ba, papatayin mo pa ba ako?"*

Pedrong Kastila remained silent at first, although one could easily read his already changed expression from fear to self-assurance.

The President, satisfied at the way his point has been driven, dismissed the subject of the projected murder and called his private secretary, Jose A. de Jesus, to get 50 pesos from Mrs. Quezon.

Turning to the rebel once more, the President, extending a hand, offered the money to Pedrong Kastila. *"O, kunin mo ito. Nalalaman kong ikaw ay wala."*

"Huwag na po, Presidente. Salamat po ng marami."

But the President insisted. *"Ako'y mayroon ngayon, ikaw ay wala. Kunin mo't alaala ko ito. Kung sa ibang araw ay may kailangan ka sa akin ay huwag kang matitigilang pumarito ha?"*

Nueno's account is slightly different: "He pardoned Capitan Pedro. Not only that, he gave him 50 pesos, with the promise of a monthly allowance, which was fulfilled. Capitan Pedro was so deeply impressed and emotionally moved by Quezon's kind words and commanding personality that he shed tears when we left."

Incidentally, before they left, the now safe Pedrong Kastila had the effrontery to ask Quezon, *"Maaaring ang* revolver *po ba ay mapabalik sa akin? Matagal ko pong gamit iyan."*

Quezon without thinking correctly replied, *"Aba, hindi na. Ito'y alaala mo sa akin."*

Question: Was Capitan Pedrong Kastila, Quezon's would-be assassin, the same Captain Pedro Janolino who delivered the first blow in the assassination of Antonio Luna?

The story of Doña Aurora and Quezon is well-known. Suffice it to say here that in an age of male chauvinism, where Quezon was a stupendous male macho to end all machos, he showed his respect and progressive attitude when he presented her to the Filipino people in a film clip not as his wife but as "my friend, companion and partner" — which she truly was.

We may note that they are the only couple after whom one province each was named. A municipality is also named after their daughter, Maria Aurora, nicknamed Baby.

But let us go back to much earlier times. When the long arm of the Katipunan Revolution reached Baler, most of the population in that remote, isolated, very poor town fled — to no one knew where, since it was surrounded by steep mountains and the sea.

Among those who did not leave town was Doña Aurora's father, Pedro Aragon, who was implicated in the uprising, arrested and sent to Manila under guard.

Earlier, the whole Aragon family, including nine-year-old Aurora, had been held as hostages in the town church by the Spanish officer in command of the *cazadores* stationed there.

Pedro Aragon died in 1901. "For some years, in order to earn a livelihood, young Aurora toiled as a tenant in the farms of Baler, standing knee-deep in the mud. With her elder sisters she started a small vegetable garden where she could raise sweet potatoes and other vegetables.

"As their home and their lands had been confiscated by the government, they moved into a nipa hut not larger than five square-meters. In that little hovel ... the bedroom served as living room as well as kitchen. In that atmosphere of poverty and hardship, her personality began to develop. She treated rich and poor alike."[12]

As we said, Baler was a very poor isolated community, and practically everyone except the Spaniards — the friar, *guardia civil* chief, etc. — lived in a nipa hut, including the Quezons and the Aragons.

With his parents gone — his father murdered and his mother having died of tuberculosis in his small young arms — young Quezon stayed with his aunt Zeneida Aragon, his mother's sister, when he came from Manila to vacation in Baler.

When he became a well-to-do lawyer in Lucena, he asked Aunt Zeneida to join him there with her two unmarried daughters, Amparo and Aurora. He most proudly says in his autobiography that "my cousin Aurora looked very pretty. I sent her to Manila to study in Normal School."

Doña Aurora was a total partner of MLQ with whom she was in close company every day. As in the case of Pedrong Kastila shown above, the scenario of President Quezon referring himself to her was familiar to all who dealt with them in Malacañang.

She was unarguably the most respected, and the most prestigious, First Lady ever, dignified but accessible and loved in an age of cold and remote *caciques*. After MLQ passed away she immersed herself in social work while, at the same time, devoted to anything that would honor his memory. She perished that way.

Early morning of April 28, 1949. Doña Aurora, her sister Amparo and her two daughters, all devout Catholics, went to early morning mass as usual in Quezon City. She was scheduled to be present in the unveiling of a marker in honor of MLQ in their hometown of Baler, and so after church she had a quick breakfast along with the others who were to constitute her party.

Maria Zeneida, or Nini, would have been in the trip but she was not feeling well and begged off, and so did Amparo.

In the party now were Baby Quezon, Doña Aurora's son-in-law Philip Buencamino, Quezon City Mayor Ponciano Bernardo, retired Armed Forces of the Philippines chief of staff Rafael Jalandoni, some civilians, other military officers and constabulary soldiers.

They rode in a total of 13 vehicles — eleven cars and wagons, and two military jeeps full of armed PC soldiers. Because it was still summer, the heat of the sun was atrocious and the swirling dust was unbearable. Mrs. Quezon asked that the Buick sedan she was riding, which belonged to Mayor Bernardo, be made the lead vehicle.

Driving was Col. Antonio San Agustin, with Baby beside him. At the rear were Bernardo and Jalandoni, with Doña Aurora between them.

Constabulary troopers in their jeep followed Doña Aurora's car which went so far ahead. It may be conjectured the PC jeep did not keep so close to her because of the dust, and so did the other vehicles. Hence, the convoy was long and this saved the lives of the riders at the rear.

Earlier, Doña Aurora told her constabulary escorts not to wear their uniforms. As it turned out, it would not have made a difference, for the ambushers were so many, very well-armed and determined to kill.

General Jalandoni later said Doña Aurora gave the instruction for two reasons — first, she did not wish to provoke the Huks, who were in total war with the PC soldiers; second, she felt no one would attack her. It appears she was kind in her opinion of the satanic communists.

At that time, the Huk rebellion was raging full blast in Central Luzon and the lower parts of Northern Luzon, and there had been so many instances of ambuscades, massacres, encounters and battles in the area.

It was clearly dangerous for anyone, even for President Quirino himself, to travel across the wooded battlefields to so remote and isolated a place as Baler.

And yet Doña Aurora had been traversing these areas many times without incident, from Manila and sometimes from Pampanga where she had her favorite rustic farm in Arayat — a small and simple one, for the Quezons in spite of their influence never enriched themselves.

Before departing from her Quezon City house, someone referred to the Huk danger. Doña Aurora replied, somewhat jestingly, "Taruc knows my white hair and he will not hurt me."[13]

Of course Luis Taruc personally was not a ruthless murderer. Indeed, among the Huk leaders, he was the one who braved ridicule by surrendering and eventually returning to his Christian faith. But there were other Huks in the top echelon whose careers were marked by a trail of blood, whom he called the Bolsheviks, meaning the hard-line faction.

But at that time Taruc was the overall commander of the Huk forces, whose formal title was chairman of the Communist Party's "military commission." The party commands the gun, remember? But like Bonifacio, he was called the Supremo — this did not sit well with envious Huk leaders, hence many Huk atrocities of which he knew nothing about were pinned on him.

In a town in Pampanga Doña Aurora's party made a stopover. Joining in a constabulary jeep was military historian Uldarico Baclagon, whom we mentioned in chapter 1 in connection with his analysis of the Battle of Mactan.

As the convoy reached the winding road through the fringes of the forest in the Bongabong-Baler highway, he noticed that "we were on a road skirting the side of a mountain slope, with the high ground on our right, covered with forest and huge boulders.

"It was clear, at least to us PC men, that we were going through a potential enemy ambush position. I was aware of what the Huks could do to us on our way. However, the presence of Mrs. Quezon and other VIPs in the party seemed to calm our fears."[14]

Much later after the incident, investigations showed that the ambushers — whether they were Huks or plain bandits — numbered at least 100 and at most 200 bloodthirsty demons.

Before Doña Aurora's convoy arrived, they set up a blockade and rounded up the hapless passengers and drivers of buses and trucks that passed by, and herded them under some trees not far from the road. Of course, they also robbed them of their cash and jewelry, as Marxism did not forbid them from accumulating logistics in class struggle.

This seems to show that the murderers had a specific target and knew it was coming. One of the passengers rounded up was a Pampango businessman who said the ambushers were Huks because he recognized one of them as Commander Marzon, who had worked as his employee before he became a Huk.

From contemporary newspaper reports,[15] here is a reconstruction of the ambush:

Doña Aurora's car was blocked on the road by a group of armed men. The other vehicles were way behind, including the immediately following jeep of PC soldiers. General Jalandoni got off and, unaware of the imperatives of dialectical materialism, approached the sinister-looking men, saying that Mrs. Quezon was in the car.

A gunman suddenly hit him with a rifle butt on the head, and the former chief of staff of the Armed Forces of the Philippines fell unconscious like a log.

Then all hell broke loose. From the road, from the mountain slopes, seemingly from everywhere, the ambushers were firing. Specially murderous were the machine guns from emplacements on high ground on the mountainside.

Mrs. Quezon, Baby, Mayor Bernardo and Col. San Agustin died instantly, showing that the focus of the heavy firing was on them. Buencamino, barely alive, was brought to a Cabanatuan hospital where he passed away. Also killed were Col. Primitivo San Agustin, PC officers and men and Doña Aurora's cook, Pedro Payumo.

The constables managed to jump from the two PC jeeps and, hitting the dirt on both sides of the highway, exchanged fire with the murderers. The other vehicles at the rear of the convoy turned back and raced for reinforcements from the first town they reached — *poblacions* in those days of the Huk peril usually had some military contingent always on hand — who arrived not long afterwards.

But true to the Huk strategy of not engaging in prolonged firing, since they were eternal guerillas in spite of their claim of being on the strategic offensive with the capability to seize Malacañang in a few months, the criminals had retreated, leaving their Marxist dead, numbering ten.

It is difficult, it is in fact stupid, to believe that a group of mere bandits could be that many, with such high-powered guns. Even the Abu Sayyaf today would not be able to inflict a horror of similar size, devastation and cruelty.

It was at this time of the criminals' retreat that Jalandoni recovered consciousness. The rifle butt saved his life because the ambushers thought he was dead. When blamed for the security failure, the nation's former top military man said that he was only a guest in the convoy, which was true, and that the one in charge was Major Pedro Alcantara, a nephew of Mrs. Quezon.

The military unleashed 3,000 crack troops — such after-the-fact troops are always crack — to comb the areas around the place of the incident and along the Bongabong-Baler highway. Batteries of heavy guns were paraded along the empty highway, without the usual Fourth of July audience, and fighter planes flew overhead like the Blue Diamonds — all too much and too late.

After two days of undisputed territorial supremacy, their commander, none other than the legendary Col. Napoleon Valeriano, called off the hunt, saying that the murderers must have gone back to their distant mountain lairs or mixed with the population in the urban lowlands — disguised as *sabungeros* stroking their fighting cocks?

The funeral for the Quezons was naturally huge — but simple and subdued, with no necrological orations. Their remains were buried beside that of the former president.

The pretty young Baby Quezon was a much-admired leader like her father, with a feminine version of his intense but beloved temper which for decades was the subject of amused jokes. Like her mother she dressed simply, although she was very glamorous.

She would have won any election easily without her father's or family's support. She had a magnetic personality and had her own rabid following, who mourned her deeply, among them the members of the big Young Ladies Association of Charity. Sol Gwekoh called her "devoted to humanitarian service in the manner of her mother."[16]

She had spent her recent years as a law student in the University of Sto. Tomas — a formidable background to what would have been a continuing national presence. Before the ambush, she told a friend she had dreamt of her father several times.

On the week of the funeral, the *Philippines Free Press*' regular cartoon showed the souls of Doña Aurora and Baby ascending to the waiting MLQ above, while beside their tombs below were the grieving Nini and Nonong Quezon, who was then out of town and was later reported to have suffered a series of strokes. It said:

"When President Quezon died, the news came to Filipinos as more than a painful shock, almost a personal tragedy. The death of Doña Aurora came not only as a shock to Filipinos but almost an assault on their person."

The nation sympathized in an unprecedented landslide of condolences. Statesmen abroad were led in their incredulity and sorrow by US President Harry Truman, who when he appeared at the White House to make his statement was visibly shocked, and in simple, unflowery Trumanesque fashion said, "It was awful."

Old Don Sergio Osmeña, Quezon's rival and ally for 40 years, was stunned beyond measure and brooded as if he had a world to mourn. Mrs. Osmeña was beside him upon hearing the news; she tried to utter something, but to the startled notice of those present, no words came out of her lips.

Doña Aurora's provincemates in Quezon province were particularly incensed. An announcement was made that the Tayabasin would organize their own guerilla movement to pursue the perpetrators in the jungles or wherever they may be.

The one who made this announcement was a Caviteño — none other than Jose Topacio Nueno who, with the above-mentioned incident with President Quezon, must have become a rabid admirer of the Quezons.

would-be assassin lawyer

President Quirino called for "a people's war on the dissidents," an inversion of the Huks' phraseology about the people supporting their communist insurgent war — with neither the support nor the war materializing, much less their salivating seizure of state power.

Quirino at that time was in Baguio. He blamed the Huks and said, somewhat impertinently, that this was what they did in return for what the government had given them — amnesty, lands, credit facilities, schools, irrigation systems, seedlings, medicine, food relief, clothing....

Then through the following months and years, Huks were arrested who confessed participation in the dastardly crime — up to as late as 1958 when the times had so receded that no military officer craving for promotion would bother to torture them to extract a false act of contrition because the issue had simmered down.

They were captured in trickles as the years went on, in battle or in raids not necessarily connected with the desire to solve the infamous murders. The truth could not set them free; it was the reason for their continued captivity.

Many of these Huks were given their day in court. Given special media attention were five men who were tried before the Cabanatuan Court of First Instance, sala of Judge Mariano Noble, who sentenced them to death.

Some Huks on the commander level who were also captured or surrendered pointed to one Commander Paulino Viernes, alias Stalin, as the leader of the ambush. He was said to operate in the area between Quezon province and Nueva Vizcaya.

But Stalin, like his Soviet counterpart, was never brought to justice. Nobody knows what happened to him. There was an unconfirmed story that a group of tribesmen murdered and feasted on him and his companions like Humabon and his men did to the survivors of Magellan's death.

Later, like a ghost, he was said to have given the military surrender feelers! Then it was said he died in an encounter with the PC.

His body was never recovered, and who knows what really happened to him? At least it was said that the Huk leadership had classified him as "officially dead" — according to his brother who was also a Huk commander and who made these revelations upon being captured and interrogated personally by then PC chief General Manuel Cabal.

Was this to help take the government forces off Stalin's back?

Or perhaps to free the high-echelon Huk leadership from the horrendous guilt? Stalin's brother also said that before his death Stalin, who was a battalion commander in the rebel forces, had been demoted by his immediate superior, Jose de Leon alias Commander Dimasalang, for undertaking the ambush without approval by the top Huks.

As early as May 7, 1949, the *Philippines Free Press* said in its editorial, "That the Huks murdered Mrs. Quezon and her party is beyond doubt."

11. Laurel Shot, Roxas Bombed, Magsaysay Missed

Lingayen

THE JAPANESE attacked Pearl Harbor on December 7, 1941— and Clark Airbase the next day, destroying on the ground practically all of the American Air Force's planes in the Philippines. The hordes of General Homma landed in Lingayen 15 days later and immediately started marching on to Manila.

On December 24, General Douglas MacArthur met with President Quezon and top government officials in their last Cabinet meeting in the imperiled city. The president, Vice President Osmeña, Justice Secretary Jose Abad Santos and others were told to go that afternoon to Corregidor to escape the hands of Nippon.

Acting Chief Justice Jose P. Laurel wanted to go with them but Quezon told him, "No, Laurel, someone will have to meet the Japanese. The people must be given the necessary protection. Times will be hard. A big man is needed for the job. You must stay."[1]

Laurel asked what he, and the others who had to stay, must do, if the Japanese made demands. MacArthur gave the historic reply, "You can do anything but take the oath of allegiance to the Japanese. If any one does that, I will shoot him when I return."

He did return, but shot no one.

Under Japanese dominion, Laurel tried to cushion the impact of the cruel war on the people. In the process, he waged his own personal contest of nerve and wits against the conqueror and, in spite of his terrible circumstances, sometimes prevailed.

For example, at the risk of enraging the Japanese and provoking them to take his own life, he defied their instruction to order the conscription of a Filipino army to fight the Americans.

He saved the lives and liberties of many individual Filipinos from the clutches of the Japanese military police, the Kempetai, among them Manuel Roxas and Ferdinand Marcos.

When one of his officers in the presidential guard, Major Jesus Vargas, was summoned by the Kempetai to report to Fort Santiago — a horrid invitation that in all probability would lead to torture and death — President Laurel instructed his guards "not to let any Japanese get inside the palace, and get ready to shoot if neccessary."[2]

Laurel saves Marcos from Jap M. Police

In November 1943, when he attended the first inter-Asian conference in Tokyo under the auspices of the victorious Japanese, who censored all speeches to be delivered by the subjugated Asian leaders, Laurel insisted he did not have a prepared copy of his speech because he delivered his speeches extempore.

In those instances, the Japanese could have executed him immediately but the prospect did not daunt him. To emphasize the fact that he and his government, although they were supposed to operate as an independent government, were under their mercy, the Japanese ringed Malacañang with garrisons and outposts.

In 1944 some 100,000 Japanese soldiers were placed around Malacañang ostensibly to help guard it. But it could well have been used, under certain emergencies, to arrest or overwhelm him and his guards, who numbered only 300.[3] This did not bother him.

To go back to the beginning when the Japanese first arrived in Manila, the officials Quezon left with Laurel to deal with the Japanese — Jorge B. Vargas, Benigno Aquino Sr., Jose Yulo, Claro M. Recto, etc. — were appointed to new positions.

Laurel was at first made "commissioner [secretary] of justice" and concurrent "commissioner of interior." Presumably this was lower than the positions given Vargas and a few others — a state of affairs that was to be changed by the attempt to assassinate him, as we shall see.

As interior commissioner he had under his jurisdiction the government's sports and amusement sector, which at first he thought could have been the reason why there was a plot to kill him.

Let us go to Laurel's own words[4] in recalling the incident where he cheated death:

Bilang komisyoner panloob, pinamahalaan ko rin ang mga laro at libangan. Ang departamentong panloob ay may nakahiwalay na dibisyong nangangasiwa sa mga laro at libangan. Sa naturang dibisyong ito kami nagkaroon ng pagkakataong maalagaan ang mga pinalayang bilanggo ng digmaan.

Pagdating ko mula sa Mindanao ay kinailangan kong magpasya sa isang kasong may kinalaman sa pandaraya sa isang karera ng kabayo sa San Lazaro Hippodrome.

Itinalaga kong dagliang magsiyasat si Colonel Telesforo Martinez, isang matapat at makatarungang beteranong noon ay puno ng dibisyon ng kaayusang pangmadla.

Isinumite niya sa akin ang ulat at nang natanggap ko ay iniutos ko ang pagtitiwalag sa mga tagahatol, pagpapawalang-karapatan sa isang hinete — hindi *ko matandaan ang mga detalye — kinansela ko ang karera, at iniutos ang pagsasauli sa publiko ng mga halagang kasangkot sa pinagtalunan.*

Ipinagbigay-alam sa akin na hindi nasiyahan sa aking kapasyahan ang mga taong labis na naapektuhan nito.

Umagang-umaga ng Hunyo 5, 1943, samantalang naglalaro ako ng golf sa Wack-Wack Country Club *sa* Mandaluyong, *kasama sina* Dr. Nicanor Jacinto, *pangulo ng* Far Eastern University *na si* Nicanor Reyes, *Dekano* Leoncio B. Monzon, Liling Roces, Aurelio Montinola Sr. *at* Enrique Katigbak — *dalawa kaming pangkat — ay pataksil akong binaril sa likuran, humigit-kumulang sa 12 o 15 yarda mula sa Tee* Bilang 7 *kung saan ako nakatayo.*

Sa tulong [ng mga kasamahan ko] ay binuhat ako at dinala sa isang kotse. Isinugod ako sa Philippine General Hospital *at doon ay ginamot ng mga doktor na sina* Antonio Sison, Nicanor Jacinto, Ramon Macasaet, Januario Estrada, Fortunato Guerrero, Col. Ishii *at iba pa.*

Namalagi ako sa pagamutan ng may dalawang buwan.

According to President Laurel, there was an intense furor as to why an attempt was made to take his life. He continued his account:

"Ako man sa aking sarili ay hindi ko nalalaman ang dahilan. Ang ibang palagay ay dahil sa pangyayaring kaugnay ng naganap sa San Lazaro na nabanggit sa naunang talata. Ang [ibang] paniwala ay maka-Hapones ako."

In those days, some Filipino guerillas had the policy of trying to assassinate those whom they perceived to be pro-Japanese. The idea that this was the reason why someone shot Laurel was, says Teodoro Agoncillo, "a colossal misunderstanding."[5]

To continue with Laurel's own words:

Labis kong ipinagdamdam ang duwag at pataksil na pagtatangka sa aking buhay nguni't higit na nadama ko ang kirot ng damdamin sa bintang na ako'y maka-Hapones. Hindi ako maka-Hapones.

Bukod pa sa roon, ako'y nasa pamahalaan nang labag sa aking kalooban at bagama't nananatili ako sa aking tungkulin ay dahil sa tiyak na tagubilin ni Pangulong Quezon.

Sa kaibuturan ng aking puso ay hindi ko maaaring mahalin ang mga Hapones nang higit sa aking sariling kababayan.

Ang isa pang dahilan (ang pangyayari sa San Lazaro) ay maaaring totoo nguni't tila hindi ito pinag-ukulan ng pagpapahalaga ng mga militar na Hapones at mga Pilipinong may kapangyarihang sibil. Isina-isantabi rin ang motibong personal sapagkat wala akong personal na kaaway.

Dahil sa aking tungkulin sa komisyong tagapagpaganap na siyang ahensiya sibil na binuo ng mga makapangyarihang militar na Hapones, inaresto ng Kempetai *ang isang bilang ng mga tao at pagkaraan ng ilang araw ay nalathala ang mga larawan ng apat o limang taong ipinapatay o ipinabaril dahil sa pagtangka sa aking buhay.*

Sinabi ko sa pulis militar, sa pamamagitan ni Kapitan Yanase, *na hindi ako naniniwalang ang mga naturang tao ang may kagagawan ng krimen, at ang natuklasan ng* Manila Police *sa pamumuno ni* Colonel Torres *ay tila higit na makatwiran.*

Tumutukoy ito sa isang "Little Joe" *na siyang may kasalanan. Si* Little Joe *ay may malaking pagkakahawig sa lalaking nagtangka sa aking buhay sa* Wack Wack Golf.

Nang lumaon ang naturang Little Joe *ay dadakpin sana ng* Kempetai *nguni't sinabi ko sa kanila na hindi ko natitiyak na siya nga ang may kinalaman — at natagpuan na nila at ipinabaril ang mga may kasalanan nang hindi isinangguni sa akin. Si* Little Joe *ay hindi dapat na ipabaril.*

Ang saloobin kong ito ay nakaabot sa kaalaman ng ilang tao at tumanggap ako ng isang liham na walang lagda na pumupuri sa "kalakihan ng aking puso."

Was this anonymous letter from Little Joe himself, or from one of Little Joe's relatives and friends?

Sa katotohanan, bilang pagtanggap ng pananagutang tulungan ang aking mga kababayan upang makaligtas at mapabuti ang kanilang kalagayan, hindi ko nanaising maging dahilan ako ng kamatayan o paghihirap ng sinuman sa kanila.

Kinokondena ko ang karuwagan at kataksilan nguni't iginagalang ko ang ideolohiyang pulitikal ng mga taong nasadlak sa kawalang-pag-asa sa isang sitwasyong may ginagampanan akong mahalagang bahagi.

President Laurel's forgiving Little Joe was an act of redemptive grace. Of past comments about his role during the Japanese Occupation, let us note what President Quezon said to President Laurel's son, Sotero, in a personal letter:

"*Kilala ko si* Dr. Laurel *nang personal at ako'y nagkaroon ng malapit na kaugnayang opisyal sa kanya sa loob ng maraming taon. Naniniwala akong ginagawa niya ang matapat*

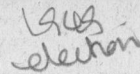
niyang pinaniniwalaang pansamantalang makabubuti sa mga mamamayang Pilipino, at hindi dahil siya'y naging isang kasangkapan ng mga Hapones."[6]

Actually, this should not be a matter only of *paniniwala*. The evidence, the record, shows that he did not seek the presidency, it was thrust to him by the Japanese, and that he tried his best to alleviate his countrymen's plight.

Before the war broke out he had determined to devote his life to the practice of law. And when the Japanese came they did not immediately choose him for the top post. But his brush with death changed his life.

> *Maging ano man ang dahilan o motibo sa pagbaril sa makin sa* Wack Wack, *nakatawag ako ng pansin ng publiko. Kamangha-mangha ang aking pagkaligtas.*
>   *Ang mga taong nakakikilala sa akin, ang ginawa kong mga pagpapakasakit, ang aking pansariling* record *pampubliko, ang aking kaunting reputasyong natamo sa mahigit na 35 taon kong paglilingkod pangmadla ay lalong tumawag ng pansin sa mga nangangasiwang Hapones.*

Ironically, the assassination attempt and all these called the attention of the Japanese to his stature — and made them decide to choose him to be the Filipinos' sacrificial lamb.

Even while he was still bedridden in the hospital, the Japs appointed him head of the commission to draft a constitution and prepare plans for the establishment of the Second Philippine Republic. In the hospital room across his own he presided over a meeting of the commisson that included such historic names as Emilio Aguinaldo, Roxas, Recto, Aquino, Paredes, Yulo, Vargas, Osias, Madrigal, Avancena, Arranz, Briones, Sison, De las Alas, Tirona.

And later, the wartime National Assembly unanimously elected him president.

That he was nominated four years after the war, in 1949, by the Nacionalista Party to be its candidate for president was vindication enough, regardless of his narrow loss in the election, which was one of the dirtiest and most notorious ever.

The conduct of the widely condemned election so heated up the Batangueños that they prepared for a revolt, starting to stockpile arms in the mountains and elsewhere. But Laurel himself calmed them down, saying in his characteristic prose that the presidency was not worth a revolution.

His full vindication came with his topping the senatorial polls in 1951, and spending the rest of his life as a most respected elder statesman.

The next president targeted for assassination was Manuel A. Roxas.

In the 1960s and the 1970s, the name Roxas was carried by his son, Gerardo, or "Gerry," who was also a senatorial topnotcher. Like his father he was president of the

Liberal Party — and being also gifted was touted to be a future president, the only one who could beat Ninoy Aquino in the scheduled Liberal Presidential National Convention of 1973, which never came because Marcos declared martial law in 1972.

The new generation of Filipinos in those two decades was hardly aware of the gigantic proportions of the first Manuel Roxas when he was alive, simply because had they been told about it sufficiently, they would have scarcely believed he had such extraordinary brilliance and diverse talents.

Roxas was the country's first number one bar topnotcher. In his youth he was secretary to Chief Justice Cayetano Arellano, and as it was the idiom or lingo then, he lived and breathed and ate and slept with the law.

Later he became a political wizard who lived and breathed and ate and slept with politics, starting as governor of Capiz, with destiny vibrations so intense that at 30 years old he was elected Speaker of the House. He was a stunning refutation of the statement that youth is wasted on the young.

His floor performance in the 1934 Constitutional Convention — delivered by the best English-speaking tongue before the sensational advent of Raul Manglapus — produced rhetorical gems and flourishes that are so much a pleasure to read even now.

He was himself so widely read — and in an oratorically-inclined age few dared to match wits with him because of his debating prowess and eloquence as one of the two greatest orators of the era, the other being Manuel L. Quezon.

He was keenly respected as a knowledgeable official, with a scholarly repertoire so vast that when Quezon became president he appointed Roxas not to a position worthy of his legal, political and constitutional background but as — secretary of finance!

And he served in that arcane capacity continuously for almost six years, up to the outbreak of the war — when MacArthur, adept in discovering extraordinary talent, made him an army major and his aide.

Again, he showed a hidden talent when, at the height — or depth — of the Fil-American forces' heroic but bloodied resistance struggle in Bataan and Corregidor, he organized an effort that brought to these hungry, dysentery-ravaged malarial troops 30,000 sacks of rice from his home province of Capiz aboard the ship *Legaspi* — along with 160,000 eggs and other food.[7]

For this vital service at a most critical hour — which was sneaky and witchlike although it was done without the benefit of a broom — Roxas was promoted to the rank of colonel.

Later, in 1944, the Japanese appointed him chief of BIBA, or Bigasang Bayan, which was in charge of the procurement and distribution of rice to the civilian population, especially in Manila — assuming there was any left after the Japanese armies had eaten up and hoarded much of the supply.

Before this appointment, he had been captured in Mindanao while inspecting USAFFE troops, and placed in a prison camp along with 10,000 despondent others, says a historian — a very huge camp whose size should be verified.

President Quezon, in exile in the United States, was so worried about Roxas' fate, wondering in how many centuries the nation could produce another Roxas — unmindful of previous estimates by others that it would take one century (only one?) for the country to produce another Rizal.

At first Roxas refused to collaborate with the Japanese. There was a Japanese officer who was specifically assigned the task of persuading Roxas to collaborate — again a tribute to Roxas' special importance even in Jap eyes.

His name was Lt. Col. Nobuhiko Jimbo, a rare Catholic from an almost homogeneously Shintoist nation whose soldiers engaged in atrocities — for they were not Christians? Because of their tradition of ancestor worship, the Japanese up to now would never admit, out of mandatory reverence for their fathers, that their wartime leaders were in point of historical fact barbarous aggressors.

For his patriotic obstinacy, Roxas was sentenced to die by firing squad. But good old Jimbo, who had become his good friend and admirer, exerted all efforts to save him, and somehow succeeded in holding off his execution.

No less than the head of the Japanese military administration in the Philippines, one General Hayasi, unable to comprehend the importance of a Filipino who was in every civilized respect his superior, was so outraged why no report of Roxas' execution had reached him. So he issued another order to carry out the execution.

Along with a Cabinet member, Roxas was taken in a car to the place of execution. The Cabinet member was so frightened and started to be hysterical. A supercool Roxas told him to calm down and accept their fate, adding with Zenlike capability to ignore their own plight and instead "look at the [beautiful] flowers."

Luckily, Jimbo had persuaded no less than the Japanese commander in chief, General Homma, to overrule the execution order and in the nick of time they were taken back to prison with body and soul still together.

In the weeks ahead Roxas feigned illness in order to discourage further efforts by the Japanese to ask him to serve their government. But they did not cease trying. So every time the Japanese went to his house with a doctor to examine his supposedly failing health, Roxas, before he had his house door opened by his domestic help to the unwanted guttural guests, would run up and down the staircase.

Therefore, when the Japanese doctor examined him, he was sweating. And his pulse had a much faster rate than normal. He was really "sick."

When Roxas became president, he heard that Col. Jimbo had been taken prisoner in Tsinan, Northern China, by Chiang Kai-shek's forces on charges of being a war criminal. Immediately Roxas wrote Chiang, saying Jimbo was a good, humane and decent man. Note in the second sentence below how overt but subtle Roxas was in his phraseology in his letter, considering the charges against Jimbo:

> On one occasion he risked his life by disobeying an order issued for my execution and made a successful appeal at a later time for the rescinding of the order. This action was not based specially on a personal esteem for me, although he had that, too, but on a repugnance for the senseless cruelty and murder madness which possessed his commanders and associates.

Chiang, bewitched by Roxas' reference to Jap barbarity from which the Chinese had suffered more than any other people, appreciated the nuances of benign poetic justice and proved equal to the presidential appeal.

He released Jimbo, who was of course grateful. Jimbo more than a year later writhed in sadness upon learning of Roxas' death. In 1952 he wrote a small but sincere pamphlet telling his story about his friend Roxas, which was also a tribute, still extant in the files of the National Library.

Near the end of the war in 1944, when MacArthur landed in Leyte and the Japanese retreated to Baguio, they brought with them as virtual prisoners Laurel, Recto, Aquino, Vargas — and Roxas.

That it was not only Quezon but MacArthur who regarded Roxas as of incalculable value is evident from the following fact: While Adolf Hitler was ruminating the rescue by German commandos from Italy of the captured Benito Mussolini — and they succeeded — MacArthur ordered a special operation that also succeeded in rescuing Roxas from his Japanese guards in Baguio.

Under cover of darkness, he was brought to Tubao, La Union, then to San Fernando in Pampanga and then to Manila where he had a happy reunion with MacArthur, who promoted him on the spot to the rank of brigadier general. For doing nothing but allowing himself to be rescued?

Because in the last many months he had finally yielded and worked for the Jap-sponsored Republic, he was accused as one of the collaborators. But how could this accusation prosper when the greatest foe of collaborators — MacArthur himself who ordered many Filipino leaders arrested and jailed on charges of collaboration — masterminded the rescue of Roxas?

Not only that, MacArthur openly supported Roxas in his presidential election contest against the great noncollaborator Don Sergio Osmeña. Now was this poetic injustice?

Not so, Roxas himself claimed, because even while working for the Jap-sponsored Republic, he was actually running secretly the whole Filipino guerilla movement! Some could not believe this, but MacArthur himself acknowledged it. In any case, like Laurel and a few others, he was under mortal duress, and it is unfair, and wrong, to judge him adversely.

Roxas was President only for less than two years, his term cut short in 1948 by cardiac arrest. But it could have been shortened more than a year earlier, on a near-fatal day in March 1947, during a political rally in Plaza Miranda.

The Roxas government had negotiated an agreement with the Americans where the latter was to be given "parity" in the exploitation of the Philippines' natural resources. This meant that Americans would have the same rights as Filipinos in engaging in mining, logging, fishing and such other lines of business that involved the development or taking or grabbing of the country's natural wealth.

This new agreement was against the Constitution, which had reserved the right to exploit Philippine natural resources exclusively to Filipinos. Therefore, it had to be ratified by the people in a plebiscite. President Roxas led the campaign for its approval.

Among intellectuals, nationalists and some imperiled or deprived Filipino businessmen, this "parity" amendment was very unpopular. In fact it was despised. It was viewed as a wholesale surrender of sovereignty and a canine submission to ruthless pressure from the Americans at a time when the country was still recovering from the wounds and warts of war.

But America had always been popular to the great masses of Filipino citizens and, with the Roxas government's full-scale drive, its overwhelming approval in the plebiscite was expected.

On the eve of balloting day that March of 1947, Roxas led the proparity rally in Plaza Miranda. Unknown to anyone, there was a man who had dark and dangerous designs against Roxas. In his police confession later he described Roxas as one who had deceived the 18 million Filipinos by failing to fulfill his political promises and consigning the nation to a deplorable state.

In the confession, which was in Tagalog, he said, "he had only one life and only one God, and if he should accomplish his mission [to kill Roxas] he would have done a patriotic act."[8]

His name was Julio Guillen, a widower from Tondo, who owned a barber shop, a hardware store and several pieces of real property. He told a nephew to help him write his last will and testament in the municipal building of Caloocan.

He asked the same favor from the renowned writer Amado V. Hernandez who typed the will, writers being among the very few who had typewriters in those days, usually Remington or Underwood or some other rickety contraption probably whisked from a beached naval ship in Tacloban after the Leyte landing. In addition, Guillen wrote a last-farewell note.

Parenthetically, Hernandez, a true patriot on grounds other than the Guillen connection, is now formally lionized, justly, as a national artist duly proclaimed by the government; he had fought valiantly and with integrity for the cause of the workingman all his life, even suffering incarceration for it. Naturally he was against parity.

In his decision to kill the president, Guillen said he expected to be killed in turn by the presidential guards whether he was successful or not. Hence, the last will and testament and his own sort of "Mi Ultimo Adios."

He bought a pistol for the purpose, but someone stole it in an early version of *agaw-armas*. Later he was able to acquire two fragmentation hand grenades for the same plot. He waited for Roxas to arrive in the proparity rally in Plaza Guipit in Paco but the president was a no-show.

In a later assassination attempt more than 20 years later, this time on Ferdinand Marcos, the would-be assassins hid their bomb in a flower pot on the stage where Marcos was to speak. In his case, Guillen hid his grenades early in the morning also in a flower pot — not on stage but on Plaza Miranda's ground some five meters from the platform.

Note also that the Plaza Miranda bombers in 1971 who nearly wiped out the Liberal Party candidates hurled two fragmentation hand grenades.

When Roxas arrived that night, Guillen confessed he entertained the notion of killing him upon getting out of his car, but he, Guillen, was surrounded with so many people. Later, as the president delivered his bombastic speech, he still did not act. Roxas could spellbind even an assassin.

The strong-voiced Roxas, with his speech over, returned to his seat amid thundering applause. As Carlos P. Romulo shook Roxas' hand, Guillen reached for one grenade and stood on a rattan chair — the light, serviceable kind that is usually used even today to seat crowds in a political rally — and moved to throw it at Roxas.

In an almost tragicomic turn not unfamiliar to Charlie Chaplin movies, the chair broke and Guillen crashed to the ground. Undeterred, he picked himself up and threw the grenade anyway. The *Philippines Free Press* reported:

Death was only three yards away. The man who wanted to kill the President had aimed well. The hand grenade had made a swift curve in the air and landed almost at the President's feet.

Senate President Jose Avelino kicked it away. Brig. Gen. Mariano Castañeda gave the grenade, almost ready to explode, another kick. It fell on the ground under the platform. There it blew up, hurting at least seven men.[9]

Roxas survived because Avelino, the Samar political leader of what-are-we-in-power-for fame, and Castañeda, the burly general, were alive and kicking. Next day in the hospital, one of the wounded, photographic journalist "Fatso" Maglalang, died.

Back to the rally. When Guillen's grenade exploded, pandemonium broke loose as people panicked and scampered away in all directions. Naturally fearing a second grenade or more, Roxas and the other officials continued to duck. The First Lady, Doña Trinidad, became highly emotional and was calmed by the president himself.

Quickly a cordon of policemen and MPs surrounded and escorted them to the presidential car — for a swift ride to nearby Malacañang.

The assassin, running away wild-eyed like John Wilkes Booth, chose Quezon Boulevard as his venue of escape. He took a left turn at Raon and then rode a jeepney at Evangelista on his way to the last place he should have gone to — his home. Somehow the police caught him there, probably having followed him. Otherwise, how did they know it was him?

As investigators considered the angle that some communist group, a motley crew of oppositionists or Roxas' personal enemies may have masterminded the deed, Guillen insisted that he was alone, "solo" as he said, in the plot and act — which was true.

Had the grenade exploded on stage rather than under it, among those who may have been wiped out besides President and Mrs. Roxas, Romulo, Avelino and Castañeda, were Manila Mayor Valeriano Fugoso and Congressman Hermenigildo Atienza.

Guillen was charged with murder for the death of Maglalang, frustrated murder, and serious physical injuries. During the investigation, Guillen "calmly said that if he escaped or is released, he would try and kill President Roxas again."[10]

The authorities, of course, never gave him the chance either of escape or of release, or of running for election under the Nacionalista Party, or of having his life story filmed by Sampaguita Pictures. Rot in jail, he did.

With not much material on which to base a personal psychological study of the convolutions of Guillen's mind, an editorial writer contented himself with the sweeping statement that, irrational though his blaming of Roxas for the state of 18 million Filipinos was, "it is no more unreasonable than the arrogant obsession of the would-be assassin that on him rested the responsibility to set things aright. Colossal vanity!"[11]

The one who would have succeeded to the presidency had Guillen succeeded in his assassination try, Vice President Elpidio Quirino, was not in the rally; he was in his home place of Vigan. He became president anyway when Roxas died of a heart attack in only a year's time.

Now we come to the next assassination target, Ramon Magsaysay, who was scheduled for extermination at least twice. We say "at least" because it is reasonable to believe that there were more than two attempts, since he was the nemesis of the Huks who had a standing policy of killing high government officials they hated if and when the opportunity arose.

We may tend to categorize our presidents in terms of fixed political periods. Hence, Aguinaldo was of the Revolutionary epoch; Quezon, Osmeña and Laurel were of colonial times; Roxas, Quirino, Magsaysay, Garcia, Macapagal and Marcos were of the postwar era of the Third Republic; then Cory Aquino, Ramos and now Estrada of the postdictatorial period.

But Roxas and Quirino, psychologically speaking, did not belong to the postwar Third Republic as they are usually classified on the basis of chronology. They belonged to the old prewar colonial school of Quezon and Osmeña, who were born in the 19th century and rose with them during the Commonwealth era, with the same *cacique* style and worldview, the same laborious political lexicon, the same tedious stentorian oratory and misplaced *Castilaloy* machismo.

Ramon Magsaysay was the first president born in the 20th century, in 1907, with an entirely different personal psychology and political upbringing from the old Quezon-Osmeña crop.

We shall discuss him briefly on two points before we deal with his confrontations with death: first, his response to the immemorial problem of graft and corruption and, second, his social revolution in behalf of the common man, or the "*tao.*"

Historian Horacio de la Costa noted in the 1960s that the issue of graft and corruption had continuously dominated every election in the country, presidential or midterm, from 1946. He did not live to see it survive him for decades without the slightest waning; indeed it worsened to cosmic proportions.

The issue of corruption still eviscerates the nation today — and, as sure as the sun will rise tomorrow, will continue to do so for decades into the future.

Magsaysay stands in history as the president who was the most financially upright personally, and his term was the least characterized by government venality. The two factors are connected — if the president is honest, more officials are honest; if the president is a crook, many become crooks. It's leadership by example.

If a president demands from BIR regional directors a quota of 50 million pesos each to be turned over to him in cash right in Malacañang every month, then all the BIR agents down the line will have to collect it anomalously and pile up a portion of it under their own mattresses.

And justices and judges, policemen, customs officials, forest and coast guards, congressional and local legislators and so on, will find it easier to receive bribe money at the expense of the public weal.

Magsaysay was personally never stained with the slightest suspicion of venality.

When he died, he had only a few hundred pesos in his bank account. He had no house of his own, and his wealthy friends contributed individual amounts so that Mrs. Luz Banzon Magsaysay and the children could have a residence. He paid out of his own shallow pocket the expenses for the modest birthday parties of his children in Malacañang.

He dressed down a subordinate for suggesting that there was a way to buy a car for his son Junior Magsaysay and legitimately avoid paying customs duties.

He warned his relatives not to engage in business with the government, and in those days it was a punishment, not an advantage, to be related to the president. An uncle of his who had had a minor contract approved under the previous president silently seethed in anguish when Magsaysay ordered it cancelled — for no reason other than that he was his uncle!

It is said every president has his cronies. Magsaysay had none — absolutely, without any doubt.

When no less than his executive secretary innocently and harmlessly recommended a minor relative of Mrs. Magsaysay to a minor post in the foreign office in Washington, Magsaysay fired him!

The president observed a very strict code of personal integrity and ethics that stunned officialdom and amazed the people themselves. In an article written for an American magazine by prominent US Supreme Court Justice William O. Douglas, he was quoted to say he would jail his own father — whom he dearly loved — if he stole a single centavo from the government.

The words reverberated in the Philippines. And the people heard him gladly.

But unlike other presidents who always claimed success, he openly admitted failure in his fight against graft and corruption, although he had significantly reduced it.

A few weeks before his death, he ruefully conceded to his aides while commenting on some top officials of his own Nacionalista Party whose craving for ill-gotten wealth he was holding at bay, "My example has fallen on barren ground."

But his presidency was a brief, shining moment.

Like Aguinaldo, Cory and Joseph Estrada, Magsaysay had no pretensions to intellectual glory. In fact, before Erap, he was the butt of jokes for his fractured English and lack of erudition.

As early as when he ran for representative of Zambales, his intelligence was belittled. His rival told the voters to vote for himself and not for Magsaysay because, while Magsaysay did not finish an academic degree and was only a humble mechanic, he was a great lawyer — and this was true because he was known in the capital as such — who "ate with the law, drank with the law and slept with the law." Therefore, he should be elected congressman to make the law.

Magsaysay nevertheless defeated him, became an outstanding congressman as honored by the *Philippines Free Press*, and became a great president — while his rival went on eating with the law, drinking with the law and sleeping with the law.

As defense secretary, he restored morale and discipline to the abusive Armed Forces officers and men; almost single-handedly kept the 1951 midterm election peaceful and orderly after the notorious 1949 presidential elections; and broke the back of the Huk rebellion — for which he was placed on the cover of *Time* magazine.

But the greatest legacy of Magsaysay was his convincing commitment to the cause of the common man, which led to some kind of a revolution in social consciousness and electoral power politics.

The centuries-old subjugation of the Indio under Spanish rule has had its effect up to the present day when tillers of the soil are derogated and discriminated against due to their poverty, which has kept them ignorant, poor, undernourished, dirty — and without hope.

During the Commonwealth era and the postwar years, peasants and laborers were neoslaves who were trampled down. They held absolutely no economic or political power, and not the slightest shade of social respectability.

Magsaysay started to change all that, the consequences of his awesome initiative still vibrating up to contemporary times when the government has no choice but to put priority to the welfare of the masses, even if only for acoustic purposes to garner votes.

The word *tao* usually means "peasant," but it may apply also to workers, artisans, janitors, house painters, bus conductors, *jueteng* collectors, fishpond caretakers, bowling pinboys, domestic helpers, motorized *banca* crewmen, printing press reel mounters, *pandesal* or *bitsukoy* delivery boys, jeepney barkers, little-league pimps, *dama* players in the barbershop, countryside hillbillies, anyone who belongs to the low classes. One from the elite or the middle class, even if proficient in Taoism, cannot be called *tao*.

In its plural form, *tao* means the vast majority of the toiling masses.

As a private person in his early life, Magsaysay already showed preference for the *tao* in his personal conduct. In his early years he was some kind of foreman or lowly manager of a rickety transportation company when he berated his bus drivers who smugly passed by poor people on the highway waving for a ride.

He once dressed himself up in peasant's disguise — and such was his physical makeup or frame that, with proper sartorial downgrading, he could indeed be mistaken for a tiller of the soil — and tried to stop a speeding bus of the company for which he worked. When the driver ignored his signal he angrily pursued and accosted him and gave him a vigorous tongue-lashing.

From then on his drivers were more polite to peasants than to middle class passengers — after all, one of them, lurking silently in a corner seat, could turn out to be their foreman Magsaysay.

When in Malacañang as president, he made senators and governors wait in line with delegations of poorly dressed peasants from remote areas! It was not because he reckoned that on the basis of the precinct-level principle of one-man, one-vote, the masses were more important. It is tenable, in fact truthful, to say he really felt for them.

Of course, land reform took a giant stride during his administration.

Magsaysay was the first presidential candidate to campaign directly to the people, shaking as many hands as he could, embracing even the unembraceable while dreaming the possible dream and fighting the beatable foes like Huks and Liberals, pressing the innumerable masses in the flesh individually for hours and hours, mixing comfortably with crowds of peasants and workers, of the common people, of the *tao*.

He was the first Cabinet member who shocked the milieu when he went around attending to his official duties dressed in polo shirt. Today, some desperate candidates for senator, if only to win, may be willing to wear *bahag*, but no thanks anyway because it is not politically mandatory.

Besides, it would be visually offensive owing to the fact that none of them has engaged in wholesome bodybuilding, an unsightly phenomenon that could be offset by structural vote buying in Mindanao or by an election jingle over DZMM.

Magsaysay triggered gigantic waves of national goodwill and rejoicing as it seemed that the good news, as in the case of the prophet Isaias and the Gospels themselves, was being proclaimed to the poor, the dispossessed and the downtrodden, and that the kingdom of the *tao* was at hand.

Whether as a guerilla leader fighting the atrocious Japs, as congressman for his native Zambales, as defense secretary, as presidential candidate and as president, he was informal and easy and incredibly accessible, departing from the accustomed political ways of pomposity, grandiloquence and intimidation which the old native Filipino politicians had inherited from the old colonial masters and *caciques*.

His presidential election victory over reelectionist President Quirino was a landslide of stupendous proportions. He lost in only two provinces — Quirino's Ilocos Sur and in Ilocos Norte. This was better than the imperious hurricane Quezon who lost in four. Magsaysay's style — which was also his substance — changed for good the practical techniques of electoral campaigning in the Philippines.

From then on, candidates for public office from president to governor and congressman and mayor have had to dance a piece of the Magsaysay Mambo — that is, please the masses, the *tao*, with personal attention. Otherwise the *tao* would dump them and they would lose at the precincts. The *tao* for the first time after centuries of colonial degradation, for the first time after independence, could no longer be ignored.

Magsaysay was truly a living legend here and abroad, his image abetted by American media, whose impact on Filipino readers suffering from colonial mentality approximated that of Scriptures. He was called "Man of the Masses," and all sorts of politicians, the able and the incompetent, the honest and the crooked, the grand and the pip-squeak, even the vote buyer and the terrorist, tried to have themselves called the same.

But the original has never been reproduced.

The masses are still as poor as ever. But regardless of the practical or material results, at least the Magsaysay revolution to highlight the importance of the *tao* in the national life had transpired, and Philippine politics has never been the same again. It was a case where one man tried, and he made a difference.

It is the impression today that Magsaysay was kind and gentle. Not always.

When he was a congressman, he had a rift with General Mariano Castañeda, Armed Forces chief of staff, the burly one we mentioned above who had kicked the grenade off Roxas' feet. Castañeda rebuffed Magsaysay's personal request to appoint his recommendee as provincial commander of his province or turf of Zambales, which it was the recognized prerogative of a congressman to do.

The nationally renowned Castañeda, for no known reason, rubbed it in by calling the then political lightweight Magsaysay to his face as "a meddling *politico*."[12]

Magsaysay, incensed, surged with clenched fists at Castañeda to assault him but the proverbial cooler heads intervened. Later in the day, while Magsaysay and his friends, among them the bulldozer Congressman Floro Crisologo, were drinking milk from contented cows at the old Selecta restaurant in Azcarraga, now Recto Avenue, who sat at the table beside them but Castañeda and his armed military aides.

Magsaysay was not discomfited by the provocation, whether intended or accidental. Unmindful of the immemorial legacy of human mortality, without a single thought of his happy moments with his beauteous wife Luz and his kids, from whom he could have been permanently separated by a single temperamental act, and most certainly without any thought either of what had happened to Antonio Luna, he stood up with menacing eyes, his hands in his pockets as if to draw out two pistols, and approached Castañeda.

The startled Crisologo, himself not a stranger to armed confrontations in the grievous kingdom of Ilocoslandia, whence Ferdinand Marcos had also sprung with the Nalundasan case, restrained him with a whisper and a tight embrace as the burly General Castañeda left with his official lackeys, recognizing that prudence is the better part of pandemonium.

Castañeda picked the wrong foe. Magsaysay only a few days later was appointed by President Quirino as defense secretary, thus becoming Castañeda's administrative superior. Quickly Magsaysay fired the burly general with a one-liner, from which there was no salvation.

This outraged the members of the general staff — the chiefs of the army, navy, air force and constabulary, who were all Castañeda's men, and whose equivalent in the United States was no less than the Joint Chiefs of Staff, who in previous times could conspire to kill a president if they wanted to without the slightest punishment. They immediately protested their burly general's ouster. A historian narrates:

Magsaysay barged into the meeting of the general staff one fine morning at Camp Murphy [Camp Aguinaldo]. He was going out on a tour of a nearby Huk-infested province, wearing khaki clothes and with two .45 Colt pistols strapped around his waist.

Half a dozen bodyguards, armed with Thompson submachine guns and automatic carbines, entered the staff room with him. These were former members of the Zambales guerilla outfit whom he had selected as his personal guards, for he was not yet certain of the loyalty of the army and feared a coup on the part of the former chief of staff.

"Gentlemen," he announced, "I heard you were all planning to resign as a protest over the relief of General Castañeda. Is that right?"

The staff officers were caught by surprise and thrown off balance; they could not stammer a denial. "That's fine," Magsaysay said. "For your information I am reorganizing the general staff under your new chief, Major General Duque.'"[13] *fires Castañeda + joint chiefs of staff*

And, some time later, to demonstrate full control, he fired them all.

When the wife and children of a fired officer bravely went to the defense office and pleaded to Magsaysay to reinstate him or else they would go hungry, the Magsaysay who was legendary in his kindness towards lowly personnel refused, saying that by being merciful he could never impose discipline in the Armed Forces.

This must have tormented him. Ninoy Aquino, his assistant when he was president, recalled that each time a prisoner in Muntinlupa was scheduled to be executed in the electric chair the next morning, Magsaysay would walk to and fro in Malacañang's hallways deep into the night, torn by the choice of letting the prisoner live — or die.

Next morning, he would always call off the execution. In his term, not one prisoner was executed.[14] He would have alienated today's Alfredo Lim and Reynaldo Jaylo.

The first attempt to assassinate Magsaysay sort of started on his first day as defense secretary. President Quirino referred to him the case of one Huk, Taciano Rizal — not, it may be noted, Paciano Rizal, although Taciano was indeed related to the Calamba Rizals of the national hero. A Liberal official from Batangas had alerted Malacañang that this Taciano, alias Commander Arthur, wanted to surrender.

Having been earlier frustrated a number of times, and feeling betrayed by the Huk response to his failed amnesty edict, Quirino was sick and tired of dealing with Huks and did not want to bother.

The new defense secretary agreed to meet with Rizal — with only one bodyguard — in a dilapidated house in Tondo. The young communist revealed that the Huks were ready to overthrow the government, and had "a cache of 100,000 firearms hidden in caves."[15]

Magsaysay listened without comment as the Huk assailed the government as corrupt and rotten, did not care about the masses, and did not deserve to be supported.

Magsaysay did not argue with the Huk. He said that being a Rizal the Huk had "the blood of great patriots flowing in your veins"; that if Jose Rizal were alive he would be supporting the government in the effort to preserve law and order; that without law and order there could be no progress; that he should emulate his great-granduncle (not Andres Bonifacio?—Ed.).

After two hours they ended the discursive but dangerous tête-à-tête, agreeing to meet again, in Sampaloc. Unknown to Magsaysay, an assassin, a notorious gunman named Nick Pamintuan, had been assigned to kill him that night. Taciano was a treacherous plotter.

escapes assassination

But Pamintuan's jeep developed engine trouble, and when he arrived his would-be victim had left 30 minutes earlier.

It appears that Taciano Rizal did not tell his fellow Huks, who were clearly involved in the planning of the first meeting, about the second meeting. Magsaysay may have softened him; this time there was no plan to kill the defense secretary, who at the start bluntly asked Rizal for the names of the members of the Huk politburo.

Rizal said, truthfully as it later turned out, that he did not know them. Magsaysay was not deterred by the low rank of the man. In a third meeting the lowly Rizal asked for money to buy a car, claiming that he needed it to know the addresses of certain people, presumably politburo members.

Magsaysay, refusing still to be discouraged by this new letdown, "promptly gave him 6,000 pesos without asking for a receipt, [feeling that] he had to trust Rizal completely to gain his confidence even if it meant having trouble with the government auditors later on."

That was Magsaysay, who hated red tape as much as he despised abusive constables. Besides, why think of the auditorial requirements of the COA in a life-and-death negotiation?

Many days passed and Rizal did not get in touch. Magsaysay's own military aides concluded their boss had been duped. After all, who could trust a communist? But he maintained his "hunch" was correct. Indeed, Rizal showed up late one night, like a conspirator's recurrent wet dream.

This time he said he had decided to work with Magsaysay and help capture the politburo members, pleading for complete secrecy to protect his life and that of his family.

He revealed that a certain woman would go from one house to another in the city carrying food in baskets which contained hidden secret orders. She was the Huks' communications coordinator in Manila. By following her daily movements, government agents were able to identify all the top communists in the city, including women and children they used as couriers.

On the historic night of October 17, 1950, a fast-moving network of 21 military teams armed with search warrants raided 21 houses and captured 105 slumbering communists, the stunned members of the politburo included. The raids also yielded 42,000 pesos — not bad for Magsaysay's precarious 6,000-peso investment — and mimeographing machines, radio transmitters, plans for a general uprising in the next two years.

The rise of the Huk insurgency had ended, its fall had begun.

In one of the raids that night, Magsaysay's would-be assassin, Nick Pamintuan, managed to escape carrying a submachine gun. The raiding team, because of bureaucratic recidivism, had knocked on the wrong door.

Having been warned by the next-door commotion, he slipped out from the back of the house in which he was hiding like a pest, like the diaphanous *ipis* that usually come out when the lights had been turned off in a middle class apartment unit.

Cornered in another place later, the deluded communist biped, as thoughts of his loving mother vaguely wafted for the last time through his feverish mind, shot it out with government agents, and perished as a sacrificial offering on the altar of Marxist dialectics, although more directly from the implacable application of Newtonian physics. Surely poetic justice for one who would have killed Magsaysay treacherously.

Magsaysay's contempt for danger showed again in a trip to Mindanao to accept the surrender of Maranaw leader Datu Tawan Tawan. Along with Senator Tomas Cabili, who could speak Maranaw, he went straight to Tawan Tawan's lair in Kapatagan valley.

Historian and national artist Carlos Quirino writes:

There were speeches, of course, in Maranaw which Magsaysay didn't understand at all. And he literally squirmed in his seat at the thought of what could possibly happen. "What if Tawan Tawan decides to liquidate us?" he asked himself.

He finally breathed a sigh of relief as he saw the Muslim crowd break into smiles and clap their hands after Tawan Tawan's speech. "I guess everything's going to be all right," he muttered to himself, and smiled right back at the friendly sea of faces.[16]

It was not a Filipino source, but the same US Supreme Court Justice William O. Douglas mentioned above, who first told the story of another Huk, Tomas Santiago, alias Manila Boy, who "came to assassinate Secretary Magsaysay but instead surrendered to become the latter's follower. Although the main story was substantially correct, it had reached legendary proportions: Manila Boy was said to have been so convinced of Magsaysay's lofty motives after seeing him at his desk at army headquarters that the regenerated Huk pulled out from his pockets several hand grenades (big pockets they were) and a dagger with these words:

"Secretary, here are my grenades and dagger — I came to kill you but I have changed my mind. Let me work for you instead."

Security guards in the defense secretary's office would have immediately spotted and arrested Manila Boy. In all likelihood, his surrender was pre-arranged, and Magsaysay must have acquiesced to a touch of the dramatic, for he fully appreciated the publicity value of such a scene.[17]

Of course, among Filipino journalists of the time, Magsaysay from the beginning was the butt of jokes for being a publicity hound.

Three decades later, House Speaker Ramon Mitra remembered an incident he witnessed when he was a young reporter for the old *Manila Chronicle*. On that occasion President Magsaysay was listening in conversation with the great Claro M. Recto, who was his leading critic. Magsaysay looked humble as he appeared to try to catch every word uttered by Recto, whom he allowed to speak without interruption for many minutes as if Recto was a Greek oracle.

Then Magsaysay saw from the corner of his eye that a news photographer was about to shoot their picture. Even when today's phrase, "photo-op," did not yet exist, Magsaysay suddenly took a formidable aggressive stance, raising a clenched fist as if to stress a point in a lecture to Recto, and waited for the lightbulb to flash.

Unfortunately, the photographer had some trouble with his camera and took a long time to press the button. Yet Magsaysay never put down his raised fist. He kept it in the air for many seconds, as if in suspended animation, and it was only when the bulb flashed, recalled Mitra laughing, that Magsaysay put down his arm and reassumed the posture of listening most humbly to Recto.

And then there was one Pablito Gepana, alias Commander Milan, a dreaded rebel. He was known as Pretty Boy Killer "for his deadly proficiency in wielding firearms," not much different from Pretty Boy Floyd of Al Capone times.

He surrendered to Magsaysay saying he wanted to help the government. Pretty Boy Killer became the conduit also for the surrender of Jesus Nava, Panay politburo member, and 16 other Visayan Huks. Magsaysay, accompanied by two of his officers, went unarmed to meet them at Villa Beach in Iloilo City. One of his two escorts was Col. Ismael Lapus, who recalled:

"The Huks always insisted that in meetings of this sort we come unarmed. Naturally we never knew if we would be double-crossed and an ambush planned for us.

Everytime one of the Huks would close the bolt of his automatic rifle while cleaning it, I'd give an inward jump and wonder if a shot would next be heard."[18]

Magsaysay showed no fear, although he, too, may have been jumpy. When Nava surrendered his .45 pistol, Magsaysay returned it to him, saying, "You're with us now, here's your gun back."

Magsaysay was not around when a meeting between military officers and men and Panay's Huks turned bloody. It was supposed to be a surrender, but somehow the band of 45 Huks and ex-Huks and the military people started shooting one another at close range.

Was there bad faith or was it just a precautionary measure when the government soldiers, before the scheduled meetings, were actually coached who exactly among the Huks and ex-Huks would each one of them shoot within a second if the meeting turned deadly?

In that meeting 22 Huks perished and only one government soldier died — only because his thigh wound could not be treated in the mountain lair where they met, and developed gangrene, and the poor soldier expired before he could receive medical attention in the lowlands.

What Magsaysay's assassins failed to do, a plane crash did. But even this was suspected to be the result of sabotage. Why did some people wish to think that Magsaysay had to die from assassination, even by way of an "accident?"

Some, like the communists, said that it was the CIA which masterminded the plane crash. But who believed them? The Philippine government's indefinite verdict: Magsaysay's plane crashed either because of pilot error or instrument malfunction — or metal fatigue.

In any case, Magsaysay died as he had lived — in the service of his people.

12. The Kamikaze Attack on Mrs. Marcos

THE MOST visible lady in Philippine history has been Cory Aquino. Before she came to the scene, however, the limelight was hogged by Imelda Marcos as First Lady for a long time, from 1966 to February 1986, or for almost 20 years!

Through the years, with her involuntary exit from the pedestal of power up to the present when a new millennium has started, Imeldific could still take the limelight once in a while — at will — by simply saying a thing or two to media.

Imelda was dislodged by Cory from her first place in the sun even before Marcos' term ended. This was when Cory became the sensational opposition presidential candidate against Ferdinand Marcos.

Some may even say that Cory started to outshine Imeldific after the Ninoy assassination, when the biggest crowds that time gathered in Manila in oceanic proportions, with Cory as the lead personality.

In her presidential election campaign her drawing power surged forth to biblical dimensions, and a magazine put her on its cover with the title, "Cory of the Multitudes."

Imelda wanted to become president after Ferdinand. Failing in that, she wanted to be president after Cory. She ran for president in 1992, placing fifth in a field of seven candidates.

Cory in her time was not only the most visible, she was also the most powerful, woman ever — and more powerful than any man, being the president.

Imelda, in her years as First Lady starting way back in 1966, took not only the Philippines but the international scene by storm. In that famous first official visit with President Marcos to the United States, the Americans were startled by her beauty, from President Johnson to New York City Mayor John Lindsay, to ordinary Americans who gathered at the lobby of the Waldorf Towers to take a look at her, to newspaper editors who gave her more coverage than President Marcos!

For example, the *New York Post* published her photograph on its front page — with the blurb, "For a look at Mrs. Marcos' husband, please turn the page."[1]

A joint session of the United States Congress, where Ferdinand Marcos was about to deliver an address, gave her an unprecedented standing ovation when she was mentioned as one of the guests in the gallery — with the applause lasting for an incredible period of three minutes.

One may verify this from the newspapers[2] — they really said three minutes. And considering that on TV, for example, a mere ten seconds of applause is already very long, those three minutes may have seemed like an eternity. It is difficult to find an American president who got the same length of applause!

In Broadway, before the showing of *Man from La Mancha*, whose theme song much later became some kind of an anthem for the slain Ninoy Aquino, the audience also applauded when her name was announced.

Imelda at the reception for publishers and editors met *Life* magazine editor Henry Moscow who had featured her on the magazine's cover. Upon seeing her personally, he said that *Life*'s cover photograph did not do her justice. Nevertheless, he added, that particular issue — both the US and international editions — increased in sales by a total of half a million copies.

Of course, 20 years later, Cory Aquino, no less, enchanted and enraptured the US Congress, also in joint session, with a spectacular speech which triggered repeated rounds of tremendous applause, shaking the American Capitol building and penetrating even the far reaches of the cosmos.

As president, Cory traveled to some nations as an extraordinary political celebrity. She captivated her hosts who gaped curiously at her, wondering how this gentle, homely, dignified woman could challenge a well-entrenched dictatorship and be brought to power by a great people who adored her name above all names except the Virgin Mary and Mother Teresa.

Cory was distinctly honored to sit in the first row of the presidents and prime ministers of the world who attended in Paris the climax of the historic bicentennial celebrations of the French Revolution.

Imelda also had her great moments in her early years in power as the first-rate overseas diplomat and negotiator of the Marcos administration.

In 1969, she went to Rome to attend the investiture by Pope Paul VI of Waray Bishop Julio Rosales as cardinal, along with 32 other bishops from many lands. Nick Joaquin wrote of what happened in Rome:

Then Mrs. Marcos arrived and the Philippines really made the scene. The hotel Excelsior, where she stayed, flew the Philippine flag in her honor. Whenever she appeared in public, the Romans wondered if she was some empress from the Orient and in her wake swelled a cry in crescendo, "Bella, Bella,

Tripoli 2greement

Bellisima!" The Romans said that Mrs. Marcos brought the good weather. She came, she saw, she conquered.[3]

Imelda's writer!

Imelda, said Queen Sirikit of Thailand, was "like a Greek goddess." In 1975, she visited Cuba and her writer, Ileama Maramag, reported to the Filipino home readers:

"During the dinner, Fidel Castro and Mrs. Marcos were seated across each other in the long table. Now and then he would be caught with intent glances at the First Lady. Giving Mrs. Marcos penetrating looks, he said, 'This is a different kind of diplomacy!' "

With King Hassan in Morocco, what was scheduled as a routine diplomatic reception lasted for two hours as a personal conversation. At the end the monarch impulsively reached out for his traditional cape, the burnous. It is a royal mantle symbolizing friendship and protection, which he had given only once in his 18-year reign. Now he gave it to Imeldific.

Is this the reason why the Marcoses have always been welcome in Morocco, even if King Hassan had long gone?

In 1977, she negotiated the Tripoli Agreement with Khaddafi. Of course, she often spent time on the telephone with President Marcos in Manila, who guided her. Once, the final draft caused a furor because what Khaddafi thought was "provincial," Mrs. Marcos took as "provisional."

When Khaddafi gave his final conditions, she wrote them down word for word and showed the draft to the Libyan dictator so there would be no misunderstanding, after which she passed on the draft to Marcos over the telephone.

Imelda went to all the continents in no less than 50 diplomatic missions, meeting with leaders too numerous to all mention, from Mao Tse-tung to Lee Kuan Yew to the shah of Iran to five American presidents to Latin American *politicos* and generals to Saudi sheiks and royalty to Moscow's topmost leaders like Andropov, Brezhnev and Kosygin.

At home she caused the building of the Cultural Center, the Heart Center, the Lung Center, the Kidney Center, Bliss Housing, LRT, Folk Arts Center, Film Center, Nayong Pilipino, so many Human Settlements buildings in the provinces, etc.

In political campaigns, she was called Marcos' secret weapon, although it was an open secret. Politically she showed a stamina and elan that are yet unsurpassed by other women.

And courage. Once her helicopter nearly crashed on the beach in Barangay Balogo, Calatrava, Romblon, but she showed no concern that her life was endangered.

It was getting dark, being dusk. She proceeded to transfer to her backup helicopter without the slightest ruffle, still smiling graciously and pausing to shake hands with the poor half-naked fishermen who had run to the scene after hearing the descending chopper's troubled engine vibrations.

In 1973 Isabelo Crisostomo wrote:

In spite of Marcos' personal charisma, campaign machinery, the helicopter, the computer and foreign opinion pollsters. Serging Osmeña [Marcos' opponent in the 1969 presidential contest] could have given him a good fight if Serging had someone to match Imelda.

For it was Imelda who, as in 1965 [against Macapagal] would give Marcos countless votes. She has not lost her bewitching appeal. While she merely sang or delivered five-minute passages in 1965, in 1969 she went campaigning on her own, accompanied only by some Blue Ladies, distributing goodies and making hour-long speeches. Her enchanting style is said to have softened the Opposition.

Hour-long speeches? You bet. She also talked at length in convocations and seminars, even in interviews. This was not always the case in the first few years of the Marcos rule, when she was perceived as shy. But after daily practice for years, she got used to all sorts of situations and subjects, including government activities, programs, policies, etc., that she became so well-informed and fluent.

For example, in a recital in New York, she talked — extemporaneously — to an American audience on the arts and music. In a meeting with government ministers in Manila she gave a lecture, without notes, on media projection. Before delegates to a livelihood conference she discoursed on human motivation vis-à-vis government systems. And in a talk with an Italian minister she bathed him with statistics on Philippine trade with European countries.

Newsweek, however, once reported:

Mrs. Marcos' worldview can have a distinctly eccentric bend. She frequently draws bizarre diagrams with squares, circles and triangles to help make her points. And at one memorable meeting in Manila with American scientists in January 1982, Mrs. Marcos said in all seriousness:

"There is a hole in outer space through which cosmic forces beam down on these [Philippine] islands. They are stronger than anywhere else and that is why we have so many good faith healers. My scientists tell me that we could use these forces to protect the United States from ballistic missiles."

Said one of the American scientists in attendance, "She is self-confident and articulate...."

Her clout was unprecedented. In 1980, for example, she easily gathered on short notice for a simple meeting at the Philippine Center in New York City eleven ambassadors and more consuls — a display of power and command that could not lag behind anything Cleopatra mustered in ancient Egypt.

At home, of course, there were many who obeyed her more speedily than they did Marcos. And it may not be amiss to say there were times when Marcos himself deferred to Imelda, not merely out of gentlemanliness but out of political wisdom.

In her public career, Imelda's forte was outward do-goodism in the face of turmoil. In the women's liberation movement then raging, the adversary notion of which she repeatedly rejected, her example rendered the women libbers' efforts as a proselytism without joy or merit.

With her hyperactive regimen, she conserved her energies, appearing fresh even after the tightest schedules, by being the object rather than the source of indignation. With her long experience in the art of absorbing brickbats, she was unharried by regular damnations exhaled by her political enemies and critics, of whom she had a surplus.

Even before their hasty exit from Malacañang, in those days when their political triumphs seemed endless, the Marcoses resolutely bore the mandatory burden of those who craved authoritarian powers — the problems and the perils came with the territory — and thus collided with their own people.

They knew this occupational hazard, and they had to engage in political forensics to the depths of personal malediction and the heights of discursive apoplexy.

Marcos and Imelda were natural political partners, operating with an awesome combination of precision and passion. Their enemies they considered as monstrous ogres whom they confronted with conjugal tenacity — Ferdinand reached out for the jugular and held it at bay while Imelda proceeded to wrap up the veins and the capillaries.

And so it was with tenacity, too, that she tried to break with her arms and fingers the bolo blows of a would-be assassin who frontally attacked her in a public function.

The day was December 7, 1972, the anniversary of the Pearl Harbor bombing. It was less than three months after the Marcos declaration of martial law.

Everybody was still adjusting to the new life under authoritarian rule, which somewhat resembled the Japanese Occupation at least in terms of a curfew that restrained the population's taste for boulevard alcoholism and nightclub psychedelia.

As usual, Mrs. Imelda Marcos braced for another day of public functions in spite of the civil tension. She was to grace the occasion that afternoon in her Nayong Pilipino where awards would be made in connection with her nationwide campaign for cleanliness and beautification.

The rites at Nayong Pilipino proceeded smoothly, with Mrs. Marcos on stage receiving one by one the awardees and shaking hands with them. Her guards, naturally, were not on the stage but a short distance away, for who would think any attempt on her life would be made in that most friendly environment.

South Cotabato won the grand prize for being the model province in terms of parks and plazas, with the municipality of Kiamba adjudged the cleanest. Its delegation went up the stage to receive their award. Among them was a man in all-black suit and pants who pretended to be part of the group.

When his turn came before the First Lady, he whipped out a bolo and made two determined thrusts at her. A split second before the attack, as photographs later showed, she was looking sideways and did not see the bolo already leveled horizontally a few inches away from her abdominal region.

She was quick enough to parry with her arms and fingers the first blow. The hospital report later said she suffered lacerations at the back of her right hand, on the right forearm, across the index finger and the ring finger of the right hand.

In short, without help from anyone, she defended herself. She fell down from the second thrust.

Quickly, 22-year-old Linda Amor Robles of the Department of Education, who was secretary of the cleanliness committee, covered Mrs. Marcos with her own body and suffered a huge three-inch wound on her back. The First Family a week later, when Imelda could walk around with a sling around her arm, visited her in the hospital.

Tourism Secretary Jose Aspiras also shielded Mrs. Marcos by taking some of the blows. He sustained a head wound that took nine stitches. Others who tried to cover her were Social Welfare Secretrary Aldaba Lim and Josefa Aquino, the wife of Highways Commissioner Baltazar Aquino.

The would-be assassin, diverted from the fallen First Lady, continued to hack wildly until he was shot dead by guards who had jumped upstage. The whole scenario happened before a shocked, unbelieving television audience around the country who were watching the awarding ceremonies.

Mrs. Marcos was immediately flown by helicopter to the 9th floor of the Makati Medical Center. Shortly afterwards, President Marcos speedily came to her side, grim and unsmiling, and soon he ordered the scene replayed again and again.

Because they had no equipment or tape at the hospital, a television station replayed it for him on the air, and Filipinos saw the many replays themselves for hours.

Marcos' anger mounted as he watched them, sometimes banging his fist with tremendous force on a tabletop. He asked why the assailant was killed — he should have been captured alive to tell the whole story, since it was possible someone ordered him to do the job, which may have been a conspiracy.

In Stalin's regime, the would-be assassin would have been used as witness to incriminate innocent people and send them to death.

It was said Marcos interrogated the guards who shot down the bolo wielder, for it was not impossible that one of them was part of the plan and shot the assassin to silence him. Later on Marcos told reporters he was satisfied that the guards could not be blamed for immediately killing the man.

On television, the president assured the nation that the First Lady was safe and recovering. He said he wished he were there when the incident happened.

He added that when he declared martial law "we knew we would pay the price, but I cannot forgive myself that she herself had to pay it."[4] But instead of being daunted, he said, he would even more resolutely proceed with his program "to eradicate and eliminate all threats against the stability of our society and to push through the [martial law] reformist program."

The newspapers later showed Marcos kneeling before a priest saying mass at the hospital chapel.

Information Minister Francisco Tatad announced his theory that the would-be assassin was not alone. More problematically, he said that "three conspirators detained in the assassination plot had confessed that some members of the group are still in Manila,"[5] and that the target had always been both the president and the First Lady!

To buttress this theory, Tatad stated that at 3:30 p.m. — the attack on Imelda happened two hours later, at 5:36 p.m. — a call had been received at the palace asking if the president would be at the Nayong Pilipino ceremonies. He said "the call was unusual for no media announcement had been made" of the affair.[6]

Tatad's tacit suggestion, apparently, was that assassination plotters would be so incompetent that they would take their cue from media only — not from participants in the affair or moles who monitored events on their own.

A wave of arrests followed. Many Muslims in Manila were said to have been rounded up — after all, the Muslims were resisting martial law. And the assassination attempt was made ostensibly from among the Cotabato awardee group.

In those days, the country was still reeling from the novelty of living under martial law. One of the most sensitive topics was the security of Marcos and Imelda.

There was talk about all sorts of dangerous eventualities and soon Marcos issued a decree penalizing rumormongering.

As information minister, Tatad tried to do his duty. In a speech before a business conference, he discussed the assassination attempt. He pointed out that if there was anyone who saved Mrs. Marcos from assassination, it was Mrs. Marcos herself because of her quickwittedness.

Tatad later expanded the range of assassination targets by saying that the three Marcos children — Imee, Bongbong who was then in London, and Irene — were included in assassination plots.

Or they may be kidnapped to force the release of political prisoners and the resignation of President Marcos.

He said that a total of 85 persons had been arrested and were being kept in 14 safehouses in Greater Manila[7] by Metrocom, CIS and other security men. He announced — the first time the government did so — that in the two years preceding the declaration of martial law, there had been seven assassination attempts on President Marcos. Note the use of the mystical number 7.

This was an announcement that would in a few weeks be supported by a government press release detailing the assassination plots, as we will see in the next chapter. Tatad in his speech focused not on the First Lady but on Marcos:

> We have not entirely subdued the political passions, the bitterness and the violence that have long sought to claim the life of our President in the hands of his enemies.
>
> [Enemies] will persist in the belief that their goals can be achieved by putting an end to the lives of our leaders. They will persist in the belief that their control of government can only be founded on the death of the President. For we can dispossess all men of their weapons but can never completely purge all men of their hate.

He continued by saying that Marcos' enemies thought that the First Lady's death "would transform the President into a tyrant who would decree and institute all manners of repression to negate the gains achieved during the last ten months.

"The President would be so deranged as a leader and blindly let loose an anger that would destroy everything on its path and ultimately make his life and office meaningless to the very people who have given him support. [But] there will be no anger, no bitterness, no violence that will sweep away the good that we have sown or built."[8]

Such elaborate words.

Imelda's personal physician, Dr. Raul Fores, said she would be staying in the hospital for a few days. Unlike in the EDSA Revolution 14 years later, the Americans were very much concerned about Mrs. Marcos. President Nixon called, saying "America is shocked and dismayed...and thankful she was able to weather this attempt at assassination."[9]

An American expert, Dr. Bob Chase, was flown in from the United States to look into the repair of the tendons in the right forearm and middle finger of the right hand. Among the early visitors were Ambassador Henry Byroade and Senator Charles "Chuck" Percy, future contender for the Republican nomination for president, who said he saw the incident on TV.

Percy said, correctly, "I am happy she did not lose her mind and her reflexes were quick."[10]

Imelda was as self-possessed as Jacqueline Kennedy in an unexpected moment of danger. It may be recalled that the latter defied the prospect of being hit by bullets as she tried to help President Kennedy. She maintained her presence of mind and did not seek cover in the car — she even exposed herself by pulling from the outside a secret service agent at the height of the shooting.

Bulletin Today columnist Apolonio Batalla titled his column, "Imelda: She's More than a First Lady," and wrote somewhat impertinently:

"It may be, as Malacañang hinted, that a political reason lies behind the attempt, since the transformation of society even how bloodless the process is bound to have repercussions."[11]

From Brazil, UPI quoted Imelda's sister, a Catholic nun, Sr. Bellarmine, expressing grief and offering prayers to "our dearest Imelda." Mrs. Tien Suharto, her friend and wife of the Indonesian president, communicated her sympathies, saying the attempt was "not the way to topple President Marcos. It is very bad." Another reaction:

Rangoon, Dec. 9 (UPI) — A government-owned newspaper, in a rare comment on foreign affairs, today denounced the assassination attempt Thursday on Philippine First Lady Imelda Marcos.

"Since the attempt has been linked to a rightist plot, one suspects the hand of President Marcos' enemies among civil servants who got sacked under charges of corruption and wealthy oligarchs who were financially hurt by his economic measures," the English-language *Working People's Daily* said.

"But whoever tried to take his bitterness or hatred out on the wife was responsible for a shameful dastardly act that deserves to be denounced in the strongest possible manner," it said.

The daily said it was "appalled by the barbarity of the assassination attempt which is all the more reprehensible for its stark brutality at a member of the fair sex."

To the consternation of enemies of the martial law regime, whether innocent or not, the government-controlled media kept up a barrage of publicity about a possible conspiracy to assassinate not only Mrs. Marcos but the president.

Was this a prelude to outright accusations of assassination, trial, sentencing and execution? The conspiracy angle occupied and preoccupied the regime's newspapers as the would-be killer was identified.

He was one Carlito Dimailig, single, of Calaca, Batangas, one of nine children of Francisco Dimailig. Tatad said Carlito was "quiet and shy" and "susceptible to suggestion," according to sworn statements gathered from some arrested persons.

By December 12, five days after the attempt, the progovernment *Bulletin Today* on its front page said:

Probers obtained evidence that the would-be assassin Carlito Dimailig was part of a conspiracy and evidently under the influence of drugs when he attacked the First Lady.

Testimony of people close to Dimailig as gathered by the investigators disclosed that he attended "several meetings with unknown persons."[13]

Hala ka....

Government probers added they found pills in the dead man's pockets. "The pills discovered on the person of the slain would-be assassin were reportedly the type that could drive a man to frenzy. He was believed to have obtained the drugs from those persons with whom he had been meeting in previous days."[14]

Even the poor dead man's father was now quoted in the same news story to have said that his son "could not have acted alone." That was Carlito's way?

On December 13 —six days after the assassination attempt — all the news stories about Carlito and the horrible incident vanished from the newspapers. Not a single line was subsequently written or published about it, not even in opinion columns or in editorials or in features.

This incident that dominated the front pages was completely erased and forgotten — because the conspiracy angle could not be sustained? On December 13, the news that appeared on the front pages were:

Apollo astraunauts in the second moon walk say lunar rocks are geologists' paradise; aliens are warned not to meddle in the constitutional prebiscite; Marcos decrees new property taxes; Bagatsing demotes 148 policemen for lack of qualifications; there is a sharp rise in RP tourist traffic; cold front breathes across Luzon; judge declares a mistrial in the Pentagon Papers case; and Paris peace negotiators agree on limited troop pullout from Vietnam.

ENDNOTES

Chapter 1. The First Conspirators

1. From Pigafetta's account. See Uldarico Baclagon, *Philippine Campaigns* (Manila: Graphic House, 1952); Sofronio Alip, *Political and Cultural History of the Philippines* (Manila: Alip & Sons, 1963); Teodoro Agoncillo and Milagros Guerrero, *History of the Filipino People* (Quezon City: Garcia Publishing House, 1971).
2. Horacio de la Costa, *Readings in Philippine History* (Manila: Bookmark, 1965), p. 17.
3. Nick Joaquin, *Manila My Manila* (Manila: City of Manila, 1990), p.19.
4. *Filipinos in History*, vol. I (Manila: National Historical Institute, 1989), p. 263.
5. Joaquin, p. 26.
6. Ibid.
7. *Filipinos in History*, vol. II (Manila: National Historical Institute, 1989), p. 220.
8. Emilio Aguinaldo and Vicente Albano Pacis, *A Second Look at America* (New York: Robert Speller & Sons, 1957), p. 124.
9. Baclagon, p. 5.
10. Bernal Diaz, *The Conquest of New Spain,* ed. and tr. by J. M. Cohen (Middlesex: Penquin, 1975).
11. De la Costa, p. 15.
12. Gabriel Fabella, "The Role of Aguinaldo in History," *Historical Bulletin,* vol. viii, January–December, 1969, nos. 1–4, pp. 26–27.

Chapter 2. The Tondo Conspiracy

1. O. D. Corpuz, *The Roots of the Filipino Nation* (Quezon City: AKLAHI Foundation, 1989), p. 113.
2. Ibid, p. 112.
3. Ibid, p. 115.
4. Gregorio F. Zaide and Sonia Zaide, *The Philippines: A Unique Nation* (Quezon City: All Nations Publishing Co., 1994), p. 182.
5. Corpuz, p. 116.
6. Joaquin, p. 11.
7. Leandro Tormo Sanz, *A Town the Franciscans Built*, tr. by Antonio Soriano (Manila: Historical Conservation Society, 1971), p. 5.
8. Fray San Antonio, "The Philippine Chronicles," tr. by Pedro Picornell (Manila: Casalinda/National Conservation Society/TheFranciscan Fathers, 1977), p. 28.
9. Corpuz, p. 117.
10. Ibid.

Chapter 3. The Sumuroy Assassination

1. Zaide and Zaide, p. 181.
2. Ibid., p. 184.
3. Renato Constantino, *A Past Revisited* (Quezon City: Constantino, 1974), p. 92.
4. Ernest Gruening, *Mexico and Its Heritage* (New York: Greenwood Press, 1968), p. 230.
5. Elsie S. Ramos, "Tayabas: 1578–1907," masteral thesis, University of the Philippines, 1992.
6. Corpuz, p. 131.

Chapter 4. The Diego Silang Assassination

1. David Routledge, *Diego Silang and the Origins of Philippine Nationalism* (Diliman, Quezon City: Philippine Center for Advanced Studies, 1979).
2. Corpuz, p. 336.
3. Routledge, p. 15.
4. Ibid., pp. 18–19.
5. Agoncillo and Guerrero, p. 181.
6. De la Costa, p. 91.
7. Routledge, p. 16.
8. Ibid., p. 17.
9. Ibid., p. 19.
10. Ibid., p. 23.
11. Ibid., p. 19.
12. Ibid., p. 27.
13. Ibid., p. 32.
14. Ibid., pp. 35–36.
15. Neni Sta. Romana Cruz, *Gabriela Silang* (Manila: Tahanan Book for Young Readers, 1992), pp. 28-30.
16. Ibid., p. 30.
17. Ibid., p. 7.
18. Ibid., p. 9.
19. Constantino, pp. 107–112.
20. Ibid., pp. 110–111.

Chapter 5. The Extermination of Hermano Pule

1. Corpuz, p. 488.
2. Reynaldo Ileto, *Pasyon and Revolution* (Quezon City: Ateneo de Manila University Press,1970), p. 31.
3. Ramos.
4. Tormo, p. 97.
5. *Lucban Quadcentennial Souvenir Program,* 1978, p. 84.
6. Ileto, p. 32.
7. Ibid., pp. 50–51.
8. Ibid.
9. Ramos.
10. Tormo, pp. 97–98.
11. Corpuz, 489.
12. Ibid.
13. Emma Helen Blair and James Alexander Robertson, *The Philippine Islands,* vol. 52 (Cleveland, Ohio: A.R. Clark, 1903–1909), pp. 167–169.
14. Jesus C. Olega, "Ang Mahiwagang Pagkamatay sa Unang Bayani ng Lalawigan ng Tayabas," *Tayabas Direktoryo at Kasaysayan* (Tayabas, 1938), p. 11.
15. *Historical Data,* vol. 85, compiled by The National Library. In 1951 President Elpidio Quirino issued a decree ordering public school teachers in the Philippines to write a history of the barrios and towns where they were assigned as teachers. The result was a collection of more than 250 volumes which encompassed all provinces at that time and an overwhelming majority of municipalities and barrios.
16. Agoncillo and Guerrero, p. 123.
17. Corpuz, p. 492.
18. Tormo, p. 100.
19. Corpuz, p. 491.

20. *Lucban Quadcentennial Program,* p. 85.
21. Olega, p. 14.
22. Agoncillo and Guerrero, p. 195.
23. Santiago V. Alvarez, *The Katipunan and the Revolution,* tr. by Carolina S. Malay (Quezon City: Ateneo de Manila University Press, 1996).
24. Constantino.
25. Blair and Robertson, p. 93–94. Tormo, p. 97.
26. Corpuz, p. 488.
27. Zaide, p. 199.
28. Tormo, p. 98.
29. Reynaldo Ileto, *Filipinos and Their Revolution* (Quezon City: Ateneo de Manila University Press, 1998), p. 86.
30. Corpuz, p. 491.
31. Tormo, p. 100.
32. Ibid.
33. Ibid.
34. Ileto, *Filipinos and...,* p. 47.
35. Tormo, p. 100.
36. Ibid.
37. Ramos.
38. Ileto, p. 62.
39. Corpuz, p. 492.
40. Teodoro A. Agoncillo, *Malolos: Crisis of the Republic* (Quezon City: University of the Philippines Press, 1960) p. 225.
41. Corpuz, p. 492.
42. Ibid., p. 493.
43. Joaquin, p. 91.
44. De la Costa, p. 145.
45. Zaide, p. 199.
46. Joaquin, p. 91.

Chapter 6.   The Ultimate in Intrigue: The Extirpation of Burgos

1. Sol Gwekoh, *Gomes, Burgos and Zamora* (Quezon City: National Book Store, 1974).
2. Dagohoy started his revolt when the Jesuit parish priest in his hometown in Bohol would not bless the dead body of his brother who was killed in a duel, a death that in those days was banned from the sacrament by the Church.
3. Nick Joaqun, *A Question of Heroes* (Navotas: Filipinas Foundation, 1977), p. 15.
4. Gwekoh, pp. 135–136.
5. Ibid., p. 44.
6. Ibid., p. 68.
7. Ibid., p. 121.
8. Joaquin, pp. 20–21.
9. The Regidor account was taken by Gwekoh from Wenceslao Retana, *Vida y Escritos del Dr. Jose Rizal* (Madrid, 1907) p. 454, in Gwekoh, p. 109.

Chapter 7. Bonifacio Obliterated

1. Emilio Aguinaldo, *Mga Gunita ng Himagsikan* (Manila: National Centennial Commission/Cavite Historical Association, A.T.S. and Associates, 1998).
2. Constantino, p. 199.
3. Agoncillo and Guerrero, p. 242.

4. Alvarez, p. 70.
5. Aguinaldo, p. 47.
6. Alvarez, p. 82.
7. Aguinaldo, p. 179.
8. Artemio Ricarte, *Memoirs of the Revolution* (Manila: National Historical Institute, undated), p. 23.
9. Alvarez, pp. 98-99.
10. Cesar Adib Ma, *Apolinario Mabini: Revolutionary* (Manila: National Historical Institute, 1993), p. 23.

Chapter 8. Noriel Devastated, Del Pilar Execrated
1. Aguinaldo, pp.260–261.
2. Orlina A. Ochosa, *Pio del Pilar and Other Heroes* (Quezon City: New Day Publishers, 1997).
3. Ibid.
4. Aguinaldo, p. 44.
5. *Filipinos in History*, vol. IV (Manila: National Historical Institute, 1994), p. 238.
6. Agoncillo, p. 142.
7. Ibid., p. 344.
8. Ibid., p. 374.
9. Amzi B. Kelly, *The Killing of General Noriel* (Manila: Historical Conservation Society, 1987), p. 4.
10. Ibid., p. 5.
11. Ibid., p. xi.
12. Ibid.
13. Ibid., p. 6.
14. Filipinos in History, vol. II (Manila: National Historical Institute, 1994), p. 241.
15. Ochosa, p. 36.
16. Ibid., p. 49.
17. Ibid., p. 56.
18. Ibid., p. 70.
19. Ibid., p. 76.
20. Ibid.
21. Ibid., p. 114.
22. Ibid., pp. 120-121.
23. Ibid., pp. 122-123.

Chapter 9. How They Liquidated Luna
1. Vivencio Jose, *The Rise and Fall of Antonio Luna* (UP Diliman: Filipiniana Reprint Series, 1972).
2. Same, see Chapter 16, "Death in the Afternoon," pp. 341–355; Chapter 17, "Epilogue to Disaster," pp. 357–377.
3. Ambeth Ocampo, *Luna's Moustache* (Pasig City: Anvil, 1997), p. 19.
4. Corpuz, vol. II, p. 415.
5. Jose, p. 354.
6. Ibid., p. 355.
7. Ibid., pp. 365-377.
8. Ibid., p. 367.
9. Ibid., p. 46.
10. Manuel F. Martinez, *Aquino V. Marcos: The Grand Collision* (Manila: Martinez, 1984), p. 99.

11. Jose, p. 69.
12. Alejandrino, p. 116.
13. Corpuz, vol. II, p. 450.

Chapter 10. Mission Possible: Assassinate Quezon

1. Douglas MacArthur, "Message of the General of the Army," *Historical Bulletin,* vol. XXII, January–December, 1978, p. 242.
2. Olega.
3. Manuel L. Quezon, *The Good Fight* (New York: D. Appleton–Century Co., 1946), p. 91.
4. Ibid., p. 90.
5. Olega.
6. Carlos Quirino, *Paladin of Philippine Freedom* (Manila: Filipiniana Book Guild, 1971), p. 173.
7. Quezon, pp. 102–104.
8. Carlos Quirino, *Quezon: Man of Destiny* (Manila: Quirino, 1935), p. 84.
9. Ibid., p. 85.
10. Sergio R. Mistica, "Manuel Quezon – A Character Sketch," in *Quezon: Thoughts and Anecdotes About His Fights* (QuezonCity: Kayumanggi Press, 1971), p.322.
11. Jose Topacio Nueno, "Quezon Forgave His Would-Be Assassin," in Rivera, pp. 324–326.
12. Quirino, *Paladin...,*p. 126.
13. Editorial, *Philippines Free Press,* May 7, 1949.
14. *Manila Times,* April, 28, 1958, no pagination, from files in the Lopez Museum.
15. Ibid.
16. Ibid., November 4, 1968.

Chapter 11. Laurel Shot, Roxas Bombed, Magsaysay Missed

1. Agoncillo and Guerrero, p. 450.
2. Ricardo Trota Jose, "Rising to the Challenge of the Japanese Occupation," in *Philippine Presidents,* (Quezon City: Philippine Historical Association/New Day Publishers, 1999), p. 144.
3. Ibid.
4. Jose P. Laurel, *Talaarawan ng Digmaan* (Intramuros: Lyceum of the Philippines, 197), pp. 21–37.
5. Agoncillo and Guerrero, p. 463.
6. Letter of President Quezon to Sotero Laurel, dated September 30, 1943, in *Talaarawan*
7. Eduardo Bananal, *Presidents of the Philippines* (Manila: National Book Store, 1986), p. 70.
8. "Roxas Has Narrow Escape," *Philippines Free Press,* March 15, 1947, pp. 8–9, 41.
9. Ibid.
10. Ibid.
11. Editorial, *Philippines Free Press,* March 15, 1947.
12. Carlos Quirino, *Magsaysay of the Philippines,* (Manila: Ramon Magsaysay Memorial Society, 1958), pp. 54–55.
13. Ibid.
14. Told by Ninoy Aquino, special asssistant to Magsaysay, to friends.
15. Quirino, p. 56.
16. Ibid.
17. Ibid., pp. 81–82.

18. Ibid., p. 83.

Chapter 12. The Kamikaze Attack on Imelda

1. Martinez, p. 128. This book was written and published at great speed in the months following the assassination of Ninoy Aquino and its endnotes were not printed. The sources of this book, from which most of the quotes came, were Manila newspapers. The book was largely a tribute to Ninoy Aquino and contained critical remarks against the Marcos regime. In those days, any writer could be arrested on that basis and the printing press confiscated under the provisions of a presidential decree. Hence, the lack of endnotes. The first issue was released in 1984, printed in Hong Kong and circulated in the United States; the second in 1986, when Cory Aquino had come to power.
2. Ibid.
3. Ibid.
4. *Bulletin Today*, December 1, 1972, p. 1.
5. December 9, 1972, p. 9.
6. Ibid., December 10, p. 15.
7. Ibid.
8. Ibid., December 9, 1972.
9. Ibid.
10. Ibid., December 10, 1972, p. 15.
11. Ibid., December 11, 1972, pp. 1, 27.
12. Ibid., December 10, 1972, p. 1.
13. Ibid., December 12, 1972, p. 1.
14. Ibid., p. 9.

BIBLIOGRAPHY

Aguinaldo, Emilio. *Mga Gunita ng Himagsikan* (Manila: National Centennial Commission, Cavite Historical Assocation, A.T.S. and Associates, 1998).

Aguinaldo, Emilio and Vicente Albano Pacis. *A Second Look at America* (New York: Robert Speller & Sons, 1957).

Agoncillo, Teodoro A. *Malolos: The Crisis of the Republic* (Quezon City: University of the Philippines Press, 1960).

Agoncillo, Teodoro and Milagros Guerrero. *History of the Filipino People* (Quezon City: Garcia Publishing, 1971).

Alip, Sofronio. *Political and Cultural History of the Philippines* (Manila: Alip & Sons, 1963).

Alvarez, Santiago V. *The Katipunan and the Revolution* tr. by Carolina S. Malay (Quezon City: Ateneo de Manila University Press, 1996).

San Antonio, Fray. "The Philippine Chronicles," tr. by Pedro Picornell (Manila: Casalinda/National Conservation Society/The Franciscan Fathers, 1877).

Arillo, Cecilio. *Breakaway* (Mandaluyong: CTA & Associates, 1986).

Aruiza, Arturo. *Ferdinand E. Marcos: Malacañang to Waikiki* (Quezon City: ACAruiza Enterprises, 1992).

Baclagon, Uldarico. *Philippine Campaigns* (Manila: Graphic House, 1952).

Bananal, Eduardo. *Presidents of the Philippines* (Manila: National Book Store, 1986).

Blair, Emma Helen and James Alexander Robertson. *The Philippine Islands*, vol. 52 (Cleveland, Ohio: A. R. Clark, 1903-1909).

Constantino, Renato. *A Past Revisited* (Quezon City: Constantino, 1974).

Copeland, Lewis ed. *The World's Greatest Speeches* (New York: Dover Publications, 1958).

De la Costa, Horacio. *Readings in Philippine History* (Manila: Bookmark, 1965).

Corpuz, Onofro D. *The Roots of the Filipino Nation* (Quezon City: AKLAHI Foundation, 1989).

Cortes, Rosario Mendoza ed. *Philippine Presidents* (Quezon City: New Day Publishers, 1999).

Cruz, Neni Sta. Romana. *Gabriela Silang* (Manila: Tahanan Books, 1992).

Diaz, Bernal. *The Conquest of New Spain*, tr. by J. M. Cohen (Middlesex: Penguin, 1975).

Fabella, Gabriel. "The Role of Aguinaldo in History." *Historical Bulletin*, vol. xiii, January-December, 1969, nos. 1-4.

Gruening, Ernest. *Mexico and Its Heritage* (New York: Greenwood Press, 1968).

Gwekoh, Sol. *Gomes, Burgos and Zamora* (Quezon City: National Book Store, 1974).

Ileto, Reynaldo. *Filipinos and their Revolution* (Quezon City: Ateneo de Manila University Press, 1998).

Ileto, Reynaldo. *Pasyon and Revolution* (Quezon City: Ateneo de Manila de University Press, 1979).

Joaquin, Nick. *The Aquinos of Tarlac* (Manila: Cacho Hermanos, 1983).

Joaquin, Nick. *Manila My Manila* (Manila: City of Manila, 1990).

Joaquin, Nick. *A Question of Heroes* (Navotas: Filipinas Foundation, 1977).

Jose, Vivencio. *The Rise and Fall of Antonio Luna* (UP Diliman: Filipiniana Reprint Series, 1972).

Kelly, Amzi B. *The Killing of General Noriel* (Manila: Historical Conservation Society, 1987).

Laurel, Jose P. *Talaarawan ng Digmaan* (Intramuros: Lyceum of the Philippines, 1997).

MacArthur, Douglas. "Message of the General of the Army," *Historical Bulletin*, vol. xxii,

January-December, 1978.

Majul, Cesar Adib. *Apolinario Mabini: Revolutionary* (Manila: National Historical Institute, 1993).

Ocampo, Ambeth. *Luna's Moustache* (Pasig City: Anvil, 1997).

Ochosa, Orlina A. *Pio del Pilar and* Other *Heroes* (Quezon City: New Day Publishers, 1997).

Olega, Jesus C. Tayabas. *Direktoryo at Kasaysayan.* Tayabas, (undated).

Quezon, Manuel L. *The Good Fight* (New York: D. Appleton-Century Co., 1946).

Quirino, Carlos. *Magsaysay of the Philippines* (Manila: Ramon Magsaysay Memorial Society, 1958).

Quirino, Carlos. *Quezon: Man of Destiny* (Manila: Quirino, 1935).

Quirino, Carlos. *Paladin of Philippine Freedom* (Manila: Filipiniana Book Guild. 1971).

Ricarte, Artemio. *Memoirs of the Revolution* (Manila: National Historical Institute).

Routledge, David. *Diego Silang and the Origins of Philippine Nationalism* (Diliman, Quezon City: Philippine Center for Advanced Studies, 1979).

Rivera, Juan F. ed. *Quezon: Thoughts and Anecdotes About His Fights* (Quezon City: Kayumanggi Press, 1971).

Stuart-Santiago, Angela. *Walang Himala! Himagsikan sa EDSA* (Manila: Foundation for Worldwide People Power, 2000).

Sanz, Leandro Tormo. *A Town the Franciscans Built*, tr. by Antonio Soriano (Manila: Historical Conservation Society/The Franciscan Fathers, 1977).

Scipes, Kim. *KMU: Building Genuine Trade Unionism in the Philippines, 1980-1986.*

Taylor, Robert Lewis. *Winston Churchill* (New York: Doubleday & Co., 1965).

Zaide, Gregorio F. and Sonia Zaide. *The Philippines: A Unique Nation* (Quezon City: All Nations Publishing, 1994).

Index

Index

295-